Elementary Education Competencies & Skills

Contributors:

Section 1	Karen Sanchez, Ph.D. Elementary Education
Section 2	Mary Collins, Ph.D. Elementary Education
Section 3 and 4	Marilyn Rainear, MS Education, BA English
Section 5 and 6.1	James McGan, Ph.D. Elementary Education
Section 6.2	Kathy Schnirman, Ph.D. Special Education
Section 6.2 and 6.3	Dennis Setter, Ph.D. Elementary Education
Section 6.4 and 6.5	Frank Goldsmith, BS Education
Section 6.5	Betty Churlock, M.C.S. Computer Science
Section 6.5	Paul Bodura, MA Education, Ed. Specialist Computer Science

To Order Additional Copies:
Xam, Inc.
3646 Wylies Mill Road
Richburg, SC 29729
Toll Free   1-800-301-4647
Email: winwin1111@aol.com
Web   www.xamonline.com
EFax   1-501-325-0185
Fax: 1-803-789-7281

You will find:
- Content Review in prose format
- Bibliography
- Sample Test

XAM, INC.
Building Better Teachers

MTTC: Elementary Education Competencies & Skills
ISBN: 1-58197-202-4

Dedication

It is a general insight, which merits more attention than it receives, that teaching should not be compared to filling a bottle with water but rather to helping a flower to grow in its own way. As any good teacher knows, the methods of instruction and the range of material covered are matters of small importance as compared with the success in arousing the natural curiosity of the students and instilling their interest in exploring on their own.

Chomsky

FAMILY – the critical connection

Elementary education examinees are asked questions that cover both principles and processes. Some questions assess basic understanding of curriculum, instructional design, and assessment of student learning. You will find questions based on situations routinely faced in the classroom. Certification tests will measure knowledge of general areas such as reading/language arts, social science, math, science, art, physical education, and general information about curriculum. Licensure means that the public is satisfied that you know what to teach children. It cannot know how you will teach children until you get your opportunity.

What do you want from a teaching career? I am sure you will want to make a difference. This forward is dedicated to you and the larger questions you need to ask yourself before you teach. Go beyond what the test is asking of you. The critical connection is creating an educational identity in a child. As a whole schools are not doing a good enough job at inspiring families to participate. We know this, but how do things start turning around? Families need more nurturing from teachers to understand just how important they really are. Do we really need families doing homework with their children or is it the softer side of encouragement that needs to be defined in newsletters, examples, meetings, phone calls, teacher – parent conferences, or other communications at ball games, assemblies, etc.?

Why work intensively with families as a new teacher? There are many reasons why but one is that it makes your job easier. Is it in your lesson plans to work with families? What do parents and grandparents bring to the educational experience that you do not do as well as they can? Pride that comes internally from the family has a special place in a child's life. How would you measure how well you are doing in this area of family communication? These may be hard questions but lets face it, they are worth asking.

Look for a moment at the concept of pride. Do teachers realize the power of pride and the linkage of using family influence? Unconditional love is encouraging and caring and filled with friendship. When you cherish your students as the family does, you will be mastering the art of being a teacher and adding to the educational identity of your students. Always measure the student in terms of improvement rather than strictly achievement as your parent conferences are about growing pride.

When any family member gives those warm hugs and says, "Everything is OK," than comfort is the catalyst to keep self esteem in check. Trade your red markers for a smile or a wink of body language motivation. Winks are motivators of "secrets" we are keeping just between us.

Recently there was a poll that showed 60 percent of parents are paying their children to get good grades. Weigh in on that message. Speak to the parents directly on this practice. I am not asking you to come to any conclusion I may have, but rather form an opinion of your own and influence parents.

Grandparents have the gift of time to give to their grandchildren. Modeling behavior is living your words. How can you get to know family better and quicker? Here is what you have to deal with: the frequency you have communication with the family, the intensity of that communication, the duration of the experience, and time of day when it occurs. I am suggesting that you put more emphasis on the above questions to become a more effective teacher. The same is true for parents but they seem to have less time than grandparents in some cases. Perhaps we are looking at changing the reality of what parents think of their time and availability. They could give more and while your methods classes may have put emphasis on expectations with your role teacher to child it apparently walks softer with the teacher parent role. Maybe we should think about expectations for the parents and grandparents.

Imagine how proud I am of my intellectually gifted grandmother, Marion Mooney, born 1896. She was a first grade teacher in Massachusetts in 1919 and a college graduate which was a terrific accomplishment for women in those days. Of course she could not marry and be a teacher at the same time so her career was abruptly ended after just one year. I have an educational identity because of her. I am lucky and of course think of the many students who do not have such models. How do we make each child become a flower that is watered and grown from within? Where are the sources of the water?

If you ask the simple questions, who parents loved, who did they trust, and why were they fulfilled in life you will be looking at your students. Have your students write essays about their grandparents are cultivate those feelings of connections. You see they have the time to give to their grandchildren that is so special.

Here is what you might see in the home that has the love of a grandparent. My grandmother could beat the pants off me in scrabble and would always reach for the dictionary when she did not know how to spell a word. That taught me how to acquire knowledge when I did not know it. She was modeling behavior for me.

Grandparents have an unhurried day and time to just to talk. They speak of the past. It is the child's personal history lesson. Those memories are forming an educational identity that will last. See if your students can relate in an unhurried way some of these delights where we can watch every moment unfold. The stay at home parent will always be cherished. Who has ever regretted staying at home and nurturing their child?

Can your students draw the hands of their grandparents that take them across the street into the playground or draw their eyes that show humor, joy, or sorrow? It is OK to get gum from Grandpa....it never runs out it seems. They giggle and tickle and tap you on their knees. What a delightful way to gain emotional intelligence.

When you admire someone and they tell you, "You can be anything you set your sights on" it has credibility. The importance of hope and dreams cannot be underestimated. Potential when positive is valued when it comes from family in a lasting way. If this seems obvious as much as bringing a number two pencil to the test it is not practiced enough. We all know the damage of labeling child. They live up to labels many times rather than shaking them. The dinner table is where families would speak of these issues. Perhaps we should spend a percentage of our week dedicated to thinking of how we can motivate parents. What lesson plan have you ever written that incorporates these thoughts? If we have identified this as one of the problems, the teacher –parent motivation link, what cohesive plan do we have to make progress? Email is one way to send out messages that is done more and more. Parents like this method of communication as one of many ways to keep current.

Things do not always work out as planned and it is family that seems to understand better than anybody else. The comfort to deal with life's ups and down is a large part of the family responsibility. I am not suggesting that it is exclusively their responsibility but rather they have impact with this issue.

My Dad claims to have been a C plus student. He was taught in college by the Jesuits and his moral development was superior. That message came through to me by his example. He tells me he took twelve years of Latin. By his example education was valued. I was not allowed to be dummy. He wanted me to take the harder courses. Note the family influence in what curriculum to follow. How do we as teachers work with parents so they put more thought into what classes their children take?

It was better to try the challenge than to miss the experience. Improvement was always the path. Attitude creates altitude is something that has been correctly stated. It is all about improvement. Most improved awards hold a place as high as most outstanding student award because it is not implied that the most outstanding student gave his or her best.

Perceptions of what a teacher is comes from the past. Family is the past, present, and future of a child. You will only be privileged to know the child one year but be in their memories for a lifetime. You are next year's teacher link.

Parent's consistency of involvement makes all the difference; one time it can be a ballgame, next a visit to the guidance department, or bringing your child to school with all their projects in tow.

How are things changing for today's student?

Where did educational information come from to educate those born in the half quarter of the 1900's? Walter Cronkite covered D-Day and delivered the nightly news for 40 years. His tag line is "And that's the way it is". He took us through the Kennedy assassination and the Regan presidential election. From 1962 to 1981 he anchored the CBS Evening news. Most of you taking the teacher certification test will be the direct descendents of the Walter Cronkite generation. You may have watched TV or read books and carried a book in your back pocket.

What is different today is that there has been a media explosion. There are more TV channels, web sites, and magazines then you could ever read. Access is not the issue. The question is do they spend any time absorbing the material? Isn't that what the family experiences I described above provided? Contrast that with AOL news which is headlines and graphics to skim. News on TV is brief and sound-bites expose but do not develop complete and integrated understanding.

When towns go to only one newspaper the dangerous trend can limit our ability to have understanding of all sides of the issues. With overcrowding in our schools do students have the opportunity to absorb more meaning to the material or are they just skimming more material posed in chapters of ever increasing and competitive world of publishing? Are families working so hard that they can't get to their kids ballgames or see the teachers and collaborate anymore. No, you must not let that happen. The purpose of these last few pages was to let you see my vision of just how important life is, and how precious this union between schools, parents, and students are on their educational identity.

So, as you begin to review content for the teacher certification test you will become certified. You are the system. Education needs to be absorbed and analyzed and criticized so that it may be applied to lives with meaning. The alternative is just a bunch of facts. Life is about love and your career as teacher will glow when you do not take the place of family but become part of their families for a year.

About XAM Publishing
<u>The Difference is Clear</u>

XAM states that **THE DIFFERENCE IS CLEAR**. Our only products are for teacher certification and therefore we are branding our name on being the specialist in certification at a realistic detailed level. If you have a question you may call our company directly and speak to us. We hope you will find it refreshing to find a company that can answer most of your certification questions without referral. Official written notification of your personal certification requirements come directly from the Department of Education for your state. Please be sure you are taking the correct tests for that particular state.

THE DIFFERENCE IS CLEAR that XAM guides develop one study guide for almost every subject category for the PRAXIS II single subject tests. One book will only have one subject with all the various undergraduate components listed as topics.

THE DIFFERENCE IS CLEAR because XAM target market is identifiable and selective. XAM is trying to refresh teacher candidates that are fully qualified to sit for tests and simply want the voluminous amount of material collected for them. For those candidates the material is hopefully easy. XAM hopes you say more often than not, "I remember that". If there is a weakness in one section of your background we provide more in depth guides for the following subjects at www.XAMonline.com you may find it helpful to at least go on line where we provide the table of contents for free.

Humanities (Fine Arts)	ISBN 158197-0285
Social Science	ISBN 158197-017x
English	ISBN 158197-0552
Math	ISBN 158197-0153
General Science	ISBN 158197-0544

Teachers who have opted out for a few years and are now returning to the profession will find the material challenging but achievable. You stand to gain the most points from using this type of material

Alternative teachers with good content knowledge will perhaps be strong in several areas but weak in others. XAM makes study guides at the middle school level available online, at XAMonline.com that can go farther than this text. Professors are encouraged to list this ISBN for your students to purchase along with senior level coursework. Additionally, since actual teaching experience is not in the alternative teacher's educational background we highly recommend getting ISBN 158197-0048 Principals of Learning and Teaching. Special education is ISBN158197-0021.

Elementary Education for Praxis are similar to other individual state tests .

Test name	Field 0011:
Number of questions	110 questions
Time	2 hours
Format :	Multiple Choice

Content Categories

1. Reading and language arts, curriculum, instruction, and assessment	38 questions
2. Math curriculum, instruction, and assessment	22 questions
3. Science curriculum, instruction, and assessment	11 questions
4. Social Studies, curriculum, instruction and assessment	11 questions
5. Arts and Physical Education curriculum, instruction, and assessment	11 questions
6. General information about curriculum, instruction, and assessment	17 questions

You will see other formats such as four essays in 0012 or a different emphasis of content on 0014 but basically the above areas are the target topics.

COMPETENCY 1.0

READING

Helen Keller (1880 – 1968) was a deaf and blind woman famous for her exhilarating breakthrough with her teacher.

I was like an unconscious clod of earth. There was nothing in me except the instinct to eat, and drink, and sleep...Then suddenly, I knew not how or where or when, my brain felt the impact of another mind, and I awoke to language, to knowledge, to love... My teacher, Anne Mansfield Sullivan, had been with me nearly a month and she had taught me the names of a number of objects. She put them into my hand, spelled their names on her fingers and helped me to form the letters; but I had not the faintest idea what I was doing... One day she handed me a cup and formed the letters w-a-t-e-r, she said I looked puzzled and persisted in confusing the two words, spelling cup for water and water for cup... In despair she led me out to the ivy covered pump house and made me hold the cup under the spout while she pumped. With her other hand she spelled w-a-t-e-r emphatically. I stood still, my whole body's attention fixed on the motions of her fingers as the cool stream flowed over my hand. All at once there was a sense of something remembered. It was as if I had come back to life after being dead. I understood that what my teacher was doing with her fingers meant that the cold something that was rushing over my hand was water; and with other people by these hand signs...That first revelation was worth all those years I had spent in the dark, soundless imprisonment. That word water dropped into my mind like the sun in a frozen winter world.

Helen Keller

COMPETENCY 1.0 UNDERSTAND SKILLS AND STRAGIES INVOLVED IN READING FOR VARIOUS PURPOSES

SKILL 1.1   Understanding the stated or implied main idea of a passage

The main idea of a passage or paragraph is the basic message, idea, point concept, or meaning that the author wants to convey to you, the reader. Understanding the main idea of a passage or paragraph is the key to understanding the more subtle components of the author's message. The main idea is what is being said about a topic or subject. Once you have identified the basic message, you will have an easier time answering other questions that test critical skills.

Main ideas are either *stated* or *implied*. A *stated main idea* is explicit: it is directly expressed in a sentence or two in the paragraph or passage. An *implied main idea* is suggested by the overall reading selection. In the first case, you need not pull information from various points in the paragraph or passage in order to form the main idea because it is already stated by the author. If a main idea is implied, however, you must formulate, in your own words, a main idea statement by condensing the overall message contained in the material itself.

SKILL 1.2   Analyze the use of language to create a mood in a given passage

The *tone* of a written passage is the author's attitude toward the subject matter. The tone (mood, feeling) is revealed through the qualities of the writing itself and is a direct product of such stylistic elements as language and sentence structure. The tone of the written passage is much like a speaker's voice; instead of being spoken, however, it is the product of words on a page.

Often, writers have an emotional stake in the subject; and their purpose, either explicitly or implicitly, is to convey those feelings to the reader. In such cases, the writing is generally subjective: that is, it stems from opinions, judgments, values, ideas, and feelings. Both sentence structure (syntax) and word choice (diction) are instrumental tools in creating tone.

Tone may be thought of generally as positive, negative, or neutral. Below is a statement about snakes that demonstrates this.

   Many species of snakes live in Florida. Some of those species, both poisonous and non-poisonous, have habitats that coincide with those of human residents of the state.

The voice of the writer in this statement is neutral. The sentences are declarative (not exclamations or fragments or questions). The adjectives are few and nondescript—*many, some, poisonous* (balanced with *non-poisonous*). Nothing much in this brief paragraph would alert the reader to the feelings of the writer about snakes. The paragraph has a neutral, objective, detached, impartial tone.

Then again, if the writer's attitude toward snakes involves admiration or even affection the tone would generally be positive:

> *Florida's snakes are a tenacious bunch. When they find their habitats invaded by humans, they cling to their home territories as long as they can, as if vainly attempting to fight off the onslaught of the human hordes.*

An additional message emerges in this paragraph: The writer quite clearly favors snakes over people. The writer uses adjectives like *tenacious* to describe his/her feelings about snakes. The writer also humanizes the reptiles, making them brave, beleaguered creatures. Obviously the writer is more sympathetic to snakes than to people in this paragraph.

If the writer's attitude toward snakes involves active dislike and fear, then the tone would also reflect that attitude by being negative:

> *Countless species of snakes, some more dangerous than others, still lurk on the Urban fringes of Florida's towns and cities. They will often invade domestic spaces terrorizing people and their pets.*

Here, obviously, the snakes are the villains. They *lurk,* they *invade*, and they *terrorize.* The tone of this paragraph might be said to be distressed about snakes.

In the same manner, a writer can use language to portray characters as good or bad. A writer uses positive and negative adjectives, as seen above, to convey the manner of a character.

COMPETENCY 2.0

READING INSTRUCTION

My heart is singing for joy this morning. A miracle has happened! The light of understanding has shone upon my little pupil's mind, and behold, all things are changed!

Anne Sullivan, Helen Keller's Teacher

" "Scholarly" "

 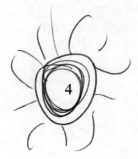

COMPETENCY 2.0 UNDERSTANDING THE SKILLS AND STRATEGIES INVOLVED IN TEACHING READING

SKILL 2.1   Beginning reading approaches

Methods of teaching beginning reading skills may be divided into two major Approaches—code-emphasis and meaning emphasis. Both approaches have their supporters and their critics. Advocates of code-emphasis instruction point Out that reading fluency depends of accurate and automatic decoding skills, while advocates of meaning emphasis favor this approach for teaching comprehension. Teachers may decide to blend aspects of both approaches to meet the individual needs of their students.

Bottom-up or Code Emphasis Approach:

- Letter-sound regularity is stressed.

- Reading instruction begins with words that consist of letter or letter combinations that have the same sound in different words. Component letter-sound relationships are taught and mastered before introducing new words.

- **Examples**—phonics, linguistic, modified alphabet, and programmed reading series such as the Merrill Linguistic Reading Program and DISTAR Reading

Top-Down or Meaning-Emphasis Model

- Reading for meaning is emphasized from the first stages of instruction

- Programs begin with words that appear frequently, which are assumed to be familiar and easier to learn. Words are identified by examining meaning and position in context and are decoded by techniques such as context, pictures, initial letters, and word configurations. Thus, a letter may not necessarily have the same sound in different words throughout the story.

- **Examples**: Whole language, language experience, and individualized reading programs.

Other approaches that follow beginning reading instruction are available to help teacher's design reading programs. Choice of approach will depend on the student's strengths and weaknesses. No matter what approach or combination of approaches is used, the teacher should encourage independent reading and build activities into the reading program that stimulate students to practice their skills through independent reading.

ELEMENTARY EDUCATION   5

SKILL 2.2   Developmental reading approaches

Developmental reading programs emphasize daily, sequential instruction. Instructional materials usually feature a series of books, often basal readers, as the core of the program.

1. *Basal Reading*

Basal reader series form the core of many widely used reading programs from preprimers through eighth grade. Depending on the series, basals may be meaning-emphasis or code-emphasis. Teacher manuals provide a highly structured and comprehensive scope and sequence, lesson plans, and objectives. Vocabulary is controlled from level to level and reading skills cover word recognition, word attack, and comprehension.

Advantages of basal readers are the structured, sequential manner in which reading is taught. The teacher manuals have teaching strategies, controlled vocabulary, assessment materials, and objectives. Reading instruction is in a systematic, sequential, comprehension-oriented manner.

Many basal reading programs recommend the <u>directed reading activity procedure:</u> for lesson presentation. Students proceed through the steps of motivation, preparation for the new concepts and vocabulary, guided reading and answering questions that give a purpose or goal for the reading: development of strength's through drills or workbook, application of the skills, and evaluation.

A variation of the directed reading method is <u>directed reading-thinking,</u> where the student must generate the purposes for reading the selection, form questions, and read the selection. After reading, the teacher asks questions designed to get the group to think of answers and justify the answers.

Disadvantages of basal readers are the emphasis on teaching to a group rather than the individual. Critics of basal readers claim that the structure may limit creativity and not provide enough instruction on organizational skills and reading for secondary content levels. Basals, however, offer the advantage of a prepared comprehensive program, and may be supplemented with other materials to meet individual needs.

2. *Phonics Approach*

Word recognition is taught through grapheme-phoneme associations, with the goal of teaching the student to independently apply these skills to new words. Phonics instruction may be synthetic or analytic. In synthetic method, letter sounds are learned first before the student goes on to blending the sounds to form words. The analytic method teaches letter sounds as integral parts of words.

The sounds are usually taught in the sequence: vowels, consonants, consonant blends at the beginning of words (e/g/. b; and dr), and consonant blends at the ends of words (e.g., ld and mp), consonant and vowel digraphs (e.g., ch and sh), and diphthongs (au, oy).

Critics of the phonics approach point out that the emphasis on pronunciation may lead to the student focusing more on decoding that comprehension. Some students may have trouble blending sounds to form words, and others my become confused with words that do not conform to the phonetic "rules". However, advocates of phonics say that the programs are useful with remedial reading and developmental reading. Examples of phonics series are Science Research Associates' *Merrill Phonics* and DLM's *Cove School Reading Program*.

3. *Linguistics Approach*

In many programs, the whole-word approach is used, meaning that words are taught in word families and as a whole (e.g., cat, hat, rat, pat). The focus is on words instead of isolated sounds. Words are chosen on the basis of similar spelling patterns and irregular spelling words are taught as sight words. Examples of programs using the linguistics approach are SRA *Basic Reading Series* and *Miami Linguistic Readers* by D.C. Heath.

Some advantages of this approach are that the student learns that reading is talk written down, and develops a sense of sentence structure. The consistent visual patterns of the lessons guide students from familiar words to semi-regular to irregular words. Reading is taught by association with the student's natural knowledge of his own language. Disadvantages are the extremely controlled vocabulary and word by word reading is encouraged. Others criticize the programs for the emphasis on auditory memory skills and the use of nonsense words in the practice exercises.

4. *Whole Language Approach*

In the whole language approach, reading is taught as a holistic, meaning-oriented activity and is not broken down into a collection of skills. This approach relies heavily on literature or printed matter selected for a particular purpose. Reading is taught as part of a total language arts program, and the curriculum seeks to develop instruction in real problems and ideas. Two examples of whole language programs are *Learning through Literature* (Dodds & Goodfellow) and *Victory!* (Brigance)

Phonics is not taught in a structured, systematic way. Students are assumed to develop their phonetic awareness through exposure to print. Writing is taught as a complement to reading. Writing centers are often part of this program as students learn to write their own stories and read them back, or follow along a cassette of a book while reading along with it.

While the integration of reading with writing is an advantage of the whole language approach, the approach has been criticized for the lack of direct instruction in specific skill strategies. For students with learning problems, more direct instruction may be needed to help students learn the word recognition skills necessary to achieve comprehension.

5.   *Language Experience Approach*

The language experience approach is similar to whole language in that reading is considered as a personal act, literature is emphasized, and students are encouraged to write about their own life experiences. The major difference is that written language is considered a secondary system to oral language, while whole language sees the two as structurally related. Language experience approach is used primarily with beginning readers, but can also be used with older elementary and with older students for corrective instruction. Reading skills are developed along with listening, speaking, and writing skills. The materials are made up of the student's experiences. The philosophy of language experience states:

*   What students think about, they can talk about
*   What students say, they can write or have someone write
*   What students have written or have written for them, they can read.

Development of a language experience story follows this sequence:

Students dictate a story to the teacher in a group activity. Ideas for stories can originate from students' artwork, news events, personal experiences, or creative ideas. Topic lists, word cards, or idea lists can also be used to generate topics and ideas for a class story.

The teacher writes down the story in a first draft and the students read them back. The language patterns are the patterns of the students, and they learn to read their own written thoughts. The teacher provides guidance on word choice, sentence structure, and the sounds of the letters and words.

The students edit and revise their story on an experience chart. The teacher provides specific instruction in grammar, sentence structure, and spelling when the need appears, rather than using a specified schedule.

As the students progress, they create their individual story books, adding illustrations if they choose. The story books are placed in folders to share with others. Progress is evaluated in terms of the changes in the oral and written expression, as well as mechanics. There is no set method of evaluation student progress, which is one disadvantage of language experience. However, the emphasis on student experiences and creativity stimulates interest and motivation, which is an advantage of the approach.

6. *Individualized Reading Approach*

The students select their own reading materials from a variety of materials according to interest and ability, progress is self paced. Word recognition and comprehension are taught, as the student needs them. The teacher's role is to diagnose errors and prescribe materials, although the final choice is up to the student. The individual work can be supplemented by group activities with basal readers and workbooks for specific reading skills. The lack of systematic check of developmental skills and emphasis on self-learning may be a disadvantage for students with learning problems.

SKILL 2.3 **Recognize the hierarchy of the developmental stages of reading in instruction.**

During the preschool years, children acquire cognitive skills in oral language that they apply later on to reading comprehension. Reading aloud to young children is one of the most important things that an adult can do because they are teaching children how to monitor, question, predict, and confirm what they hear in the stories. Reid (1988, p. 165) described four metalinguistic abilities that young children acquire through early involvement in reading activities:

1. *Word consciousness.* Children who have access to books first can tell the story through the pictures. Gradually they begin to realize the connection between the spoken words and the printed words. The beginning of letter and word discrimination begins in the early years.
2. *Language and conventions of print.* During this stage children learn the way to hold a book, where to begin to read, the left to right motion, and how to continue from one line to another.

3. *Functions of print.* Children discover that print can be used for a variety of purposes and functions, including entertainment and information.

4. *Fluency.* Through listening to adult models, children learn to read in phrases and use intonation.

Mercer and Mercer divide the reading experience into two basic processes: word recognition and word and idea comprehension. Reading programs may differ in how and when these skills are presented.

WORD RECOGNITION	WORD AND IDEA COMPREHENSION
Configuration	Vocabulary Development
Content Analysis	Literal Comprehension
Sight Words	Inferential Comprehension
Phonics Analysis	Evaluation or Critical Reading
Syllabication	Appreciation
Structural Analysis	
Dictionary Analysis	

SKILL 2.4   Constructing meaning from text

The purpose of reading is to convert visual images (the letters and words) into a message. Pronouncing the words is not enough; the reader must be able to extract the meaning of the text. When people read, they utilize four sources of background information to comprehend the meaning behind the literal text (Reid, p. 166-171).

1. *Word Knowledge:* Information about words and letters. One's knowledge about word meanings is *lexical knowledge*—a sort of dictionary. Knowledge about spelling patterns and pronunciations is *orthographic knowledge.* Poor readers do not develop the level of automatically in using orthographic knowledge to identify words and decode unfamiliar words.

2. *Syntax and Contextual Information.* When children encounter unknown words in a sentence, they rely on their background knowledge to choose a word that makes sense. Errors of younger children therefore are often substitutions of words in the same syntactic class. Poor readers often fail to make use of context clues to help them identify words or activate the background knowledge that would help them with comprehension. Poor readers also process sentences word by word, instead of "chunking" phrases and clauses, resulting in a slow pace that focuses on the decoding rather than comprehension. They also have problems answering wh-(Who, what, where, when, why) questions as a result of these problems with syntax.

3. *Semantic Knowledge:* This includes the reader's background knowledge about a topic, which is combined with the text information as the reader tries to comprehend the material. New information is compared to the background information and incorporated into the reader's schema. Poor readers have problems with using their background knowledge, especially with passages that require inference or cause-and-effect.

4. *Text Organization:* Good readers are able to differentiate types of text structure, e.g., story narrative, exposition, compare-contrast, or time sequence. They use knowledge of text to build expectations and construct a framework of ideas on which to build meaning. Poor readers may not be able to differentiate types of text and miss important ideas. They may also miss important ideas and details by concentrating on lesser or irrelevant details.

SKILL 2.5   Characteristics of good readers

Research on reading development has yielded information of the behaviors and habits of good readers vs. poor readers. Some of the characteristics of good readers are:

*   They think about the information that they will read in the text, formulate questions that they predict will be answered in the text, and confirm those predictions from the information in the text.

*   When faced with unfamiliar words, they attempt to pronounce them using analogies to familiar words.

*   Before reading, good readers establish a purpose for reading, select possible text structure, choose a reading strategy, and make predictions about what will be in the reading.

*   As they read, good readers continually test and confirm their predictions, go back when something does not make sense, and make new predictions.

COMPETENCY 3.0

LANGUAGE ARTS

It is the supreme art of the teacher to awaken joy in creating expression and knowledge.

Albert Einstein

COMPETENCY 3.0 APPLY VOCABULARY SKILLS TO DETERMINE THE MEANING OF WORDS IN GIVEN CONTEXT

SKILL 3.1   Using word structure or context to determine the meaning or meanings of an unfamiliar word

Word meanings in context are definitions that you determine based on information from the surrounding text, such as other words, phrases, sentences and/or paragraphs.

You can use words you already know to pieces together possible meanings. You can use root words, antonyms, and word forms to help determine the meaning of an unfamiliar word.

Root words

Look at word parts to determine the meaning if you are stumped. For example:

> If you learn that _chronological order_ means arranged by order of occurrence in time, and you know that _speedometer_ measures speed, you know that a _chronometer_ is an instrument for measuring time.

Antonyms

Sometimes antonyms, opposites or contrasts, can illuminate the meaning of an unfamiliar word. For example:

> If you know that something _delayed_ arrives late, then you can determine the meaning of _expedite_ in the following sentence: _To avoid the delay, Julius sent the package months early to expedite its arrival._

Word forms

Sometimes a very familiar word can appear as a different part of speech, as in the examples below:

> You may have heard that _fraud_ involves a criminal misrepresentation, so when it appears as the adjective form _fraudulent_ ("He was suspected of fraudulent activities") you can make an educated guess.

> You probably know that something out of date is _obsolete_; therefore, when you read about "built in _obsolescence_," you can detect the meaning of the unfamiliar word.

SKILL 3.2   Using context clues to determine the intended meaning of a word with multiple meanings

The context for a word is the written passage that surrounds it. Sometimes the writer offers synonyms—words that have nearly the same meaning. Context clues can appear within the sentence itself, within the preceding and/or following sentence(s), or in the passage as a whole.

Sentence clues

Definition
Often, a writer will actually define a difficult or particularly important word for you the first time it appears in a passage. Phrases like *that is, such as, which is,* or *is called* might announce the writer's intention to give just the definition you need. Occasionally, a writer will simply use a synonym (a word that means the same thing) or near-synonym joined by the word *or*. Look at the following examples:

> The <u>credibility</u>, *that is to say the believability, of the witness was called into question by evidence of previous perjury.*

> *Nothing would <u>assuage</u> or lessen the child's grief.*

Punctuation

Punctuation at the sentence level is often a clue to the meaning of a word. Commas, parentheses, quotation marks and dashes tell the reader that a definition is being offered by the writer.

> *A tendency toward <u>hyperbole</u>, extravagant exaggeration, is a common flaw among persuasive writers.*

> *Political <u>apathy</u>—lack of interest—can lead to the death of the state.*

Explanation

A writer might simply give an explanation in other words that you can understand, in the same sentence:

> *The <u>xenophobic</u> townspeople were suspicious of every foreigner.*

Writers also explain a word in terms of its opposite at the sentence level:

> *His <u>incarceration</u> was ended, and he was elated to be out of jail.*

Adjacent sentence clues

The context for a word goes beyond the sentence in which it appears. At times, the writer uses adjacent (adjoining) sentences to present an explanation or definition:

> *The 200 dollars for the car repair would have to come out of the <u>contingency</u> fund. Fortunately, Angela's father had taught her to keep some money set aside for just such emergencies.*

> Analysis: The second sentence offers a clue to the definition of *contingency* as used in this sentence: "emergencies." Therefore, a fund for contingencies would be money tucked away for unforeseen and/or urgent events.

Entire passage clues

On occasion, you must look at an entire paragraph or passage to figure out the definition of a word or term. In the following paragraph, notice how the word *nostalgia* undergoes a form of extended definition throughout the selection rather than in just one sentence.

> *The word <u>nostalgia</u> links Greek words for "away from home" and "pain." If you're feeling <u>nostalgic</u>, then, you are probably in some physical distress or discomfort, suffering from a feeling of alienation and separation from love ones or loved places. <u>Nostalgia</u> is that awful feeling you remember the first time you went away to camp or spent the weekend with a friend's family—homesickness, or some condition even more painful than that. But in common use, <u>nostalgia</u> has come to have more sentimental associations. A few years back, for example, a <u>nostalgia</u> craze had to do with the 1950s. We resurrected poodle skirts and saddle shoes, built new restaurants to look like old ones, and tried to make chicken a la king just as mother probably never made it. In TV situation comedies, we recreated a pleasant world that probably never existed and relished our <u>nostalgia</u>, longing for a homey, comfortable lost time.*

COMPETENCY 4.0

LITERATURE

The mediocre teacher tells. The good teacher explains. The superior teacher demonstrates. The great teacher inspires.

William Arthur Ward

COMPETENCY 4.0 UNDERSTAND LITERATURE FR0M AROUND THE WORLD

SKILL 4.1   Understanding differences among genres of literature

The major literary genres include allegory, ballad, drama, epic, epistle, essay, fable, novel, poem, romance, and the short story.

Allegory: A story in verse or prose with characters representing virtues and vices. There are two meanings, symbolic and literal. John Bunyan's *The Pilgrim's Progress* is the most renowned of this genre.

Ballad: An *in media res* story told or sung, usually in verse and accompanied by music. Literary devices found in ballads include the refrain, or repeated section, and incremental repetition, or anaphora, for effect. Earliest forms were anonymous folk ballads. Later forms include Coleridge's Romantic masterpiece, "The Rime of the Ancient Mariner."

Drama: Plays – comedy, modern, or tragedy - typically in five acts. Traditionalists and neoclassicists adhere to Aristotle's unities of time, place and action. Plot development is advanced via dialogue. Literary devices include asides, soliloquies and the chorus representing public opinion. Greatest of all dramatists/playwrights is William Shakespeare. Other dramaturges include Ibsen, Williams, Miller, Shaw, Stoppard, Racine, Moliére, Sophocles, Aeschylus, Euripides, and Aristophanes.

Epic: Long poem usually of book length reflecting values inherent in the generative society. Epic devices include an invocation to a Muse for inspiration, purpose for writing, universal setting, protagonist and antagonist who possess supernatural strength and acumen, and interventions of a God or the gods. Understandably, there are very few epics: Homer's *Iliad* and *Odyssey*, Virgil's *Aeneid*, Milton's *Paradise Lost*, Spenser's *The Fairie Queene*, Barrett Browning's *Aurora Leigh*, and Pope's mock-epic, *The Rape of the Lock*.

Epistle: A letter that is not always originally intended for public distribution, but due to the fame of the sender and/or recipient, becomes public domain. Paul wrote epistles that were later placed in the <u>Bible</u>.

Essay: Typically a limited length prose work focusing on a topic and propounding a definite point of view and authoritative tone. Great essayists include Carlyle, Lamb, DeQuincy, Emerson and Montaigne, who is credited with defining this genre.

Fable: Terse tale offering up a moral or exemplum. Chaucer's "The Nun's Priest's Tale" is a fine example of a *bete fabliau* or beast fable in which animals speak and act characteristically human, illustrating human foibles.

Legend: A traditional narrative or collection of related narratives, popularly regarded as historically factual but actually a mixture of fact and fiction.

Myth: Stories that are more or less universally shared within a culture to explain its history and traditions.

Novel: The longest form of fictional prose containing a variety of characterizations, settings, local color and regionalism. Most have complex plots, expanded description, and attention to detail. Some of the great novelists include Austin, the Brontes, Twain, Tolstoy, Hugo, Hardy, Dickens, Hawthorne, Forster, and Flaubert.

Poem: The only requirement is rhythm. Sub-genres include fixed types of literature such as the sonnet, elegy, ode, pastoral, and villanelle. Unfixed types of literature include blank verse and dramatic monologue.

Romance: A highly imaginative tale set in a fantastical realm dealing with the conflicts between heroes, villains and/or monsters. "The Knight's Tale" from Chaucer's *Canterbury Tales*, *Sir Gawain and the Green Knight* and Keats' "The Eve of St. Agnes" are prime representatives.

Short Story: Typically a terse narrative, with less developmental background about characters. May include description, author's point of view, and tone. Poe emphasized that a successful short story should create one focused impact. Great short story writers include: Hemingway, Faulkner, Twain, Joyce, Shirley Jackson, Flannery O'Connor, de Maupasssant, Saki, Edgar Allen Poe, and Pushkin.

SKILL 4.2   Recognizing characteristic features of works of well-known authors or works associated with a given place and time

There are four major time periods of writings. They are neoclassicism, romanticism, realism, and naturalism. Certain authors, among these Chaucer, Shakespeare, Whitman, Dickinson, and Donne, though writing during a particular literary period, are considered to have a style all their own.

Neoclassicism: Patterned after the greatest writings of classical Greece and Rome, this type of writing is characterized by balanced, graceful, well-crafted, refined, elevated style. Major proponents of this style are poet laureates, John Dryden and Alexander Pope. The eras in which they wrote are called the Ages of Dryden and Pope. The self is not exalted and focus is on the group, not the individual, in neoclassic writing.

Romanticism: Writings emphasizing the individual. Emotions and feelings are validated. Nature acts as an inspiration for creativity; it is a balm of the spirit. Romantics hearken back to medieval, chivalric themes and ambiance. They also emphasize supernatural, Gothic themes and settings, which are characterized by gloom and darkness. Imagination is stressed. New types of writings include detective and horror stories (Poe) and autobiographical introspection (Wordsworth and Thoreau). There are two generations in British Literature: First Generation includes William Wordsworth and Samuel Taylor Coleridge whose collaboration, *Lyrical Ballads*, defines romanticism and its exponents. Wordsworth maintained that the scenes and events of everyday life and the speech of ordinary people were the raw material of which poetry could and should be made. Romanticism spread to the United States, where Ralph Waldo Emerson and Henry David Thoreau adopted it in their transcendental romanticism, emphasizing reasoning. Further extensions of this style are found in Edgar Allan Poe's Gothic writings. Second Generation romantics include the ill-fated Englishmen Lord Byron, John Keats, and Percy Bysshe Shelley. Lord Byron and Percy Bysshe Shelley, who for some most typify the romantic poet (in their personal lives as well as in their work), wrote resoundingly in protest against social and political wrongs and in defense of the struggles for liberty in Italy and Greece. The Second Generation romantics stressed personal introspection and the love of beauty and nature as requisites of inspiration.

Muckracking?

Realism: Unlike classical and neoclassical writing, which often deal with aristocracies and nobility or the gods, realistic writers deal with the common man and his socio/economic problems in a non-sentimental way. Muckraking, social injustice, domestic abuse, and inner city conflicts are examples of writings by writers of realism. Realistic writers include Stephen Crane, Ernest Hemingway, Thomas Hardy, George Bernard Shaw, and Henrik Ibsen.

Naturalism: This is realism pushed to the maximum, writing which exposes the underbelly of society, usually the lower class struggles. This is the world of penury, injustice, abuse, ghetto survival, hungry children, single parenting, and substance abuse. Émile Zola was inspired by his readings in history and medicine and attempted to apply methods of scientific observation to the depiction of pathological human character, notably in his series of novels devoted to several generations of one French family.

Literature also varies by the author's location and heritage. Below are several different examples of locations throughout the world and their well-known authors and their literature accomplishments.

Central American/Caribbean Literature

The Caribbean and Central America encompass a vast area and cultures that reflect oppression and colonialism by England, Spain, Portugal, France, and The Netherlands. The Caribbean writers include Samuel Selvon from Trinidad and Armado Valladres from Cuba. Central American authors include the novelist, Gabriel Garcia Marquez, (*A Hundred Years of Solitude*) from Columbia, as well as the 1990 Nobel Prize winning poet, Octavia Paz, (*The Labyrinth of Solitude*) from Mexico and feminist Rosarian Castillanos (*The Nine Guardians*), also Mexican. Carlos Solorzano, a dramatist, whose plays include Dona Beatriz, The Hapless, The Magician, and The Hands of God, represents Guatemala.

South American Literature

Chilean Gabriela Mistral was the first Latin American writer to win the Nobel Prize for literature. She is best known for her collections of poetry, *Desolation* and *Feeling*. Chile was also home to Pablo Neruda who, in 1971, also won the Nobel Prize for literature for his poetry. His 29 volumes of poetry have been translated into more than 60 languages attesting to his universal appeal. *Twenty Love Poems* and *Song of Despair* are justly famous. Isabel Allende is carrying on the Chilean literary standards with her acclaimed novel, *House of Spirits*. Argentinean Jorge Luis Borges is considered by many literary critics to be the most important writer of this century from South America. His collections of short stories, *Ficciones*, brought him universal recognition. Also from Argentina,

Silvina Ocampo, a collaborator with Borges on a collection of poetry, is famed for her poetry and short story collections, which include *The Fury* and *The Days of the Night*.

Noncontinental European Literature

Horacio Quiroga represents Uruguay, and Brazil has Joao Guimaraes Rosa, whose novel, *The Devil to Pay*, is considered first rank world literature.

Continental European Literature

The Anglo-Saxon period spans six centuries but produced only a smattering of literature. The first British epic is *Beowulf,* anonymously written by Christian monks many years after the events in the narrative supposedly occurred. This Teutonic saga relates the triumph three times over monsters by the hero, Beowulf. "The Seafarer," a shorter poem, some history, and some riddles are the rest of the Anglo-Saxon canon.

The Medieval period introduces Geoffrey Chaucer, the father of English literature, whose *Canterbury Tales* are written in the vernacular, or street language of England, not in Latin. Thus, this famous story is said to be the first work of British literature. Next, Thomas Malory's *Le Morte d'Arthur* calls together the extant tales from Europe as well as England concerning the legendary King Arthur, Merlin, Guenevere, and the Knights of the Round Table. This work is the generative work that gave rise to the many Arthurian legends that stir the chivalric imagination.

The Renaissance, the most important period since it is synonymous with William Shakespeare, begins with importing the idea of the Petrarchan or Italian sonnet into England. Sir Thomas Wyatt and Sir Philip Sydney wrote English versions. Next, Sir Edmund Spenser invented a variation on this Italian sonnet form, aptly called the Spenserian sonnet. His masterpiece is the epic, *The* Fairie *Queene*, honoring Queen Elizabeth I's reign. He also wrote books on the Red Cross Knight, St. George and the Dragon, and a series of Arthurian adventures. Spencer was dubbed the Poet's Poet. He created a nine-line stanza, eight lines iambic pentameter and an extra-footed ninth line, an alexandrine. Thus, he invented the Spencerian stanza as well.

William Shakespeare, the Bard of Avon, wrote 154 sonnets, 39 plays, and two long narrative poems. The sonnets are justifiably called the greatest sonnet sequence in all of literature. Shakespeare dispensed with the octave/sestet format of the Italian sonnet and invented his three quatrains, one heroic couplet format. His plays are divided into comedies, history plays, and tragedies. Great lines from these plays are more often quoted than from any other author. The Big Four tragedies, Hamlet, *Macbeth*, *Othello*, and *King Lear* are acknowledged to be the most brilliant examples of this genre.

John Milton's devout Puritanism was the wellspring of his creative genius that closes the remarkable productivity of the English Renaissance. His social commentary in such works as *Aereopagitica*, *Samson Agonistes*, and his elegant sonnets would be enough to solidify his stature as a great writer. It is his masterpiece based in part on the Book of Genesis that places Milton very near the top of the rung of a handful of the most renowned of all writers. *Paradise Lost*, written in balanced, elegant Neoclassic form, truly does justify the ways of God to man. The greatest allegory about man's journey to the Celestial City (Heaven) was written at the end of the English Renaissance, as was John Bunyan's *The Pilgrim's Progress*, which describes virtues and vices personified. This work is, or was for a long time, second only to the *Bible* in numbers of copies printed and sold.

The Jacobean Age gave us the marvelously witty and cleverly constructed conceits of John Donne's metaphysical sonnets and, as well as his insightful meditations, his version of sermons or homilies. "Ask not for whom the bell tolls", and "No man is an island unto himself" are famous epigrams from Donne's *Meditations*. His most famous conceit is that which compares lovers to a footed compass traveling seemingly separate, but always leaning towards one another and conjoined in "A Valediction Forbidding Mourning."

Ben Johnson, author of the wickedly droll play, *Volpone,* and the Cavalier *carpe diem* poets Robert Herrick, Sir John Suckling, and Richard Lovelace also wrote during King James I's reign.

The Restoration and Enlightenment reflect the political turmoil of the regicide of Charles I, the Interregnum Puritan government of Oliver Cromwell, and the restoring of the monarchy to England by the coronation of Charles II, who had been given refuge by the French King Louis. Neoclassicism became the preferred writing style, especially for Alexander Pope. New genres, such as *The Diary of Samuel Pepys*, the novels of Daniel Defoe, the periodical essays and editorials of Joseph Addison and Richard Steele, and Alexander Pope's mock epic, *The Rape of the Lock*, demonstrate the diversity of expression during this time.

Writers who followed were contemporaries of Dr. Samuel Johnson, the lexicographer of *The Dictionary of the English Language*. Fittingly, this Age of Johnson, which encompasses James Boswell's biography of Dr. Johnson, Robert Burns' Scottish dialect and regionalism in his evocative poetry and the mystical pre-Romantic poetry of William Blake usher in the Romantic Age and its revolution against Neoclassicism.

The Romantic Age encompasses what is known as the First Generation Romantics, William Wordsworth and Samuel Taylor Coleridge, who collaborated on *Lyrical Ballads,* which defines and exemplifies the tenets of this style of writing. The Second Generation includes George Gordon, Lord Byron, Percy Bysshe Shelley, and John Keats. These poets wrote sonnets, odes, epics, and narrative poems, most dealing with homage to nature. Wordsworth's most famous other works are "Intimations on Immortality" and "The Prelude." Byron's satirical epic, *Don Juan*, and his autobiographical Childe

Harold's Pilgrimage are irreverent, witty, self-deprecating and, in part, cuttingly critical of other writers and critics. Shelley's odes and sonnets are remarkable for sensory imagery. Keats' sonnets, odes, and longer narrative poem, *The Eve of St. Agnes*, are remarkable for their introspection and the tender age of the poet, who died when he was only twenty-five. In fact, all of the Second Generation died before their times. Wordsworth, who lived to be eighty, outlived them all, as well as his friend and collaborator, Coleridge. Others who wrote during the Romantic Age are the essayist, Charles Lamb, and the novelist, Jane Austin. The Bronte sisters, Charlotte and Emily, wrote one novel each, which are noted as two of the finest ever written, *Jane Eyre* and *Wuthering* Heights. Marianne Evans, also known as George Eliot, wrote several important novels: her masterpiece, *Middlemarch*, and *Silas Marner*, *Adam Bede*, and *Mill on the Floss*.

The Victorian Period is remarkable for the diversity and proliferation of work in three major areas. Poets who are typified as Victorians include Alfred Lord Tennyson, who wrote *Idylls of the King*, twelve narrative poems about the Arthurian legend, and Robert Browning who wrote chilling dramatic monologues, such as "My Last Duchess," as well as long poetic narratives such as *The Pied Piper of Hamlin*. His wife Elizabeth wrote two major works, the epic feminist poem, *Aurora Leigh*, and her deeply moving and provocative *Sonnets* from *the Portuguese* in which she details her deep love for Robert and his startling, to her, reciprocation. Gerard Manley Hopkins, a Catholic priest, wrote poetry with sprung rhythm. (See Glossary of Literary Terms in 4.2). A. E. Housman, Matthew Arnold, and the Pre-Raphaelites, especially the brother and sister duo, Dante Gabriel and Christina Rosetti, contributed much to round out the Victorian Era poetic scene. The Pre-Raphaelites, a group of 19th-century English painters, poets, and critics reacted against Victorian materialism and the neoclassical conventions of academic art by producing earnest, quasi-religious works. Medieval and early Renaissance painters up to the time of the Italian painter Raphael inspired the group. Robert Louis Stevenson, the great Scottish novelist, wrote his adventure/history lessons for young adults. Victorian prose ranges from the incomparable, keenly woven plot structures of Charles Dickens to the deeply moving Dorset/Wessex novels of Thomas Hardy, in which women are repressed and life is more struggle than euphoria. Rudyard Kipling wrote about Colonialism in India in works like *Kim* and *The Jungle Book* that create exotic locales and a distinct main point concerning the Raj, the British Colonial government during Victoria's reign. Victorian drama is mainly a product of Oscar Wilde whose satirical masterpiece, *The Importance of Being Earnest*, farcically details and lampoons Victorian social mores.

The early twentieth century is mainly represented by the towering achievement of George Bernard Shaw's dramas: *St. Joan*, *Man and Superman*, *Major* Barbara, and *Arms and the Man* to name a few. Novelists are too numerous to list, but Joseph Conrad, E. M. Forster, Virginia Woolf, James Joyce, Nadine Gordimer, Graham Greene, George Orwell, and D. H. Lawrence comprise some of the century's very best.

Twentieth century poets of renown and merit include W. H. Auden, Robert Graves, T. S. Eliot, Edith Sitwell, Stephen Spender, Dylan Thomas, Philip Larkin, Ted Hughes, Sylvia Plath, and Hugh MacDarmid. This list is by no means complete.

Germany

German poet and playwright, Friedrich von Schiller, is best known for his history plays, *William Tell* and *The Maid of Orleans*. He is a leading literary figure in Germany's Golden Age of Literature. Also from Germany, Rainer Maria Rilke, the great lyric poet, is one of the poets of the unconscious, or stream of consciousness. Germany also has given the world Herman Hesse, (*Siddartha*), Gunter Grass (*The Tin Drum*), and the greatest of all German writers, Goethe.

Scandinavia

Scandinavia has encouraged the work of Hans Christian Andersen in Denmark who advanced the fairy tale genre with such wistful tales as "The Little Mermaid" and "Thumbelina." The social commentary of Henrik Ibsen in Norway startled the world of drama with such issues as feminism (*The Doll's House* and *Hedda Gabler*) and the effects of sexually transmitted diseases (The Wild Duck and *Ghosts*). Sweden's Selma Lagerlof is the first woman to ever win the Nobel Prize for literature. Her novels include *Gosta Berling's Saga* and the world-renowned *The Wonderful Adventures of Nils*, a children's work.

Russia

Russian literature is vast and monumental. Who has not heard of Fyodor Dostoyevski's *Crime and Punishment* or *The Brothers Karamazov*? These are examples of psychological realism. Dostoyevski's influence on modern writers cannot be overly stressed. Tolstoy's *War and Peace* is the sweeping account of the invasion of Russia and Napoleon's taking of Moscow, abandoned by the Russians. This novel is called the national novel of Russia. Further advancing Tolstoy's greatness is his ability to create believable, unforgettable female characters, especially Natasha in *War and Peace* and the heroine of *Anna Karenina* . Puskin is famous for great short stories; Anton Chekhov for drama, (*Uncle Vanya, The Three Sisters, The Cherry Orchard*); Yvteshenko for poetry (*Babi Yar*). Boris Pasternak won the Nobel Prize (*Dr. Zhivago*). Aleksandr Solzhenitsyn (*The Gulag Archipelago*) is only recently back in Russia after years of expatriation in Vermont. Ilya Varshavsky who creates fictional societies that are dystopias, or the opposite of utopias, represents the genre of science fiction.

France

France has a multifaceted canon of great literature that is universal in scope, almost always championing some social cause: the poignant short stories of Guy de Maupassant; the fantastic poetry of Charles Baudelaire (*Fleurs de Mal*); the groundbreaking lyrical poetry of Rimbaud and Verlaine; and the existentialism of Jean-Paul Sartre (*No Exit, The Flies, Nausea*), Andre Malraux, (*The Fall*), and Albert Camus (*The Stranger, The Plague*), the 1957 Nobel Prize for literature recipient. Drama in France is best represented by Rostand's *Cyrano de Bergerac*, and the neo-classical dramas of Racine and Corneille (*El Cid*). Feminist writings include those of Sidonie-Gabrielle Colette known for her short stories and novels, as well as Simone de Beauvoir. The great French novelists include Andre Gide, Honore de Balzac (*Cousin Bette*), Stendel (*The Red and the Black*), the father/son duo of Alexandre Dumas (*The Three Musketeers* and *The Man in the Iron Mask*. Victor Hugo is the Charles Dickens of French literature having penned the masterpieces, *The Hunchback of Notre Dame* and the French national novel, *Les Miserables*. The stream of consciousness of Proust's *Remembrance of Things Past*, and the Absurdist theatre of Samuel Beckett and Eugene Ianesco (*The Rhinoceros*) attest to the groundbreaking genius of the French writers.

Slavic nations

Austrian writer Franz Kafka (*The Metamorphosis, The Trial,* and *The Castle*) is considered by many to be the literary voice of the first-half of the twentieth century. Representing the Czech Republic is the poet Vaclav Havel. Slovakia has dramatist Karel Capek (*R.U.R*). Romania is represented by Elie Weisel (*Night*), a Nobel Prize winner.

Spain

Spain's great writers include Miguel de Cervantes (*Don Quixote*) and Juan Ramon Jimenez. The anonymous national epic, *El Cid*, has been translated into many languages.

Italy

Italy's greatest writers include Virgil, who wrote the great epic (The Aeneid); Giovanni Boccaccio (*The Decameron*); Dante Alighieri (*The Divine Comedy*); and Alberto Moravia.

Ancient Greece

Greece will always be foremost in literary assessments due to its Homer's epics, *The Iliad* and *The Odyssey*. No one, except Shakespeare, is more often cited. Add to these the works of Plato and Aristotle for philosophy; the dramatists Aeschylus, Euripides, and Sophocles for tragedy, and Aristophanes for comedy. Greece is not only the cradle of democracy, but of literature as well.

Africa

African literary greats include South Africans Nadine Gordimer (Nobel Prize for literature) and Peter Abrahams (*Tell Freedom: Memories of Africa*), an auto-biography of life in Johannesburg. Chinua Achebe (*Things Fall Apart*) and the poet, Wole Soyinka, hail from Nigeria. Mark Mathabane wrote an autobiography *Kaffir Boy* about growing up in South Africa. Egyptian writer, Naguib Mahfouz, and Doris Lessing from Rhodesia, now Zimbabwe, write about race relations in their respective countries. Because of her radical politics, Lessing was banned from her homeland and The Union of South Africa, as was Alan Paton whose seemingly simple story, *Cry, the Beloved Country*, brought the plight of blacks and the whites' fear of blacks under apartheid to the rest of the world.

Far East

Asia has many modern writers who are being translated for the western reading public. India's Krishan Chandar has authored over more than 300 stories. Rabindranath Tagore won the Nobel Prize for literature in 1913 (*Song Offerings*). Narayan, India's most famous writer (*The Guide*), is highly interested in mythology and legends of India. Santha Rama Rau's work, *Gifts of Passage*, is her true story of life in a British school where she tries to preserve her Indian culture and traditional home.

Revered as Japan's most famous female author, Fumiko Hayashi (*Drifting Clouds*) by the time of her death had written more than 270 literary works. The classical Age of Japanese literary achievement includes the father Kiyotsugu Kan ami and the son Motokkiyo Zeami who developed the theatrical experience known as No drama to its highest aesthetic degree. The son is said to have authored over 200 plays, of which 100 still are extant.

In 1968 the Nobel Prize for literature was awarded to Yasunari Kawabata (*The Sound of the Mountain, The Snow Country*) considered to be his masterpieces. His Palm-of-the-Hand Stories take the essentials of Haiku poetry and transform them into the short story genre.

Katai Tayama (*The Quilt*) is touted as the father of the genre known as the Japanese confessional novel. He also wrote in the "ism" of naturalism. His works are definitely not for the squeamish.

The "slice of life" psychological writings of Ryunosuke Akutagawa gained him acclaim in the western world. His short stories, especially "Rashamon" and "In a Grove," are greatly praised for style as well as content.

China, too, has given to the literary world. Li Po, the T'ang dynasty poet from the Chinese Golden Age, revealed his interest in folklore by preserving the folk songs and mythology of China. Po further allows his reader to enter into the Chinese philosophy of Taoism and to know this feeling against expansionism during the T'ang dynastic rule. Back to the T'ang dynasty, which was one of great diversity in the arts, the Chinese version of a short story was created with the help of Jiang Fang. His themes often express love between a man and a woman. Modern feminist and political concerns are written eloquently by Ting Ling, who used the pseudonym Chiang Ping-Chih. Her stories reflect her concerns about social injustice and her commitment to the women's movement.

COMPETENCY 5.0

CHILDREN'S LITERATURE

When someone is taught the joy of learning, it becomes a life-long process that never stops, a process that creates a logical individual. That is the challenge and joy of teaching.

Marva Collins

COMPETENCY 5.0 UNDERSTAND CHILDREN'S LITERATURE AND THEIR CHARACTERISTIC FEATURES

SKILL 5.1   Different genres in children's literature

Drama
Stories composed in verse or prose, usually for theatrical performance, where conflicts and emotion are expressed through dialogue and action.

Fable
Narration demonstrating a useful truth, especially in which animals speak as humans; legendary, supernatural tale.

Fairy Tale
Story about fairies or other magical creatures, usually for children.

Fantasy
Fiction with strange or other worldly settings or characters; fiction which invites suspension of reality.

Fiction
Narrative literary works whose content is produced by the imagination and is not necessarily based on fact.

Fiction in Verse
Full-length novels with plot, subplot(s), theme(s), major and minor characters, in which the narrative is presented in (usually blank) verse form.

Folklore
The songs, stories, myths, and proverbs of a people or "folk" as handed down by word of mouth.

Historical Fiction
Story with fictional characters and events in a historical setting.

Horror
Fiction in which events evoke a feeling of dread in both the characters and the reader.

Humor
Fiction full of fun, fancy, and excitement, meant to entertain; but can be contained in all genres.

Legend
Story, sometimes of a national or folk hero, which has a basis in fact but also includes imaginative material.

Mystery
Fiction dealing with the solution of a crime or the unraveling of secrets.

Mythology
Legend or traditional narrative, often based in part on historical events, that reveals human behavior and natural phenomena by its symbolism; often pertaining to the actions of the gods.

Poetry
Verse and rhythmic writing with imagery that creates emotional responses.

Realistic Fiction
Story that can actually happen and is true to life.

Science Fiction
Story based on impact of actual, imagined, or potential science, usually set in the future or on other planets.

Short Story
Fiction of such brevity that it supports no subplots.

Tall Tale
Humorous story with blatant exaggerations, swaggering heroes who do the impossible with nonchalance.

All Nonfiction

Biography/Autobiography
Narrative of a person's life, a true story about a real person.

Essay
A short literary composition that reflects the author's outlook or point.

Narrative Nonfiction
Factual information presented in a format which tells a story.

Nonfiction
Informational text dealing with an actual, real-life subject.

Speech
Public address or discourse.

SKILL 5.2   Various authors and types of children's literature

Alphabet book—A book that utilizes letters of the alphabet in different ways that may or may not tell a story. These books are often told in rhyme or alliteration.

DR. SUESS
Dr. Suess's ABC: An Amazing Alphabet Book

Classic—A book that has withstood the test of time and has been a favorite or readers for many years.

MAURICE SENDAK
Where the Wild Things Are

Concept book—An informational book that introduces a single concept such as shape, color, size, or numbers.

BILL MARTIN AND ERIC CARLE
Brown Bear, Brown Bear, What Do You See?

Counting book—A picture book that focuses on numbers and counting.

LOIS EHLERT
Fish Eyes: A Book You Can Count On

Early chapter book—Transitional fiction that is longer than a standard picture book, with fewer pictures. This type of book is generally written for grades 1-3.

MARY POPE OSBORNE
The Tree House Series

Easy reader—A book that is written for 1-2 grade levels in which phrases or sentences are repeated in the text in easily recognizable patterns.

STAN AND JAN BERENSTAIN
The Berenstain Bears & The Honey Tree
The Berenstain Bears Are A Family

Photo essay—A book that presents information on a concept or illustrates a story using photographs and text.

DORLING KINDERSLEY
My First Animal Book

Picture book—A book in which the message depends upon pictures as much or more than text.

MARGERY WILLIAMS
The Velveteen Rabbit

Read aloud—A book that works well with children when presented orally.

DR. SEUSS (THEODOR S. GEISEL)
The Cat In The Hat
Horton Hears A Who

Wordless book—A picture book that tells a story or presents material through pictures with very little or no text.

LUCY COUSINS
Flower in the Garden (My Cloth Book)

COMPETENCY 6.0

WRITING

Teachers can change lives with just the right mix of chalk and challenges.

Joyce A. Myers

COMPETENCY 6.0 UNDERSTAND SKILLS AND STRATEGIES INVOLVED IN WRITING FOR VARIOUS PURPOSES

SKILL 6.1 Analyzing factors a writer should consider when writing for a variety of audiences and purposes

In the past teachers have assigned reports, paragraphs and essays that focused on the teacher as the audience with the purpose of explaining information. However, for students to be meaningfully engaged in their writing, they must write for a variety of reasons. Writing for different audiences and aims allows students to be more involved in their writing. If they write for the same audience and purpose, they will continue to see writing as just another assignment. Listed below are suggestions that give students an opportunity to write in more creative and critical ways.

* Write letters to the editor, to a college, to a friend, to another student that would be sent to the intended audience.

* Write stories that would be read aloud to a group (the class, another group of students, to a group of elementary school students) or published in a literary magazine or class anthology.

* Write plays that would be performed.

* Have students discuss the parallels between the different speech styles we use and writing styles for different readers or audiences.

* Allow students to write a particular piece for different audiences.

* Make sure students consider the following when analyzing the needs of their audience.

    1. Why is the audience reading my writing? Do they expect to be informed, amused or persuaded?

    2. What does my audience already know about my topic?

    3. What does the audience want or need to know? What will interest them?

    4. What type of language suits my readers?

* As part of the prewriting have students identify the audience.

* Expose students to writing that is on the same topic but with a different audience and have them identify the variations in sentence structure and style.

* Remind your students that it is not necessary to identify all the specifics of the audience in the initial stage of the writing process but that at some point they must make some determinations about audience.

SKILL 6.2   Understand the steps and procedures associated with given components of the writing process

STAGES OF WRITING

Writing is a recursive process. As students engage in the various stages of writing, they develop and improve not only their writing skills, but their thinking skills as well. The stages of the writing process are as follows:

PREWRITING

Students gather ideas before writing. Prewriting may include clustering, listing, brainstorming, mapping, free writing, and charting. Providing many ways for a student to develop ideas on a topic will increase his/her chances for success.

WRITING

Students compose the first draft.

REVISING

Students examine their work and make changes in sentences, wording, details and ideas. Revise comes from the Latin word *revidere*, meaning, "to see again."

EDITING

Students proofread the draft for punctuation and mechanical errors.

PUBLISHING

Students may have their work displayed on a bulletin board, read aloud in class, or printed in a literary magazine or school anthology. It is important to realize that these steps are recursive; as a student engages in each aspect of the writing process, he or she may begin with prewriting, write, revise, write, revise, edit, and publish. They do not engage in this process in a lockstep manner; it is more circular.

TEACHING THE COMPOSING PROCESS

Prewriting Activities

1. Class discussion of the topic.
2. Map out ideas, questions, graphic organizers on the chalkboard.
3. Break into small groups to discuss different ways of approaching the topic and develop an organizational plan and create a thesis statement.
4. Research the topic if necessary.

Drafting/Revising

1. Students write first draft in class or at home.
2. Students engage in peer response and class discussion.
3. Using checklists or a rubric, students critique each other's writing and make suggestions for revising the writing.
4. Students revise the writing.

Editing and Proofreading

1. Students, working in pairs, analyze sentences for variety.
2. Students work in groups to read papers for punctuation and mechanics.
3. Students perform final edit.

SKILL 6.3   Understand the developmental stages of a writer

Remind students that as they pre-write they need to consider their audience. Prewriting strategies assist students in a variety of ways. Listed below are the most common prewriting strategies students can use to explore, plan and write on a topic. It is important to remember when teaching these strategies that not all prewriting must eventually produce a finished piece of writing. In fact, in the initial lesson of teaching prewriting strategies, it might be more effective to have students practice prewriting strategies without the pressure of having to write a finished product.

* Keep an idea book so that they can jot down ideas that come to mind.

* Write in a daily journal.

* Write down whatever comes to mind. This is called free writing. Students do not stop to make corrections or interrupt the flow of ideas. A variation of this technique is focused free writing - writing on a specific topic - to prepare for an essay.

* Make a list of all ideas connected with their topic; this is called brainstorming. Make sure students know that this technique works best when they let their mind work freely. After completing the list, students should analyze the list to see if a pattern or way to group the ideas.

* Ask the questions Who? What? When? Where? When? and How? Help the writer approach a topic from several perspectives.

* Create a visual map on paper to gather ideas. Cluster circles and lines to show connections between ideas. Students should try to identify the relationship that exists between their ideas. If they cannot see the relationships, have them pair up, exchange papers and have their partners look for some related ideas.

* Observe details of sight, hearing, taste, touch, and taste.

* Visualize by making mental images of something and write down the details in a list.

After they have practiced with each of these prewriting strategies, ask them to pick out the ones they prefer and ask them to discuss how they might use the techniques to help them with future writing assignments. It is important to remember that they can use more than one prewriting strategy at a time. Also they may find that different writing situations may suggest certain techniques.

SKILL 6.4   Comparing characteristic features and requirements associated with written materials in various modes

It becomes the responsibility of the learner to understand the various structures of written communication, in order to refine the communication process.

Basic expository writing simply gives information not previously known about a topic or is used to explain or define one. Facts, examples, statistics, cause and effect, direct tone, objective rather than subjective delivery, and non- emotional information is presented in a formal manner.

Descriptive writing centers on person, place, or object, using concrete and sensory words to create a mood or impression and arranging details in a chronological or spatial sequence.

Narrative writing is developed using an incident or anecdote or related series of events. Chronology, the 5 W's, topic sentence, and conclusion are essential ingredients.

Persuasive writing implies the writer's ability to select vocabulary and arrange facts and opinions in such a way as to direct the actions of the listener/reader. Persuasive writing may incorporate exposition and narration as they illustrate the main idea.

COMPETENCY 7.0

RESPOND TO CHILDREN'S WRITING

Many people like to read, but few enjoy writing.
Does writing need to be graded as much as felt?
Writing enables you to choose your words
more carefully where thoughts are measured
more deeply. When the critique enhances
perception then flow of thought is inspired. Find
the you that you never knew.

Sharon A. Wynne

COMPETENCY 7.0 ANALYZE WRITTEN WORK IN RELATION TO ITS STATED PURPOSE; EVALUATE AREAS IN NEED OF IMPROVEMENT; AND REVISE WRITTEN TEXTS FOR STYLE, CLARITY, AND ORGANIZATION

SKILL 7.1   **Revision strategies for improving the effectiveness of written material in relation to a given purpose**

When assessing and responding to student writing, there are several guidelines to remember.

Responding to non-graded writing (formative).

1. Avoid using a red pen.
2. Explain the criteria that will be used for assessment in advance.
3. Read the writing once while asking the question is the student's response appropriate for the assignment?
4. Reread and make note at the end whether the student met the objective of the writing task.
5. Responses should be noncritical and use supportive and encouraging language.
6. Resist writing on or over the student's writing.
7. Highlight the ideas you wish to emphasize, question or verify.
8. Suggest and encourage students to take risks.

Responding and evaluating graded writing (summative).

1. Ask students to submit prewriting and rough draft materials including all revisions with their final draft.
2. For the first reading, use a holistic method examining the work as a whole.
3. When reading the draft for the second time, assess it using the standards previously established.
4. Responses to the writing should be written in the margin and should use supportive language.
5. Make sure you address the process as well as the product. It is important that students value the learning process as well as the final product.
6. After scanning the piece a third time, write final comments at the end of the draft.

SKILL 7.2   Select effective responses to student writing.

When responding to student writing, there are a variety of approaches you can use depending on the focus and purpose of the assignment. You may want to vary the approaches.

- Analytical Evaluation identifies the qualities of a successful piece of writing and attributes point values for each aspect. The student's grade is determined by the point total. Students often like this type of evaluation since it is concrete and highlights specific strengths and weaknesses. One drawback for this type of evaluation is that it places a greater emphasis on the part rather than the whole.

- Holistic Scoring assesses a piece of writing as a whole. Usually a paper is read quickly through once to get a general impression. The writing is graded according to the impression of the whole work rather than the sum of its parts. Often holistic scoring uses a rubric that establishes the overall criteria for a certain score to evaluate each paper.

- A Performance System identifies established criteria, and as long as the student meets the acceptable level of activity, the points are awarded. This particular approach is useful for activities like journal writing.

- Portfolio Grading allows the students to select the pieces of work to be graded. Often this technique is used with writing workshops. Students often like this method because they have control over the evaluation process.

When the time comes to assign grades, keep a few things in mind.

1.   Each piece of writing should have clearly established criteria.

2.   Involve students in the process of defining the criteria. Students are more apt to understand criteria they have helped develop.

3.   Give students numerous experiences with formative evaluation (evaluation as the student is writing the piece). Give students points for the work they have done throughout the process.

4.   During the summative evaluation phase (final evaluation), students play an active role. Provide them with a form to identify the best parts of the writing and the things they would work on given more time.

5.   Focus on content, fluency and freshness of ideas with young writers. Correctness and punctuation will follow as they gain control of the language.

ELEMENTARY EDUCATION   41

SKILL 7.3   Analyzing given texts in terms of unity and organization and making appropriate revision

Gone are the days when students engage in skill practice with grammar worksheets. Grammar needs to be taught in the context of the students' own work. Listed below is a series of classroom practices that encourage meaningful context-based grammar instruction, combined with occasional mini-lessons and other language strategies that can be used on a daily basis.

* Connect grammar with the student's own writing while emphasizing grammar as a significant aspect of effective writing.

* Emphasize the importance of editing and proofreading as an essential part of classroom activities.

* Provide students with an opportunity to practice editing and proofreading cooperatively.

* Give instruction in the form of 15-20 minute mini-lessons.

* Emphasize the sound of punctuation by connecting it to pitch, stress, and pause.

* Involve students in all facets of language learning including reading, writing, listening, speaking and thinking. Good use of language comes from exploring all forms of it on a regular basis.

There are a number of approaches that involve grammar instruction in the context of the writing.

1.   Sentence Combining - try to use the student's own writing as much as possible. The theory behind combining ideas and the correct punctuation should be emphasized.

2.   Sentence and paragraph modeling - provide students with the opportunity to practice imitating the style and syntax of professional writers.

3.   Sentence transforming - give students an opportunity to change sentences from one form to another, i.e. from passive to active, inverting the sentence order, change forms of the words used.

4.   Daily Language Practice - introduce or clarify common errors using daily language activities. Use actual student examples whenever possible. Correct and discuss the problems with grammar and usage.

COMPETENCY 8.0

GRAMMAR AND MECHANICS

Learn to distinguish between constructive and destructive criticism. Precisely never sounded so good!

Jim Finnerty

COMPETENCY 8.0 APPLY KNOWLEDGE OF ENGLISH GRAMMAR AND MECHANICS IN REVISING TEXTS

SKILL 8.1 Sentence construction and making appropriate revisions

Sentence completeness

Avoid fragments and run-on sentences. Recognition of sentence elements necessary to make a complete thought, proper use of independent and dependent clauses, and proper punctuation will correct such errors.

Sentence structure

Recognize simple, compound, complex, and compound-complex sentences. Use dependent (subordinate) and independent clauses correctly to create these sentence structures.

Simple	Joyce wrote a letter.
Compound	Joyce wrote a letter, and Dot drew a picture.
Complex	While Joyce wrote a letter, Dot drew a picture.
Compound/Complex	When Mother asked the girls to demonstrate their new-found skills, Joyce wrote a letter, and Dot drew a picture.

Note: Do **not** confuse compound sentence elements with compound sentences.

Simple sentence with compound subject
Joyce and Dot wrote letters.
The girl in row three and the boy next to her were passing notes across the aisle.

Simple sentence with compound predicate
Joyce wrote letters and drew pictures.
The captain of the high school debate team graduated with honors and studied broadcast journalism in college.

Simple sentence with compound object of preposition
Colleen graded the students' essays for style and mechanical accuracy.

Parallelism

Recognize parallel structures using phrases (prepositional, gerund, participial, and infinitive) and omissions from sentences that create the lack of parallelism.

Prepositional phrase/single modifier

Incorrect: Colleen ate the ice cream with enthusiasm and hurriedly.

Correct: Colleen ate the ice cream with enthusiasm and in a hurry.

Correct: Colleen ate the ice cream enthusiastically and hurriedly.

Participial phrase/infinitive phrase

Incorrect: After hiking for hours and to sweat profusely, Joe sat down to rest and drinking water.

Correct: After hiking for hours and sweating profusely, Joe sat down to rest and drink water.

Recognition of dangling modifiers

Dangling phrases are attached to sentence parts in such a way they create ambiguity and incorrectness of meaning.

Participial phrase

Incorrect: Hanging from her skirt, Dot tugged at a loose thread.

Correct: Dot tugged at a loose thread hanging from her skirt.

Incorrect: Relaxing in the bathtub, the telephone rang.

Correct: While I was relaxing in the bathtub, the telephone rang.

Infinitive phrase

Incorrect: To improve his behavior, the dean warned Fred.

Correct: The dean warned Fred to improve his behavior.

Prepositional phrase

Incorrect: On the floor, Father saw the dog eating table scraps.

Correct: Father saw the dog eating table scraps on the floor.

Recognition of syntactical redundancy or omission

These errors occur when superfluous words have been added to a sentence or key words have been omitted from a sentence.

Redundancy

Incorrect: Joyce made sure that when her plane arrived that she retrieved all of her luggage.

Correct: Joyce made sure that when her plane arrived she retrieved all of her luggage.

Incorrect: He was a mere skeleton of his former self.

Correct: He was a skeleton of his former self.

Omission

Incorrect: Sue opened her book, recited her textbook, and answered the teacher's subsequent question.

Correct: Sue opened her book, recited from the textbook, and answered the teacher's subsequent question.

Avoidance of double negatives

This error occurs from positioning two negatives that, in fact, cancel each other in meaning.

Incorrect: Harold couldn't care less whether he passes this class.
Correct: Harold could care less whether he passes this class.

Incorrect: Dot didn't have no double negatives in her paper.
Correct: Dot didn't have any double negatives in her paper.

Correct use of coordination and subordination

Connect independent clauses with the coordinating conjunctions - *and*, *but*, *or*, *for*, or *nor* - when their content is of equal importance. Use subordinating conjunctions - although, because, before, if, since, though, until, when, whenever, where - and relative pronouns - that, who, whom, which - to introduce clauses that express ideas that are subordinate to main ideas expressed in independent clauses. (See *Sentence Structure* above.)
Be sure to place the conjunctions so that they express the proper relationship between ideas (cause/effect, condition, time, space).

Incorrect: Because mother scolded me, I was late.
Correct: Mother scolded me because I was late.

Incorrect: The sun rose after the fog lifted.
Correct: The fog lifted after the sun rose.

Notice that placement of the conjunction can completely change the meaning of the sentence. Main emphasis is shifted by the change.

Although Jenny was pleased, the teacher was disappointed.
Although the teacher was disappointed, Jenny was pleased.

The boys who wrote the essay won the contest.
The boys who won the contest wrote the essay.

Note: While not syntactically incorrect, the second sentence makes it appear that the boys won the contest for something else before they wrote the essay.

SKILL 8.2   Subject-verb agreement

A verb agrees in number with its subject. Making them agree relies on the ability to properly identify the subject.

> <u>One</u> of the boys *was playing* too rough.
> <u>No one</u> in the class, not the teacher nor the students, <u>was listening</u> to the message from the intercom.
> The <u>candidates</u>, including a grandmother and a teenager, <u>are debating</u> some controversial issues.

If two singular subjects are connected by *and* the verb must be plural.

> A *man* and his *dog* were jogging on the beach.

If two singular subjects are connected by *or* or *nor*, a singular verb is required.

> Neither <u>Dot</u> nor <u>Joyce</u> <u>has</u> missed a day of school this year.
> Either <u>Fran</u> or <u>Paul</u> <u>is</u> missing.

If one singular subject and one plural subject are connected by *or* or *nor*, the verb agrees with the subject nearest to the verb.

> Neither the <u>coach</u> nor the <u>players</u> <u>were</u> able to sleep on the bus.

If the subject is a collective noun, its sense of number in the sentence determines the verb: singular if the noun represents a group or unit and plural if the noun represents individuals.

> The <u>House of Representatives</u> <u>has adjourned</u> for the holidays.

> The House of Representatives have failed to reach agreement on the subject of adjournment.

SKILL 8.3   Using standard verb forms, pronouns, adjectives, and plural and possessive forms of nouns in context

Use of verbs (tense)

Present tense is used to express that which is currently happening or is always true.

> Randy is playing the piano.

> Randy plays the piano like a pro.

Past tense is used to express action that occurred in a past time.

> Randy learned to play the piano when he was six years old.

Future tense is used to express action or a condition of future time.

> Randy will probably earn a music scholarship.

Present perfect tense is used to express action or a condition that started in the past and is continued to or completed in the present.

> Randy has practiced piano every day for the last ten years.

> Randy has never been bored with practice.

Past perfect tense expresses action or a condition that occurred as a precedent to some other action or condition.

> Randy had considered playing clarinet before he discovered the piano.

Future perfect tense expresses action that started in the past or the present and will conclude at some time in the future.

> By the time he goes to college, Randy will have been an accomplished pianist for more than half of his life.

Use of verbs (mood)

Indicative mood is used to make unconditional statements; subjunctive mood is used for conditional clauses or wish statements that pose conditions that are untrue. Verbs in subjunctive mood are plural with both singular and plural subjects.

> If I <u>were</u> a bird, I would fly.

> I wish I <u>were</u> as rich as Donald Trump.

Verb conjugation

The conjugation of verbs follow the patterns used in the discussion of tense above. However, the most frequent problems in verb use stem from the improper formation of past and past participial forms.

> Regular verb: believe, believed, (have) believed

> Irregular verbs: run, ran, run; sit, sat, sat; teach, taught, taught

Other problems stem from the use of verbs that are the same in some tense but have different forms and different meanings in other tenses.

> I lie on the ground. I lay on the ground yesterday. I have lain down.

> I lay the blanket on the bed. I laid the blanket there yesterday. I have laid the blanket every night.

> The sun rises. The sun rose. The sun has risen.

> He raises the flag. He raised the flag. He had raised the flag.
> I sit on the porch. I sat on the porch. I have sat in the porch swing.

> I set the plate on the table. I set the plate there yesterday. I had set the table before dinner.

Two other verb problems stem from misusing the preposition *of* for the verb auxiliary *have* and misusing the verb *ought* (now rare).

> Incorrect: I should of gone to bed.
> Correct: I should have gone to bed.

Incorrect:	He hadn't ought to get so angry.
Correct:	He ought not to get so angry.

Use of pronouns

A pronoun used as a subject of predicate nominative is in nominative case.

> She was the drum majorette. The lead trombonists were Joe and he. The band director accepted whoever could march in step.

A pronoun used as a direct object, indirect object of object of a preposition is in objective case.

> The teacher praised him. She gave him an A on the test. Her praise of him was appreciated. The students whom she did not praise will work harder next time.

Common pronoun errors occur from misuse of reflexive pronouns:

Singular:	*myself, yourself, herself, himself, itself*
Plural:	*ourselves, yourselves, themselves.*
Incorrect:	Jack cut hisself shaving.
Correct:	Jack cut himself shaving.
Incorrect:	They backed theirselves into a corner.
Correct:	They backed themselves into a corner.

Use of adjectives

An adjective should agree with its antecedent in number.

> Those apples are rotten. This one is ripe. These peaches are hard.

Comparative adjectives end in -er and superlatives in -est, with some exceptions like *worse* and *worst*. Some adjectives that cannot easily make comparative inflections are preceded by *more* and *most*.

> Mrs. Carmichael is the better of the two basketball coaches.

> That is the hastiest excuse you have ever contrived.

> Candy is the most beautiful baby.

ELEMENTARY EDUCATION 51

Avoid double comparisons.

    Incorrect: This is the worstest headache I ever had.

    Correct: This is the worst headache I ever had.

When comparing one thing to others in a group, exclude the thing under comparison from the rest of the group.

    Incorrect: Joey is larger than any baby I have ever seen. (Since you have seen him, he cannot be larger than himself.)

    Correct: Joey is larger than <u>any other</u> baby I have ever seen.

Include all necessary word to make a comparison clear in meaning.

    I am as tall as my mother. I am as tall as she (is).
    My cats are better behaved than those of my neighbor.

Plurals

The multiplicity and complexity of spelling rules based on phonics, letter doubling, and exceptions to rules - not mastered by adulthood - should be replaced by a good dictionary. As spelling mastery is also difficult for adolescents, our recommendation is the same. Learning the use of a dictionary and thesaurus will be a more rewarding use of time.

Most plurals of nouns that end in hard consonants or hard consonant sounds followed by a silent *e* are made by adding *s*. Some words ending in vowels only add *s*.

    fingers, numerals, banks, bugs, riots, homes, gates, radios, bananas

Nouns that end in soft consonant sounds *s, j, x, z, ch,* and *sh,* add *es.* Some nouns ending in *o* add es.

    dresses, waxes, churches, brushes, tomatoes

Nouns ending in *y* preceded by a vowel just add *s*.

    boys, alleys

Nouns ending in *y* preceded by a consonant change the *y* to *i* and add *es.*

    babies, corollaries, frugalities, poppies

Some nouns plurals are formed irregularly or remain the same.

>   sheep, deer, children, leaves, oxen

Some nouns derived from foreign words, especially Latin, may make their plurals in two different ways - one of them Anglicized. Sometimes, the meanings are the same; other times, the two plurals are used in slightly different contexts. It is always wise to consult the dictionary.

>   appendices, appendixes   criterion, criteria
>   indexes, indices   crisis, crises

Make the plurals of closed (solid) compound words in the usual way except for words ending in *ful* which make their plurals on the root word.

>   timelines, hairpins, cupsful

Make the plurals of open or hyphenated compounds by adding the change in inflection to the word that change in number.

>   fathers-in-law, courts-martial, masters of art, doctors of medicine

Make the plurals of letters, numbers, and abbreviations by adding *s.*

>   fives and tens, IBMs, 1990s, *p*s and *q*s (Note that letters are italicized.)

Possessives

Make the possessives of singular nouns by adding an apostrophe followed by the letter *s* ('s).

>   baby's bottle, father's job, elephant's eye, teacher's desk, sympathizer's protests, week's postponement

Make the possessive of singular nouns ending in *s* by adding either an apostrophe or a ('s) depending upon common usage or sound. When making the possessive causes difficulty, use a prepositional phrase instead. Even with the sibilant ending, with a few exceptions, it is advisable to use the ('s) construction.

>   dress's color, species' characteristics or characteristics of the species,
>   James' hat or James's hat, Delores's shirt

Make the possessive of plural nouns ending in *s* by adding the apostrophe after the *s*.

>   horses' coats, jockeys' times, four days' time

Make possessives of plural nouns that do not end in *s* the same as singular nouns by adding 's.

>   children's shoes, deer's antlers, cattle's horns

Make possessives of compound nouns by adding the inflection at the end of the word or phrase.

>   the mayor of Los Angeles' campaign, the mailman's new truck, the
>   mailmen's new trucks, my father-in-law's first wife, the keepsakes'
>   values, several daughters-in-law's husbands

Note: Because a gerund functions as a noun, any noun preceding it and operating as a possessive adjective must reflect the necessary inflection. However, if the gerundive following the noun is a participle, no inflection is added.
The general was perturbed by the private's sleeping on duty. (The word *sleeping* is a gerund, the object of the preposition *by*.

>   *but*

The general was perturbed to see the private sleeping on duty. (The word *sleeping* is a participle modifying private.)

SKILL 8.4   Revisions involving punctuation and capitalization in a given text

The candidate should be cognizant of proper rules and conventions of punctuation, capitalization, and spelling. Competency exams will generally test the ability to apply the more advanced skills; thus, a limited number of more frustrating rules are presented here. Rules should be applied according to the American style of English, i.e. spelling *theater* instead of *theatre* and placing terminal marks of punctuation almost exclusively within other marks of punctuation.

Punctuation

Using terminal punctuation in relation to quotation marks

In a quoted statement that is either declarative or imperative, place the period inside the closing quotation marks.

> "The airplane crashed on the runway during takeoff."

If the quotation is followed by other words in the sentence, place a comma inside the closing quotations marks and a period at the end of the sentence.

> "The airplane crashed on the runway during takeoff," said the announcer.

In most instances in which a quoted title or expression occurs at the end of a sentence, the period is placed before either the single or double quotation marks.

> "The middle school readers were unprepared to understand Bryant's poem 'Thanatopsis.' "

> Early book length adventure stories like *Don Quixote* and *The Three Musketeers* were known as "picaresque novels."

There is an instance in which the final quotation mark would precede the period - if the content of the sentence were about a speech or quote so that the understanding of the meaning would be confused by the placement of the period.

> The first thing out of his mouth was "Hi, I'm home."
> *but*
> The first line of his speech began "I arrived home to an empty house".

In sentences that are interrogatory or exclamatory, the question mark or exclamation point should be positioned **outside** the closing quotation marks if the quote itself is a statement or command or cited title.

> Who decided to lead us in the recitation of the "Pledge of Allegiance"?

> Why was Tillie shaking as she began her recitation, "Once upon a midnight dreary..."?

> I was embarrassed when Mrs. White said, "Your slip is showing"!

In sentences that are declarative but the quotation is a question or an exclamation, place the question mark or exclamation point **inside** the quotation marks.

> The hall monitor yelled, "Fire! Fire!"

> "Fire! Fire!" yelled the hall monitor.

> Cory shrieked, "Is there a mouse in the room?" (In this instance, the question supersedes the exclamation.)

Using periods with parentheses or brackets

Place the period inside the parentheses or brackets if they enclose a complete sentence, independent of the other sentences around it.

> Stephen Crane was a confirmed alcohol and drug addict. (He admitted as much to other journalists in Cuba.)

If the parenthetical expression is a statement inserted within another statement, the period in the enclosure is omitted.

> Mark Twain used the character Indian Joe (He also appeared in *The Adventures of Tom Sawyer*) as a foil for Jim in *The Adventures of Huckleberry Finn*.

When enclosed matter comes at the end of a sentence requiring quotation marks, place the period outside the parentheses or brackets.

> "The secretary of state consulted with the ambassador [Powell]."

Using commas

Separate two or more coordinate adjectives, modifying the same word and three or more nouns, phrases, or clauses in a list.

Maggie's hair was dull, dirty, and lice-ridden.

Dickens portrayed the Artful Dodger as a skillful pickpocket, loyal follower of Fagin, and defendant of Oliver Twist.
Ellen daydreamed about getting out of the rain, taking a shower, and eating a hot dinner.

In Elizabethan England, Ben Johnson wrote comedy, Christopher Marlowe wrote tragedies, and William Shakespeare composed both.

Use commas to separate antithetical or complimentary expressions from the rest of the sentence.

The veterinarian, not his assistant, would perform the delicate surgery.

The more he knew about her, the less he wished he knew.

Randy hopes to, and probably will, get an appointment to the Naval Academy.

His thorough, though esoteric, scientific research could not easily be understood by high school students.

Using double quotation marks with other punctuation

Quotations - whether words, phrases, or clauses - should be punctuated according to the rules of the grammatical function they serve in the sentence.

The works of Shakespeare, "the bard of Avon," have been contested as originating with other authors.

"You'll get my money," the old man warned, "when 'Hell freezes over'."

Sheila cited the passage that began "Four score and seven years ago...." (Note the ellipsis followed by an enclosed period.)

"Old Ironsides" inspired the preservation of the U.S.S. Constitution.

Use quotation marks to enclose the titles of shorter works: songs, short poems, short stories, essays, and chapters of books. (See "Using Italics" for punctuating longer titles.)

"The Tell-Tale Heart"   "Casey at the Bat"   "America the Beautiful"

Using semicolons

Use semicolons to separate independent clauses when the second clause is introduced by a transitional adverb. (These clauses may also be written as separate sentences, preferably by placing the adverb within the second sentence.)

> The Elizabethans modified the rhyme scheme of the sonnet; thus, it was called the English sonnet.
> *or*
> The Elizabethans modified the rhyme scheme of the sonnet. It thus was called the English sonnet.

Use semicolons to separate items in a series that are long and complex or have internal punctuation.

> The Italian Renaissance produced masters in the fine arts: Dante Alighieri, author of the *Divine Comedy;* Leonardo da Vinci, painter of *The Last Supper;* and Donatello, sculptor of the *Quattro Coronati*, the four saints.

> The leading scorers in the WNBA were Haizhaw Zheng, averaging 23.9 points per game; Lisa Leslie, 22; and Cynthia Cooper, 19.5.

Using colons

Place a colon at the beginning of a list of items. (Note its use in the sentence about Renaissance Italians on the previous page.)

> The teacher directed us to compare Faulkner's three symbolic novels: *Absalom, Absalom; As I Lay Dying,* and *Light in August.*

Do **not** use a comma if the list is preceded by a verb.

> Three of Faulkner's symbolic novels are *Absalom, Absalom; As I Lay Dying,* and *Light in August.*

Using dashes

Place dashes to denote sudden breaks in thought.

> Some periods in literature - the Romantic Age, for example -
> spanned different time periods in different countries.

Use dashes instead of commas if commas are already used elsewhere in the sentence for amplification or explanation.

> The Fireside Poets included three Brahmans - James Russell
> Lowell, Henry David Wadsworth, Oliver Wendell Holmes -
> and John Greenleaf Whittier.

Use italics to punctuate the titles of long works of literature, names of periodical publications, musical scores, works of art, and motion picture television, and radio programs. (When unable to write in italics, students should be instructed to underline in their own writing where italics would be appropriate.)

> *The Idylls of the King*   *Hiawatha*   *The Sound and the Fury*
> *Mary Poppins*   *Newsweek*   *The Nutcracker Suite*

Capitalization

Capitalize all proper names of persons (including specific organizations or agencies of government); places (countries, states, cities, parks, and specific geographical areas); and things (political parties, structures, historical and cultural terms, and calendar and time designations); and religious terms (any deity, revered person or group, sacred writings).

> Percy Blythe Shelley, Argentina, Mount Rainier National Park,
> Grand Canyon, League of Nations, the Sears Towers, Birmingham,
> Lyric Theater, Americans, Midwesterners, Democrats, Renaissance,
> Boy Scouts of America, Easter, God, Bible, Dead Sea Scrolls, Koran

Capitalize proper adjectives and titles used with proper names.

California gold rush, President John Adams, French fries, Homeric epic, Romanesque architecture, Senator John Glenn

COMPETENCY 9.0

SPELLING

He knows it is never to late to learn.

COMPETENCY 9.0 UNDERSTAND SKILLS AND STRATEGIES INVOLVED IN SPELLING

SKILL 9.1   Developmental stages of spelling

Spelling instruction should include words misspelled in daily writing, generalizing spelling knowledge, and mastering objectives in progressive phases of development. Developmental stages of spelling are:

1) *Prephonemic spelling*—Children know that letters stand for a message, but they do not know the relationship between spelling and pronunciation.

2) *Early phonemic spelling*—Children are beginning to understand spelling. They usually write the beginning letter correctly, with the rest consonants or long vowels.

3) *Letter-name spelling*—Some words are consistently spelled correctly. The student is developing a sight vocabulary and a stable understanding of letters as representing sounds. Long vowels are usually used accurately, but silent vowels are omitted. Unknown words are spelled by the child attempting to match the name of the letter to the sound.

4) *Transitional spelling*—This phase is typically entered in late elementary school. Short vowel sounds are mastered and some spelling rules known. They are developing a sense of which spellings are correct and which are not.

5) *Derivational spelling*—This is usually reached from high school to adulthood. This is the stage where spelling rules are being mastered.

SKILL 9.2   Instructional approaches to spelling

Rule-Based Instruction. Spelling is taught as a system of rules and generalizations. Rule-based instruction may be taught with the linguistics or phonics approach.

A) The *linguistic* approach is based on the idea that there is regularity in the phoneme/grapheme correspondence. Spelling rules, generalizations, and patterns are taught that apply to whole words, and the spelling lists are selected according to a particular pattern. (e.g. take, cake, rake, fake).

B) The *phonics approach* teaches the student to associate a sound with a particular letter or combination of letters. The student breaks the words down into syllables, pronounces each syllable, and writes the letters that represent the sound. Rules that apply to a large number of words are taught first. After the students generalize these rules, exceptions are taught.

Multisensory Approaches. Multisensory approaches to spelling are based on the principle that spelling incorporates *visual skills* (seeing the word and discriminating the letters), *auditory recognition* of the word, and *motor skills* (writing). Supporters of multisensory approaches assert that students who learn to spell using these approaches can use any of these modalities to recall the word and are better able to remember the words. Several more popular methods are described here:

1) *Fernald method.* This method is also called VAKT, because it uses visual, auditory, kinesthetic, and tactile modalities. According to this method, learning to spell involves a clear perception of the word, development of a clear visual image, and repetition of the word until the motor pattern becomes automatic. Words are taught in this sequence:

  - Teacher writes and says the word; students listen and watch.
  - Student traces the word while saying it, then writes the word down while saying it.
  - Student writes the word from memory. If the word is incorrect, the steps are repeated. If it is correct, the word is put in a file box to use in stories.
  - The tracing method may be discontinued at later stages if it is not needed.

2) *Gillingham method.* The Gillingham method teaches letter/sound correspondence with an alphabetic system. Words are learned syllable by syllable. Spelling words are studied by "simultaneous oral spelling". The teacher says the word and the student repeats the word, names the letters while writing them, and then reads the written word. The method differs from the Fernald because the words that are taught are selected according to a structural sequence, and individual letters and sounds are emphasized, rather than whole words.

3) *Cover-and-Write.* The student follows four steps in learning a word.

  - Look at the word and say it.
  - Write the word twice while looking at it.
  - Cover the word and write it again.
  - Check the spelling by looking at it.

  Repeat if needed.

Test-Study-Test. At the beginning of a spelling unit, students are given a pretest. Words that the students misspell become individual study lists. At the end of the unit, the students are tested again. Any misspelled words become the basis for the next study list. Periodic checks are conducted to determine if any word need to be reintroduced. It is recommended that students correct their own tests with the teacher's supervision. Mastery checks also include samples of the students' writing to make sure that students can spell the words in their actual writing.

Fixed and Flow Word Lists. Fixed lists present a new list of words, usually assigned on a weekly basis. The words may or may not be familiar to the students. The problem with fixed lists is that the words the student continues to misspell may be ignored or left for the student to practice as soon as the next list is assigned. In a flow list, words are dropped as the student learns to spell them and new words are added. The teacher periodically re-tests the student for retention and may add words back as needed.

Imitation Methods. The method is used with students who have not had success with traditional methods. The teacher provides an oral and written model of the target word. The student imitates the model by spelling the word and writing. The procedure is repeated until the student can write the word correctly without models and prompts.

COMPETENCY 10.0

APPROACHES TO TEACHING LANGUAGE ARTS

When someone is taught the joy of learning, it becomes a lifelong process that never stops, a process that creates a logical individual. That is the challenge and joy of teaching.

Mava Collins

COMPETENCY 10.0   IDENTIFY VARIOUS APPROACHES TO THE TEACHING OF GRAMMAR, LANGUAGE, AND USAGE

SKILL 10.1 Teaching styles

Teaching styles are an extension of learning styles. Once teachers assess how students learn, they can vary their teaching styles to accommodate students' needs. Research in the 1960's and 1970's solidified thinking about learning and teaching that had been evolving since the turn of the century. In the 1980's, several states adopted standards for student performance and began to hold teachers accountable for student progress. Formative and summative evaluation instruments were developed to enable administrators to evaluate teacher performance and to help teachers improve their teaching styles.

Six styles

1. **Task-oriented**. The teacher prescribes the resources and identifies specific performances, some of which may be individualized.

2. **Cooperation-centered**. The teacher and students plan the course of study and select resources together.

3. **Child-centered**. The student plans his own course of study based on his own interests.

4. **Subject-oriented**. Well-organized content dictates the course of study, with little regard to individual differences.

5. **Learning-centered**. This style combines both child-centered and subject-oriented approaches. The organized content and specific resources from which the student must select are prescribed.

6. **Emotionally exciting**. Not centered on any planning method, this style merely categorizes those teachers who instruct with more emotion than structure.

Concerns for the teacher

Within any of these styles, researchers identified specific element - instructional planning, personality traits, educational philosophy, attitudes toward students, teaching environments, methodology, and evaluation techniques - that could be assessed as having an impact on student learning.

As a result, in the last two decades, greater emphasis has been placed on identifying learning and teaching styles and attempting to match learner needs with the appropriate delivery methods. Teachers who have been trained and subscribe to task-oriented and subject-centered instruction are encouraged to abandon the textbook dependent or lecture approaches to learning in favor of smaller group discussion, independent study and research, and creative student projects. Teachers who have an abundance of enthusiasm, but little organization, have been encouraged to become more learning-oriented.

Early in each school year, the teacher needs to assess social, environmental, physical, and perceptual characteristics of each individual and class. This can be done informally through observation or formally with any number of learning style inventories.

The drawback of formal inventories is that adolescents aware of the inventory's purpose or youngsters who have been exposed to repeated assessments may intentionally or inadvertently miscue their responses. Many researchers and teachers prefer a hands-on approach to assessment. By trying various styles in the early weeks of a course of study, the teacher can observe the methods that work best. Using half a class as a control group or altering teaching styles with different classes during the day can result in providing improved instructional strategies and in making better recommendations for study techniques and resources for study.

COMPETENCY 11.0

LANGUAGE

DEVELOPMENT

I touch the world, I teach.

Christa McAuliffe

COMPETENCY 11.0   LANGUAGE DEVELOPMENT

SKILL 11.1   Understand the different approaches to language development

Learning approach

Early theories of language development were formulated from learning theory research. The assumption was that language development evolved from learning the rules of language structures and applying them through imitation and reinforcement. This approach also assumed that language, cognitive, and social developments were independent of each other. Thus, children were expected to learn language from patterning after adults who spoke and wrote Standard English. No allowance was made for communication through child jargon, idiomatic expressions, or grammatical and mechanical errors resulting from too strict adherence to the rules of inflection (*childs* instead of *children*) or conjugation (*runned* instead of *ran*). No association was made between physical and operational development and language mastery.

Linguistic approach

Studies spearheaded by Noam Chomsky in the 1950's formulated the theory that language ability is innate and develops through natural human maturation as environmental stimuli trigger acquisition of syntactical structures appropriate to each exposure level. The assumption of a hierarchy of syntax downplayed the significance of semantics. Because of the complexity of syntax and the relative speed with which children acquire language, linguists attributed language development to biological rather than cognitive or social influences.

Cognitive approach

Researchers in the 1970's proposed that language knowledge derives from both syntactic and semantic structures. Drawing on the studies of Piaget and other cognitive learning theorists, supporters of the cognitive approach maintained that children acquire knowledge of linguistic structures after they have acquired the cognitive structures necessary to process language. For example, joining words for specific meaning necessitates sensory motor intelligence. The child must be able to coordinate movement and recognize objects before she can identify words to name the objects or word groups to describe the actions performed with those objects. Adolescents must have developed the mental abilities for organizing concepts as well as concrete operations, predicting outcomes, and theorizing before they can assimilate and verbalize complex sentence structures, choose vocabulary for particular nuances of meaning, and examine semantic structures for tone and manipulative effect.

Socio-cognitive approach

Other theorists in the 1970s proposed that language development results from sociolinguistic competence. Language, cognitive, and social knowledge are interactive elements of total human development. Emphasis on verbal communication as the medium for language expression resulted in the inclusion of speech activities in most language arts curricula.

Unlike previous approaches, the socio-cognitive allowed that determining the appropriateness of language in given situations for specific listeners is as important as understanding semantic and syntactic structures. By engaging in conversation, children at all stages of development have opportunities to test their language skills, receive feedback, and make modifications. As a social activity, conversation is as structured by social order as grammar is structured by the rules of syntax. Conversation satisfies the learner's need to be heard and understood and to influence others. Thus, his choices of vocabulary, tone, and content are dictated by his ability to assess the language knowledge of his listeners. He is constantly applying his cognitive skills to using language in a social interaction. If the capacity to acquire language is inborn, without an environment in which to practice language, a child would not pass beyond grunts and gestures as did primitive man.

Of course, the varying degrees of environmental stimuli to which children are exposed at all age levels creates a slower or faster development of language. Some children are prepared to articulate concepts and recognize symbolism by the time they enter fifth grade because they have been exposed to challenging reading and conversations with well-spoken adults at home or in their social groups. Others are still trying to master the sight recognition skills and are not yet ready to combine words in complex patterns.

Concerns for the teacher

Because teachers must, by virtue of tradition and the dictates of the curriculum, teach grammar, usage, and writing as well as reading and later literature, the problem becomes when to teach what to whom. The profusion of approaches to teaching grammar alone is mind-boggling. In the universities, we learn about transformational grammar, stratificational grammar, sectoral grammar, etc. But in practice, most teachers, supported by presentations in textbooks and by the methods they learned themselves, keep coming back to the same traditional prescriptive approach - read and imitate - or structural approach - learn the parts of speech, the parts of sentence, punctuation rules, sentence patterns. After enough of the terminology and rules are stored in the brain, then we learn to write and speak. For some educators, the best solution is the worst - don't teach grammar at all.

The same problems occur in teaching usage. How much can we demand students communicate in only Standard English? Different schools of thought suggest that a study of dialect and idiom and recognition of various jargons is a vital part of language development. Social pressures, especially on students in middle and junior high schools, to be accepted within their peer groups and to speak the non-standard language spoken outside the school make adolescents resistant to the corrective, remedial approach. In many communities where the immigrant populations are high, new words are entering English from other languages even as words and expressions that were common when we were children have become rare or archaic.

Regardless of differences of opinion concerning language development, it is safe to say that a language arts teacher will be most effective using the styles and approaches with which he/she is most comfortable. And, if he/she subscribes to a student-centered approach, he/she may find that the students have a lot to teach him/her and each other. Moffett and Wagner in the Fourth Edition of *Student-centered Language Arts K-12* stress the three letter I's : individualization, interaction, and integration. Essentially, they are supporting the socio-cognitive approach to language development. By providing an opportunity for the student to select his own activities and resources, his instruction is individualized. By centering on and teaching each other, students are interactive. Finally, by allowing students to synthesize a variety of knowledge structures, they integrate them. The teacher's role becomes that of a facilitator.

Benefits of the socio-cognitive approach

This approach has tended to guide the whole language movement, currently in fashion. Most basal readers utilize an integrated, cross-curricular approach to successful grammar, language, and usage. Reinforcement becomes an intradepartmental responsibility. Language incorporates diction and terminology across the curriculum. Standard usage is encouraged and supported by both the core classroom textbooks and current software for technology. Teachers need to acquaint themselves with the computer capabilities in their school district and at their individual school sites. Advances in new technologies require the teacher to familiarize herself with programs that would serve her students' needs. Students respond enthusiastically to technology. Several highly effective programs are available in various formats to assist students with initial instruction or remediation. Grammar texts, such as the Warriner's series, employ various methods to reach individual learning styles. The school library media center should become a focal point for individual exploration.

COMPETENCY 12.0

SPEAKING

Don't run with the ball unless you know the direction of the goal.

COMPETENCY 12.0 UNDERSTAND SKILLS AND STRATEGIES INVOLVED IN SPEAKING FOR VARIOUS PURPOSES

SKILL12.1 Using tone to convey your message

When you speak, you naturally alter the tone of your voice according to your feelings or mood, your need to communicate some message, your purpose, and your intended audience. You also use different kinds of sentences. If you want to get something across to a child, for example, you may used a different tone of voice depending on the circumstances. Let's say that you want the child to go to the library immediately. To get your message across, you might

Demand:	*Go to the library now!*
State:	*It's time to go to the library.*
Plead:	*Won't you please go to the library?*

Those are three different sentences—a command, an assertion, and a request—and you might choose any of the three depending on those circumstances and your relationship to the child. You might also deliver any one of those sentences at volumes varying from a whisper to a shout, depending on your emotional state. The point is that different audiences and different situations require different language choices—if you want your message to be effectively conveyed to the listener.

SKILL 12.2 Using connotations to convey your message

In everyday language, we attach affective meanings to words unconsciously; we exercise more conscious control of informative connotations. In the process of language development, the student must come not only to grasp the definitions of words but also to become more conscious of the affective connotations and how his listeners process these connotations. Gaining this conscious control over language makes it possible to use language appropriately in various situations and to evaluate its uses in literature and other forms of communication.

The manipulation of language for a variety of purposes is the goal of language instruction. Advertisers and satirists are especially conscious of the effect word choice has on their audiences. By evoking the proper responses from readers/listeners, we can prompt them to take action.

Choice of the medium through which the message is delivered to the receiver is a significant factor in controlling language. Spoken language relies as much on the gestures, facial expression, and tone of voice of the speaker as on the words he speaks. Slapstick comics can evoke laughter without speaking a word. Young children use body language overtly and older children more subtly to convey messages. These refinings of body language are paralleled by an ability to recognize and apply the nuances of spoken language. To work strictly with the written work, the writer must use words to imply the body language.

By the time children begin to speak, they have begun to acquire the ability to use language to inform and manipulate. They have already used kinesthetic and verbal cues to attract attention when they seek some physical or emotional gratification. Children learn to apply names to objects and actions. They learn to use language to describe the persons and events in their lives and to express their feelings about the world around them.

Semantic connotations

To effectively teach language, it is necessary to understand that, as human beings acquire language, they realize that words have <u>denotative</u> and <u>connotative</u> meanings. Generally, denotative words point to things and connotative words deal with mental suggestions that the words convey. The word *skunk* has a denotative meaning if the speaker can point to the actual animal as he speaks the word and intends the word to identify the animal. *Skunk* has connotative meaning depending upon the tone of delivery, the socially acceptable attitudes about the animal, and the speaker's personal feelings about the animal.

Informative connotations

Informative connotations are definitions agreed upon by the society in which the learner operates. A *skunk* is "a black and white mammal of the weasel family with a pair of perineal glands which secrete a pungent odor." The *Merriam Webster Collegiate Dictionary* adds "...and offensive" odor. Identification of the color, species, and glandular characteristics are informative. The interpretation of the odor as *offensive* is affective.

Affective connotations

Affective connotations are the personal feelings a word arouses. A child who has no personal experience with a skunk and its odor or has had a pet skunk will feel differently about the word *skunk* than a child who has smelled the spray or been conditioned vicariously to associate offensiveness with the animal denoted *skunk*. The very fact that our society views a skunk as an animal to be avoided will affect the child's interpretation of the word. In fact, it is not necessary for one to have actually seen a skunk (that is, have a denotative understanding) to use the word in either connotative expression. For example, one child might call another child a skunk, connoting an unpleasant reaction (affective use) or, seeing another small black and white animal, call it a skunk based on the definition (informative use).

SKILL 12.3 Applying knowledge of language conventions appropriate to a variety of social situations

Different from the basic writing forms of discourse is the art of debating, discussion, and conversation. The ability to use language and logic to convince the audience to accept your reasoning and to side with you is an art. This form of writing/speaking is extremely confined/structured, logically sequenced, with supporting reasons and evidence. A position statement, evidence, reason, evaluation and refutation are integral parts of this writing schema.

Interviewing provides opportunities for students to apply expository and informative communication. It teaches them how to structure questions to evoke fact-filled responses. Compiling the information from an interview into a biographical essay or speech helps students to list, sort, and arrange details in an orderly fashion.

Speeches that encourage students to describe persons, places, or events in their own lives or oral interpretations of literature help them sense the creativity and effort used by professional writers.

COMPETENCY 13.0

MATHEMATICS

Knowledge is power.

Francis Bacon

COMPETENCY 13.0   KNOWLEDGE OF MATHEMATICS CURRICULUM AND INSTRUCTION

SKILL 13.1   Identify basic levels of learning mathematics concepts

Reid describes four processes are directly related to an understanding of numbers: Children typically begin learning these processes in early childhood through the opportunities provided by their caretakers. Children who do not get these opportunities have difficulties when they enter school.

- Describing—characterizing an object, set, or event in terms of its attributes, such as calling all cats "kitties", whether they are tigers or house cats.

- Classifying—sorting objects, sets, or events in terms of one or more criteria, such as color, size, or shape—black cats vs. white cats vs. tabbies.

- Comparing—determining whether two objects, sets, or events, are alike or different on the basis of a specified attribute, such as differentiating quadrilaterals from triangles on the basis of number of sides.

- Ordering—comparing two or more objects, sets, or events, such as ordering children in a family on the basis of age.

Children usually begin learning about these concepts during early childhood:

- Equalizing—making two or more sets alike on an attribute, such as putting more milk in a glass so it matches the amount of milk in another glass.

- Joining—putting together two or more sets with a common attribute to make one set, such as buying packets of X-Men trading cards to create a complete series.

- Separating—dividing an object or set into two or more sets, such as passing out cookies from a bag to a group of children so that each child gets three cookies.

- Measuring—attaching a number to an attribute, such as three cups of flour or ten gallons of gas.

- Patterns—recognizing, developing, and repeating patterns, such as secret code messages, designs in a carpet or tile floor.

However, most children are not developmentally ready to understand these concepts before they enter school.

- <u>Understanding and working with numbers larger than ten</u>. They may be able to recite larger numbers, but are not able to compare or add them, for example.

- <u>Part-whole concept</u>, or the relationship of a number as part of a larger number.

- <u>Numerical notation</u>—place value, additive system, and zero symbol.

Children with learning problems often have problems with these concepts after they enter public school because they either have not had many experiences with developing these basic concepts or they are not developmentally ready to understand such concepts as part-whole, for example.

SKILL 13.2   Sequence of mathematics understanding

Children's understanding of mathematics concepts proceeds in a developmental sequence from concrete to semiabstract to abstract. Children with learning difficulties may still be at a concrete or semiabstract level while their peers are ready to work at the abstract level. This developmental sequence has implication for instruction because the teacher will need to incorporate concrete and/or semiabstract levels into lessons for students who did not master these stages of development in their mathematics background. These levels may be explained as follows:

- ❖ <u>Concrete</u>: An example of this would be demonstrating 3 + 4 = 7 by counting out three buttons and four buttons to equal seven buttons.

- ❖ <u>Semi-abstract</u>: An example would be using pictures of 3 buttons and 4 buttons to demonstrate 3 + 4 = 7.

- ❖ <u>Abstract</u>: The student solves 3 + 4 = 7 without using manipulatives or pictures.

In summary, the levels of mathematics content involve:

- Concepts: such as the understanding of number and terms
- Development of mathematics relationships
- Development of mathematics skills such as computation and measuring
- Development of problem-solving ability, not only in books, but also in the environment

SKILL 13.3   Recognize and apply knowledge of the sequential development of mathematics skills and concepts

Mathematics instruction proceeds through a sequential development of skills and concept. For each concept, instruction should proceed from concrete to semiabstract levels before moving on to the abstract level of understanding. This section discusses the skills development of mathematics instruction.

Place Value

This is the basis of our number system. Students need to know that the position of a given number determines its value in our number system. Students need to know the grouping process, the relationship between place and value of a number, that each number to the left is a multiple of 10, and that there is only one digit per position in our number system.

Addition and Subtraction

These are the first mathematics that students are expected to learn. This requires not only an understanding of place value, but knowledge of the basic addition facts. Addition is conceptualized as the union of two sets.

Subtraction is more difficult because it has three different interpretations:

a. *Taking away* a quantity from another. (John has 10 stickers. She gives 5 away to her friend Jamie. How many stickers does John have left?)

b. *Comparison*—how much more one quantity is than another. (Tom and Matt are selling chocolate bars for the school band. In the first week, Tom sold 136 chocolate bars and Matt sold 97. How many more chocolate bars has Tom sold than Matt?)

c. *Missing addend*—how much more of a quantity is needed. (Jeff is saving his money to buy a video game. The game costs $35.99 on sale. Jeff has $29.50 so far. How much more does he need to buy the video game?)

Multiplication and Division

There are different ways of interpreting these operations. Different students will find certain interpretations easier to understand than others. An understanding of the different ways of conceptualizing these operations will help the teacher adjust instruction for individual needs. Students need a mastery of addition and subtraction facts in order to do well in multiplication and division, which are extensions of these operations. The division algorithm is the most difficult for students to learn.

Multiplication may be viewed in five different ways:

1) *Repeated addition*—7 x 5 could be viewed as 7 + 7 + 7 + 7 + 7 = 35

2) *Arrays*—7 x 5 is depicted as 7 rows of 5 objects or 5 rows of 7 objects, like rows of seats in a classroom

3) *Cartesian product of two sets*—This interpretation is used with problems such as, "Maria goes to Baskin Robbins for and ice cream cone. She decided to buy a two-scoop cone and has 25 flavors to choose from. How many possible combinations can Maria make?" There are 50 possible combinations because 25 choices x 2 scoops of ice cream = 50 combinations.

4) *Linear prototypes*—The problem 7 x 5 can be shown on a number line by starting with 0 and skipping 5 spaces 7 times, stopping on 35.

5) *Multiple sets*—12 x 6 can be described in a problem like this: Jamal is buying pencils for school for himself and his two brothers. He buys 6 packages of pencils. Each package has 12 pencils. How many pencils did Jamal buy? (12 x 6 = 72)

Division can be conceptualized in two ways: For a problem 32 divided by 8 = 4....

1) Measurement—the problem may be seen as 8 groups of 4. A sample problem could read, "Michelle has as 32-inch piece of yarn. She needs 8-inch pieces for her sting art project. How many pieces can she cut from the yarn?" (The yarn is measured into equal parts).

2) Partition—the problem may be seen as 8 dots in each of 4 groups. A sample problem could read "32 students go on a field trip to a museum. They are assigned to 4 tour guides for the guided tour. If the tour guides have an equal number of students in their groups, how many students are in each group?" (The total group of 32 students is broken up into 4 equal groups).

Fractions

Fractions may be interpreted as:

- *a part of the whole* (probably the most familiar)—"Stacey is sharing a mushroom pizza with 3 friends. If everyone gets an equal share, what part of the pizza will each girl get?" Answer: 1/4.

- *a subset of a parent set*—"Josh's dog had 8 puppies. 3 puppies are white with spots. What fraction of the puppies are white with spots?" Answer: 3/8.

- *a ratio*—Examples of rations could be 2 girls for every 3 boys in a class.

Decimal Fractions and Percents

Decimal fractions and percents are an extension of the place value system and common fractions. Students who have not mastered operations with common fractions will probably also have trouble with understanding decimal fractions and percents, as well as converting one to another.

Problem Solving

The skills of analysis and interpretation are necessary to problem solving. Skills necessary for successful problem solving include:

1) Identification of the main idea—what is the problem about?

2) Main question of the problem—what is the problem asking for?

3) Identifying important facts—what information is necessary to solve it?

4) Choose a strategy and an operation—how will the student solve the problem and with what operation?

5) Solve the problem—perform the computation

6) Check for accuracy of computation and compare the answer to the main question. Does is sound reasonable?

7) If solution is incorrect, repeat the steps.

Secondary Mathematics

Other topics of mathematics that are important to develop, especially as the student enters the higher grades, are spatial relationships, measurements, and patterns. Instruction in these areas allows students to discover relationships and properties of three-dimensional objects, explore the logical nature of mathematics, and build a foundation for algebra and geometry. Secondary students also need instruction in consumer mathematics (ratio, proportion, interest, percents, and consumer credit) because students will need to balance checkbooks, calculate best buys, apply for credit, compare interest rates, and budget their money. Students will need to know the mathematics involved with loans, credit cards, mortgages, and taxes.

SKILL 13.4 Approaches to error analysis

A simple method for analyzing student errors is to ask how the answer was obtained. The teacher can then determine if a common error pattern has resulted in the wrong answer. There is a value to having the students explain how they arrived at the correct as well as the incorrect answers.

Many errors are due to simple **carelessness**. Students need to be encouraged to work slowly and carefully. They should check their calculations by redoing the problem on another paper, not merely looking at the work. Addition and subtraction problems need to be written neatly so the numbers line up. Students need to be careful regrouping in subtraction. Students must write clearly and legibly, including erasing fully. Use estimation to ensure that answers make sense.

Many students' computational skills exceed their **reading** level. Although they can understand basic operations, they fail to grasp the concept or completely understand the question. Students must read directions slowly.

Fractions are often a source of many errors. Students need to be reminded to use common denominators when adding and subtracting and to always express answers in simplest terms. Again, it is helpful to check by estimating.

The most common error that is made when working with **decimals** is failure to line up the decimal points when adding or subtracting or not moving the decimal point when multiplying or dividing. Students also need to be reminded to add zeroes when necessary. Reading aloud may also be beneficial. Estimation, as always, is especially important.

Students need to know that it is okay to make mistakes. The teacher must keep a positive attitude, so the students do not feel defeated or frustrated.

SKILL 13.5   Problem solving

Problem solving strategies are simply plans of attack. Students often panic when confronted with word problems. If they have a "list" of ideas, ways to attempt a solution, they will be able to approach the problems more calmly and confidently. Some methods include, but are not limited to, draw a diagram, work backwards, guess and check, and solve a simpler problem.

It is helpful to have students work in groups. Mathematics does not have to be solitary activity. Cooperative learning fosters enthusiasm. Creating their own problems is another useful tool. Also, encourage students to find more than one way to solve a problem. Thinking about problem solving after the solution has been discovered encourages understanding and creativity. The more they practice problems, the more comfortable and positive students will feel.

COMPETENCY 14.0

MATH TERMS

The bad teacher's words fall on his pupils like harsh rain; the good teacher's, as gently as the dew.

Talmud: Ta'amotj. 7a

COMPETENCY 14.0   **USE MATHEMATICAL TERMINOLOGY AND SYMBOLS TO INTERPRET AND COMMUNICATE MATHEMATICAL IDEAS AND INFORMATION**

SKILL 14.1   Using appropriate models, diagrams, and symbols to represent mathematical concepts

Mathematical operations can be shown using manipulatives or drawings.

Multiplication can be shown using arrays.

3×4

Addition and subtractions can be demonstrated with symbols.

$$\psi \, \psi \, \psi \, \xi \, \xi \, \xi \, \xi$$
$$3 + 4 = 7$$
$$7 - 3 = 4$$

Fractions can be clarifies using pattern blocks, fraction bars, or paper folding.

Some examples of other manipulatives:

<u>Example</u>:
Using tiles to demonstrate both geometric ideas and number theory.

Give each group of students 12 tiles and instruct them to build rectangles. Students draw their rectangles on paper.

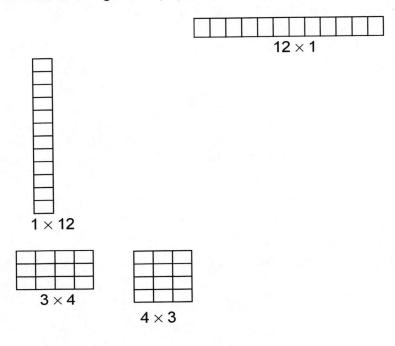

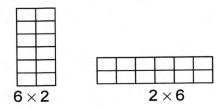

Encourage students to describe their reactions. Extend to 16 tiles. Ask students to form additional problems.

SKILL 14.2 Use appropriate vocabulary to express given mathematical ideas and relationships

Students need to use the proper mathematical terms and expressions. When reading decimals, they need to read 0.4 as "four tenths" to promote better understanding of the concepts. They should do their work in a neat and organized manner. Students need to be encouraged to verbalize their strategies, both in computation and word problems. Additionally, writing original word problems fosters understanding of math language. Another idea is requiring students to develop their own glossary of mathematical glossary. Knowing the answers and being able to communicate them are equally important.

COMPETENCY 15.0

BASIC MATH

Good teaching is one-fourth preparation and three-fourths theatre.

Gail Goodwin

COMPETENCY 15.0   **UNDERSTAND SKILLS AND CONCEPTS RELATED TO NUMBER AND NUMERATION, AND APPLY THESE CONCEPTS TO REAL-WORLD SITUATIONS**

SKILL 15.1   **Use ratios, proportion, and percents to solve problems**

A **ratio** is a comparison of two numbers. A **proportion** is a statement that two ratios are equivalent. Proportions can be solved by using cross-products.

Example: $\dfrac{n}{12} = \dfrac{7}{14}$

$n \times 14 = 7 \times 12$ Multiply to find the cross-product.
$14n = 84$

$\dfrac{14n}{14} = \dfrac{84}{14}$ Divide both sides of the equation by 14.

$n = 6$

Proportions can be used to solve word problems whenever relationships are compared. Some situations include scale drawings and maps, similar polygons, speed, time and distance, cost, and comparison shopping.

Example 1:   Which is the better buy, 6 items for $1.29 or 8 items for $1.69?

Find the unit price.

$\dfrac{6}{1.29} = \dfrac{1}{x}$ $\dfrac{8}{1.69} = \dfrac{1}{x}$
$6x = 1.29$ $8x = 1.69$
$x = 0.215$ $x = 0.21125$

Thus, 8 items for $1.69 is the better buy.

Example 2:   A car travels 125 miles in 2.5 hours. How far will it go in 6 hours?

Write a proportion comparing the distance and time.

$\dfrac{\text{miles}}{\text{hours}}$ $\dfrac{125}{2.5} = \dfrac{x}{6}$
$2.5x = 750$
$x = 300$

Thus, the car can travel 300 miles in 6 hours. Word problems involving percents can be solved by writing the problem as an equation, then solving the equation. Keep in mind that **"of"** means **"multiplication"** and **"is"** means **"equals."**

Example: The Ski Club has 85 members. 80% of the members are able to attend the meeting. How many members attend the meeting?

Restate the problem   What is 80% of 85?
Write an equation $n = 0.8 \times 85$
Solve $n = 68$

Sixty-eight members attend the meeting.

SKILL 15.2 Comparing and ordering fractions, decimals, and percents

Percent means parts of one hundred. Fractions, decimals and percents can be interchanged.

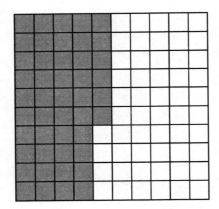

The shaded region represents 46 out of 100 or 0.46 or $\dfrac{46}{100}$ or 46%.

If a fraction can easily be converted to an equivalent **fraction** whose denominator is a power of 10 (for example, 10, 100, 1000), then it can easily be expressed as a **decimal** or **%.**

Examples: $\frac{1}{10} = 0.10 = 10\%$

$\frac{2}{5} = \frac{4}{10} = 0.40 = 40\%$

$\frac{1}{4} = \frac{25}{100} = 0.25 = 25\%$

$1 = 100\%$

Alternately, the **fraction** can be converted to a **decimal** and then a **percent** by dividing the numerator by the denominator, adding a decimal point and zeroes.

Example: $\frac{3}{8} = 8\overline{)3.000}^{\,0.375} = 37.5\%$

A **decimal** can be converted to a **percent** by multiplying by 100, or merely moving the decimal point two places to the right. A **percent** can be converted to a **decimal** by dividing by 100, or moving the decimal point two places to the left.

Examples: $0.375 = 37.5\%$
$0.7 = 70\%$
$0.04 = 4\%$
$3.15 = 315\%$

$84\% = 0.84$
$3\% = 0.03$
$60\% = 0.6$
$110\% = 1.1$
$\frac{1}{2}\% = 0.5\% = 0.005$

A **percent** can be converted to a **fraction** by placing it over 100 and reducing to simplest terms.

Examples: $32\% = \frac{32}{100} = \frac{8}{25}$

$6\% = \frac{6}{100} = \frac{3}{50}$

$111\% = \frac{111}{100} = 1\frac{11}{100}$

ELEMENTARY EDUCATION   90

SKILL 15.3   Solving problems using equivalent forms of numbers

The **exponent form** is a shortcut method to write repeated multiplication. The **base** is the factor. The **exponent** tells how many times that number is multiplied by itself.

Example: 3^4 is $3 \times 3 \times 3 \times 3 = 81$
where 3 is the base and 4 is the exponent.

x^2 is read "x squared"
y^3 is read "y cubed"

$a^1 = a$ for all values of a; thus $17^1 = 17$
$b^0 = 1$ for all values of b; thus $24^0 = 1$

When 10 is raised to any power, the exponent tells the numbers of zeroes in the product.

Example: $10^7 = 10,000,000$

Scientific notation is a more convenient method for writing very large and very small numbers. It employs two factors. The **first factor** is a **number between 1 and 10**. The **second factor** is a **power of 10**.

Example 1: Write 372,000 in scientific notation
Move the decimal point to form a number between 1 and 10; thus 3.72. Since the decimal point was moved 5 places, the power of 10 is 10^5. The exponent is positive since the decimal point was moved to the left.
$372,000 = 3.72 \times 10^5$

Example 2: Write 0.0000072 in scientific notation.
Move the decimal point 6 places to the right.
$0.0000072 = 7.2 \times 10^{-6}$

Example 3: Write 2.19×10^8 in standard form.
Since the exponent is positive, move the decimal point 8 places to the right, and add additional zeroes as needed.
$2.19 \times 10^8 = 219,000,000$

<u>Example 4</u>: Write 8.04×10^{-4} in standard form.
Move the decimal point 4 places to the left, writing additional zeroes as needed.

$$8.04 \times 10^{-4} = 0.000804$$

* Note: The first factor **must** be between 1 and 10.

SKILL 15.4   The properties of real numbers

The real number system includes all rational and irrational numbers.

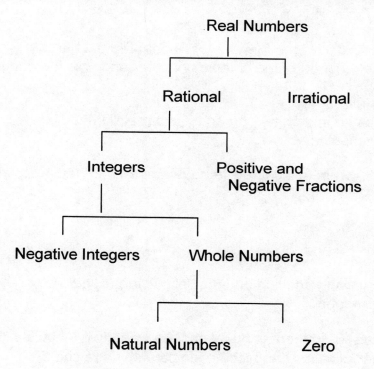

Rational numbers can be expressed as the ratio of two integers, $\frac{a}{b}$ where $b \neq 0$,   for

example $\frac{2}{3}$, $-\frac{4}{5}$, $5 = \frac{5}{1}$.

The rational numbers include integers, fractions and mixed numbers, terminating and repeating decimals. Every rational number can be expressed as a repeating or terminating decimal and can be shown on a number line.

Integers are positive and negative whole numbers and zero.
...-6, -5, -4, -3, -2, -1, 0, 1, 2, 3, 4, 5, 6, ...

Whole numbers are natural numbers and zero.
0, 1, 2, 3, ,4 ,5 ,6 ...

Natural numbers are the counting numbers.
1, 2, 3, 4, 5, 6, ...

Irrational numbers are real numbers that cannot be written as the ratio of two integers. These are infinite non-repeating decimals.
Examples: $\sqrt{5}$ = 2.2360.., pi = π = 3.1415927...

Complex numbers can be written in the form $a + bi$ where i represents $\sqrt{-1}$ and a and b are real numbers. a is the real part of the complex number and b is the imaginary part.

If $b = 0$, then the number has no imaginary part and it is a real number.
If $b \neq 0$, then the number is imaginary.

Complex numbers are found when trying to solve equations with negative square roots.

Example: If $x^2 + 9 = 0$
then $x^2 = -9$
and $x = \sqrt{-9}$ or +3i and -3i

Real numbers exhibit the following addition and multiplication properties, where $a, b,$ and c are real numbers.

Note: Multiplication is implied when there is no symbol between two variables. Thus, $a \times b$ can be written ab. Multiplication can also be indicated by a raised dot ·

Closure
$a + b$ is a real number
Example: Since 2 and 5 are both real numbers, 7 is also a real number.

ab is a real number
Example: Since 3 and 4 are both real numbers, 12 is also a real number.

The sum or product of two real numbers is a real number.

Commutative

$a + b = b + a$
Example: $5 +\ ^-8 =\ ^-8 + 5 =\ ^-3$

$ab = ba$
Example: $^-2 \times 6 = 6 \times\ ^-2 =\ ^-12$

The order of the addends or factors does not affect the sum or product.

Associative

$(a + b) + c = a + (b + c)$
Example: $(^-2 + 7) + 5 =\ ^-2 + (7 + 5)$
$\qquad 5 + 5 =\ ^-2 + 12\ = 10$

$(ab)\ c\ =\ a\ (bc)$
Example: $(3 \times\ ^-7) \times 5\ =\ 3 \times\ (^-7 \times 5)$
$\qquad ^-21 \times 5 = 3 \times\ ^-35 =\ ^-105$

The grouping of the addends or factors does not affect the sum or product.

Distributive
$a\ (b + c) = ab + ac$
Example: $6 \times (\ ^-4 + 9) = (6 \times\ ^-4) + (6 \times 9)$
$\qquad 6 \times 5 =\ ^-24 + 54 = 30$

To multiply a sum by a number, multiply each addend by the number, then add the products.

Additive Identity (Property of Zero)
$a + 0 = a$
Example: $17 + 0 = 17$

The sum of any number and zero is that number.

Multiplicative Identity (Property of One)
$a \cdot 1 = a$
Example: $^-34 \times 1 =\ ^-34$

The product of any number and one is that number.

Additive Inverse (Property of Opposites)

$a + {}^-a = 0$

<u>Example</u>: $25 + {}^-25 = 0$

The sum of any number and its opposite is zero.

Multiplicative Inverse (Property of Reciprocals)

$a \times \dfrac{1}{a} = 1$

<u>Example</u>: $5 \times \dfrac{1}{5} = 1$

The product of any number and its reciprocal is one.

COMPETENCY 16.0

LINEAR ALGEBRA

Part of teaching is helping students learn how to tolerate ambiguity, consider possibilities, and ask questions that are unanswerable.

Sara Lawrence Lightfoot

COMPETENCY 16.0   **UNDERSTAND AND APPLY THE PRINCIPLES AND PROPERTIES OF LINEAR ALGEBRAIC RELATIONS AND FUNCTIONS**

SKILL 16.1   **Analyzing mathematical relationships and patters using tables, equations, and graphs**

A first degree equation can be written in the form $ax + by = c$. To graph this equation, find either one point and the slope of the line or find two points. To find a point and slope, solve the equation for y. This gets the equation in the **slope-intercept form**, $y = mx + b$. The point $(0,b)$ is the y-intercept and m is the line's slope.

To find two points, substitute any number for x, then solve for y. Repeat this with a different number. To find the intercepts, substitute 0 for x and then 0 for y.

Remember that graphs will go up as they go to the right when the slope is positive. Negative slopes make the lines go down as they go to the right.

If the equation solves to $x =$ a constant, then the graph is a **vertical line**. It only has an x- intercept. Its slope is undefined.

If the equation solves to $y =$ a constant, then the graph is a **horizontal line**. It only has a y-intercept. Its slope is 0 (zero).

When graphing a linear inequality, the line will be dotted if the inequality sign is $<$ or $>$. If the inequality signs are either $\leq$ or $\geq$, the line on the graph will be a solid line.

Shade above the line when the inequality sign is $>$ or $\geq$. Shade below the line when the inequality sign is $<$ or $\leq$. For inequalities of the form $x > k$, $x \geq k$, $x < k$, or $x \leq k$ where k = any number, the graph will be a vertical line (solid or dotted.) Shade to the right for $>$ or $\geq$. Shade to the left for $<$ or $\leq$.

Remember: Dividing or multiplying by a negative number will reverse the direction of the inequality sign.

<u>Examples:</u>

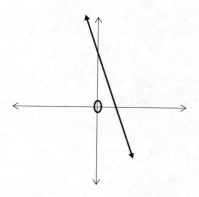

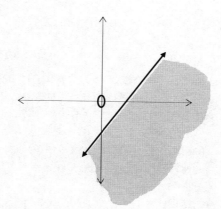

$$5x + 2y = 6$$
$$y = -\frac{5}{2}x + 3$$

$$3x - 2y \geq 6$$
$$y \leq \frac{3}{2}x - 3$$

SKILL 16.2   Derive an algebraic expression to represent a real-world relationship

<u>Example</u>: Mark and Mike are twins. Three times Mark's age plus four equals four times Mike's age minus 14. How old are the boys?

Since the boys are twins, their ages are the same. "Translate" the English into Algebra.

Let x = their age

$$3x + 4 = 4x - 14$$

$$18 = x$$

The boys are each 18 years old.

SKILL 16.3   Using algebraic functions to describe given graphs, to plot points, and to determine slopes

A **function** is a relation in which different ordered pairs have different first coordinates. (No x values are repeated.)

A first degree equation has an equation of the form $ax + by = c$. To find the slope of the line, solve the equation for y. This gets the equation into **slope-intercept form**, $y = mx + b$ where m represents the slope of the line.

To find the y-intercept, substitute 0 for x and solve for y. This is the y-intercept. The y-intercept is also the value of b in $y = mx + b$.

To find the x-intercept, substitute 0 for y and solve for x. This is the x-intercept.

<u>Example 1</u>: Find the slope and y-intercept of $3x + 2y = 14$.

$$3x + 2y = 14$$
$$2y = -3x + 14$$
$$y = -\frac{2}{3}x + 7$$

The slope of the line is $-\frac{2}{3}$, the value of m.

The y-intercept of the line is 7.

The intercepts can also be found by substituting 0 in place of the other variable in the equation.

<u>Example 2</u>: Find the x- and y-intercepts of $3x + 2y = 14$.

To find the y-intercept, let $x = 0$
$$3(0) + 2y = 14$$
$$0 + 2y = 14$$
$$2y = 14$$
$$y = 7$$

(0,7) is the y intercept.

To find the x-intercept: let $y = 0$
$$3x + 2(0) = 14$$
$$3x + 0 = 14$$
$$3x = 14$$
$$x = \frac{14}{3}$$

$(\frac{14}{3}, 0)$ is the x-intercept.

The equation of a line from its graph can be found by determining its slope and its y-intercept. To find the slope, find two points on the graph where the coordinates are integer values. Using points (x_1, y_1) and (x_2, y_2)

$$\text{slope} = \frac{y_2 - y_1}{x_2 - x_1}$$

or the change in y divided by the change in x

The y-intercept is the y-coordinate of the point where the line crosses the y-axis. The equation can be written in slope-intercept form, which is **$y = mx + b$**, where m is the slope and b is the y-intercept. To re-write the equation into some other form, multiply each term by the common denominator of all the fractions. Then rearrange terms as necessary.

If the graph is a **vertical line**, then the equation solves to
    $x =$ the x coordinate of any point on the line.

If the graph is a **horizontal line**, then the equation solves to
    $y =$ the y coordinate of any point on the line.

Examples:

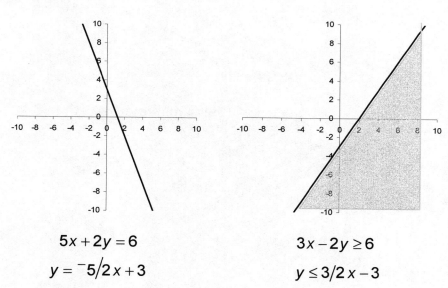

$$5x + 2y = 6$$
$$y = {}^{-}5/2\,x + 3$$

$$3x - 2y \geq 6$$
$$y \leq 3/2\,x - 3$$

SKILL 16.4   Perform algebraic operations to solve equations and inequalities

A **linear equation in one variable** can be written in the form **ax + b = 0**, where a and b are real numbers and $a \neq 0$.

An equation can be solved by performing the same operations on both sides of the equation.

Example:

$4x - 3 = {}^{-}5x + 6$	
$(4x - 3) + 3 = ({}^{-}5x + 6) + 3$	Add 3.
$4x = {}^{-}5x + 9$	Simplify.
$4x + 5x = ({}^{-}5x + 9) + 5x$	Add 5x.
$\dfrac{9x}{9} = \dfrac{9}{9}$	Simplify.
	Divide by 9.
$x = 1$	Simplify.

An **inequality** is a statement that orders two expressions. The symbols used are $<$ (less than), $>$ (greater than), $\leq$ (less than or equal to), $\geq$ (greater than or equal to) and $\neq$ (not equal to). Most inequalities have an infinite number of solutions. Methods for solving inequalities are similar to those used for solving equations, with this exception--when both sides of an inequality are multiplied or divided by a <u>negative</u> real number, the inequality sign in reversed.

Example 1:

$3x - 2 > 13$	
$(3x - 2) + 2 > 13 + 2$	Add 2.
$\dfrac{3x}{3} > \dfrac{15}{3}$	Simplify.
	Divide by 3.
$x > 5$	Simplify.

Thus the solution set is all real numbers greater than 5.

Example 2:

$x + 11 \leq 5x + 3$	
$(x + 11) - 11 \leq (5x + 3) - 11$	Subtract 11.
$x \leq 5x - 8$	Simplify.
$x - 5x \leq 5x - 8 - 5x$	Subtract 5x.
	Simplify.
$\dfrac{{}^{-}4x}{{}^{-}4} \leq \dfrac{{}^{-}8}{{}^{-}4}$	Divide by -4.
$x \geq 2$	Reverse the inequality sign.

Thus the solution set is all real numbers greater than or equal to 2.

COMPETENCY 17.0

GEOMETRY

The teacher who can make hard things easy is the educator.
Ralph Waldo Emerson

COMPETENCY 17.0   **UNDERSTAND PRINCIPLES AND PROPERTIES OF GEOMETRY AND TRIGONOMETRY, AND APPLY THEM TO MODEL AND SOLVE PROBLEMS**

SKILL 17.1 **Apply the concepts of similarity and congruence to solve real-world problems**

Congruent figures have the same size and shape. If one is placed above the other, it will fit exactly. Congruent lines have the same length. Congruent angles have equal measures.

The symbol for congruent is $\cong$.

Polygons (pentagons) ABCDE and VWXYZ are congruent. They are exactly the same size and shape.

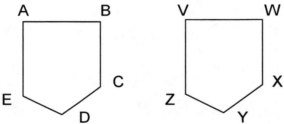

$$ABCDE \cong VWXYZ$$

Corresponding parts are those congruent angles and congruent sides, that is

corresponding angles	*corresponding sides*
$\angle A \leftrightarrow \angle V$	AB $\leftrightarrow$ VW
$\angle B \leftrightarrow \angle W$	BC $\leftrightarrow$ WX
$\angle C \leftrightarrow \angle X$	CD $\leftrightarrow$ XY
$\angle D \leftrightarrow \angle Y$	DE $\leftrightarrow$ YZ
$\angle E \leftrightarrow \angle Z$	AE $\leftrightarrow$ VZ

Two figures that have the **same shape** are **similar**. Two polygons are similar if corresponding angles are congruent and corresponding sides are in proportion. Corresponding parts of similar polygons are proportional.

Example:

Tommy draws and cuts out 2 triangles for a school project. One of them has sides of 3, 6, and 9 inches. The other triangle has sides of 2, 4, and 6. Is there a relationship between the two triangles?

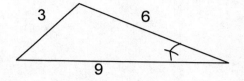   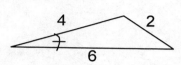

Take the proportion of the corresponding sides.

$$\frac{2}{3} \qquad\qquad \frac{4}{6} = \frac{2}{3} \qquad\qquad \frac{6}{9} = \frac{2}{3}$$

The smaller triangle is $\frac{2}{3}$ the size of the larger triangle.

SKILL 17.2   Applying knowledge of basic geometric figures to solve real-world problems involving more complex patterns

Example:

What will be the cost of carpeting a rectangular office that measures 12 feet by 15 feet if the carpet costs $12.50 per square yard?

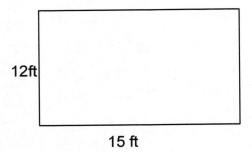

12ft

15 ft

The problem is asking you to determine the area of the office. The area of a rectangle is *length x width* = A

Substitute the given values in the equation A = *lw*

$$A = (12 \text{ ft.})(15 \text{ ft.})$$
$$A = 180 \text{ ft.}^2$$

The problem asked you to determine the cost of carpet at $12.50 per square yard.

First, you need to convert 180 ft.^{2} into yards^2.

$$1 \text{ yd.} = 3 \text{ ft.}$$
$$(1 \text{ yard})(1 \text{ yard}) = (3 \text{ feet})(3 \text{ feet})$$
$$1 \text{ yd}^2 = 9 \text{ ft}^2$$

Hence, $\dfrac{180 \text{ ft.}^2}{1} \times \dfrac{1 \text{ yd.}^2}{9 \text{ ft.}^2} = \dfrac{20}{1} \text{ yd.}^2 = 20 \text{ yd.}^2$

The carpet cost $12.50 per square yard; thus the cost of carpeting the office described is $12.50 x 20 = $250.00.

SKILL 17.3   Inductive vs. deductive reasoning

Inductive reasoning in mathematics includes making conjectures based on discoveries from observations. Deductive reasoning in mathematics includes either proving conjectures through valid inferences from assumptions or disproving conjectures by constructing counterexamples.

Emphasis is placed on the difference between supporting a mathematical conjecture and decisively establishing its truth. Students learn that the former may be done by testing additional cases but the latter is accomplished only by means of a rigorous proof.

Through a variety of exercises, puzzles, and games, students learn to:

- Recognize patterns and sequences
- Make reasonable conjectures by generalizing from patterns observed in particular cases
- Strengthen conjectures by testing additional cases
- Disprove false conjectures by formulating counterexamples

COMPETENCY 18.0

STATISTICS, MEASUREMENT, PROBABILITY

Education is not a preparation for life; education is life itself.

John Dewey

COMPETENCY 18.0 UNDERSTAND CONCEPTS RELATED TO STATISTICS, MEASUREMENT, AND PROBABILITY

SKILL 18.1 Estimate and convert measurements

To estimate measurement of familiar objects, it is first necessary to determine the units to be used.

Examples:
Length
1. The coastline of Florida   miles or kilometers
2. The width of a ribbon   inches or millimeters
3. The thickness of a book   inches or centimeters
4. The length of a football field   yards or meters
5. The depth of water in a pool   feet or meters

Weight or mass
1. A bag of sugar   pounds or grams
2. A school bus   tons or kilograms
3. A dime   ounces or grams

Capacity
1. Paint to paint a bedroom   gallons or liters
2. Glass of milk   cups or liters
3. Bottle of soda   quarts or liters
4. Medicine for child   ounces or milliliters

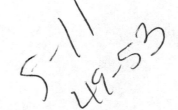

Examples: Estimate the measurements of the following objects.

length of a dollar bill	6 in.
weight of a baseball	1 pound
distance from New York to Florida	1100 km
amount of water to fill a medicine dropper	1 milliliter
length of a desk	2 meters
temperature of water in swimming pool	80° F

Depending on the degree of accuracy needed, an object may be measured to different units. For example, a pencil may be 6 inches to the nearest inch, or $6\frac{3}{8}$ inches to the nearest eighth of an inch. Similarly, it might be 15 cm to the nearest cm or 154 mm to the nearest mm.

The units of **length** in the customary system are inches, feet, yards and miles.

> 12 inches (in.) = 1 foot (ft.)
> 36 in. = 1 yard (yd.)
> 3 ft. = 1 yd.
> 5280 ft. = 1 mile (mi.)
> 1760 yd. = 1 mi.

To change from a **larger unit to a smaller unit, multiply**.
To change from a **smaller unit to a larger unit, divide**.

Example:

4 mi. = _____ yd.
Since 1760 yd. = 1 mile, multiply $4 \times 1760 = 7040$ yd.

The units of **weight** are ounces, pounds and tons.

> 16 ounces (oz.) = 1 pound
> (lb.)
> 2,000 lb. = 1 ton (T.)

Example:

$2 \frac{3}{4}$ T. = _____ lb.
$2 \frac{3}{4} \times 2,000 = 5,500$ lb.

The units of **capacity** are fluid ounces, cups, pints, quarts, and gallons.

> 8 fluid ounces (fl. oz.) = 1 cup (c.)
> 2 c. = 1 pint (pt.)
> 4 c. = 1 quart (qt.)
> 2 pt. = 1 qt.
> 4 qt. = 1 gallon (gal.)

Example1:

3 gal. = _____ qt.
$3 \times 4 = 12$ qt.

The metric system is based on multiples of <u>ten</u>. Conversions are made by simply moving the decimal point to the left or right.

kilo-	1000	thousands
hecto-	100	hundreds
deca-	10	tens
unit		
deci-	.1	tenths
centi-	.01	hundredths
milli-	.001	thousandths

The basic unit for **length** is the meter. One meter is approximately one yard.
The basic unit for **weight** or mass is the gram. A paper clip weighs about one gram.
The basic unit for **volume** is the liter. One liter is approximately a quart.

SKILL 18.2 Solving measurement problems involving volume, time, or speed

Example:

A class wants to take a field trip from New York City to Albany to visit the capital. The trip is approximately 160 miles. If they will be traveling at 50 miles per hour, how long will it take for them to get there (assuming traveling at a steady rate)?

Set up the equation as a proportion and solve:

$$\frac{50 \text{ miles}}{1 \text{ hours}} = \frac{160 \text{ miles}}{x \text{ hours}}$$

$$(160 \text{ miles})(1 \text{ hour}) = (50 \text{ miles})(x \text{ hours})$$
$$160 = 50x$$
$$x = 3.2 \text{ hours}$$

Example:

Students in a fourth grade class want to fill a 3 gallon jug using cups of water. How many cups of water are needed?

1 gallon = 16 cups of water

3 gallons x 16 cups = 48 cups of water are needed.

SKILL 18.3   Frequency, distributions, percentiles, and measures of central tendency

The arithmetic **mean** (or average) of a set of numbers is the *sum* of the numbers given, *divided* by the number of items being averaged.

Example: Find the mean. Round to the nearest tenth.
        24.6, 57.3, 44.1, 39.8, 64.5
        The sum is 230.3 ÷ 5 = 46.06, rounded to 46.1

The **median** of a set is the middle number. To calculate the median, the terms must be arranged in order. If there are an even number of terms, the median is the mean of the two middle terms.

Example 1: Find the median.
        12, 14, 27, 3, 13, 7, 17, 12, 22, 6, 16
        Rearrange the terms.
        3, 6, 7, 12, 12, **13**, 14, 16, 17, 22, 27
        Since there are 11 numbers, the middle would be the sixth number or 13.

The **mode** of a set of numbers is the number that occurs with the greatest frequency. A set can have no mode if each term appears exactly one time. Similarly, there can also be more than one mode.

Example 1: Find the mode.
        26, 15, 37, **26**, 35, **26**, 15
        15 appears twice, but 26 appears 3 times, therefore the mode is 26.

The **measures of central tendency** are the mean, median and mode. Different situations can best be described by each of these.

Example 1: Is the mean, median, or mode the best measure of central tendency for the set 135, 135, 137, 190?

        The mean is 149.25, the median is 136 and the mode is 135, therefore, the median or mode would be a better measure than the mean since they are both closer to most of the scores.

<u>Example 2:</u> The yearly salaries of the employees of Company A are $11,000, $12,000, $12,000, $15,000, $20,000, and $25,000. Which measure of central tendency would you use if you were a manager?   if you were an employee trying to get a raise?

The mean is $15,833
The median is $13,500
The mode is $12,000
The manager would probably use the mean since it is the largest amount.
The employee would most likely use the mode since is the smallest.

Percentiles divide data into 100 equal parts. A person whose score falls in the 65th percentile has outperformed 65 percent of all those who took the test. This does not mean that the score was 65 percent out of 100 nor does it mean that 65 percent of the questions answered were correct. It means that the grade was higher than 65 percent of all those who took the test.

<u>Example:</u> Graph this information on a circle graph:

Monthly expenses:

Rent, $400
Food, $150
Utilities, $75
Clothes, $75
Church, $100
Misc., $200

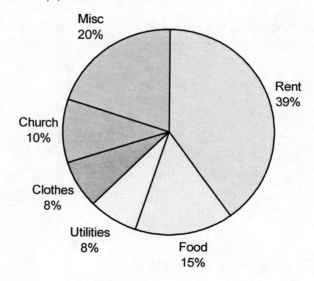

SKILL 18.4 Determine probabilities and make predictions based on probabilities

Probability measures the chances of an event occurring. The probability of an event that *must* occur, a certain event, is **one.** When no outcome is favorable, the probability of an impossible event is **zero.**

$$P(event) = \frac{\text{number of favorable outcomes}}{\text{number of possible outcomes}}$$

Example: Given one die with faces numbered 1 - 6, the probability of tossing an even number on one throw of the die is $\frac{3}{6}$ or $\frac{1}{2}$ since there are 3 favorable outcomes (even faces) and a total of 6 possible outcomes (faces).

If A and B are **independent** events then the probability both A and B will occur is the product of their individual probabilities.

Example 1: Given two dice, the probability of tossing a 3 on each of them simultaneously is the probability of a 3 on the first die, or $\frac{1}{6}$, times the probability of tossing a 3 on the second die, also $\frac{1}{6}$.

$$\frac{1}{6} \times \frac{1}{6} = \frac{1}{36}$$

Example 2: Given a jar containing 10 marbles, 3 red, 5 black, and 2 white. What is the probability of drawing a red marble and then a white marble if the marble is returned to the jar after choosing?

$$\frac{3}{10} \times \frac{2}{10} = \frac{6}{100} = \frac{3}{50}$$

When the outcome of the first event affects the outcome of the second event, the events are **dependent.** Any two events that are not independent are dependent. This is also known as conditional probability.

Probability of (A and B) = P(A) × P(B given A)

ELEMENTARY EDUCATION   113

Example: Two cards are drawn from a deck of 52 cards, without replacement; that is, the first card is not returned to the deck before the second card is drawn. What is the probability of drawing a diamond?

A = drawing a diamond first
B = drawing a diamond second

$$P(A) = \frac{13}{52} = \frac{1}{4} \qquad\qquad P(B) = \frac{12}{51} = \frac{4}{17}$$

$$P(A + B) = \frac{1}{4} \times \frac{4}{17} = \frac{1}{17}$$

COMPETENCY 19.0

SCIENCE ENVIRONMENT

In teaching children we must seek insensibly to uniting knowledge with the carrying out of that knowledge into practice.

Immanuel Kant

SKILL 19.1 Analyzing the effects of change in environmental conditions

Abiotic factors are non-living aspects of an ecosystem; soil quality, rainfall, sunlight, and temperature. Changes in climate and soil can cause effects at the beginning of the food chain, thus limiting or accelerating the growth of population.

Abiotic factors can have a dramatic impact on the food chain.

Producers are living organisms that use nonliving material, such as oxygen and other nutrients, as food. Green plants are producers and find themselves at the bottom of the food chain.

Consumers are living organisms that survive on the producers or other consumers. They do not make their own food.

> Herbivores are consumers that only eat plants.
> Omnivores are consumers that eat plants and other consumers.
> Carnivores are consumers that eat other consumers.

If the abiotic factors are not at optimal levels, the food chain can be disrupted. For example, if there is not enough rain, most plants will not survive. Herbivore, therefore, will not have an abundance of food and many of them will die. This depletes the omnivore's food source; not only from no vegetation to eat, but now there are less herbivores to eat as well. The carnivores will encounter a decrease in food supply as well with little other consumers to eat.

SKILL 19.2 Analyzing the effects of human activities on the environment

For centuries, humans have increasingly been altering the environments in which we live. Everything from driving cars to logging has had a toll on the environment.

Pollutants are impurities in the air and water that may be harmful to life. Oil is a major pollutant that can cause severe destruction of the oceans and beaches and the animal life when there is an oil spill.

Global warming is an enormous environmental issue today. Global warming is caused by the "greenhouse effect." Atmospheric greenhouse gases such as, water vapor, carbon dioxide, and other gases, trap some of the outgoing energy, retaining heat somewhat like the glass panels of a greenhouse. This occurs naturally, and without it, the temperature on earth would be too low to sustain life. The problem is when too much of these gases enter the atmosphere and enhance their heat-trapping ability, resulting in global warming. Over the past 100 years, the Earth's surface temperature has risen by 1 degree Fahrenheit, with accelerated warming occurring in the past two decades. The increase of gasses in the atmosphere is caused by the burning of combustion fuel and carbon dioxide emissions from cars and factories.

All acids contain hydrogen. Substances from factory and car exhaust dissolve in rain water, forming acid rain. When this rain falls onto stone the acids can react with metallic compounds and gradually wear the stone away.

Since radioactivity has become readily available, it has been a major concern in terms of the threat of a nuclear disaster. Radioactivity ionizes the air they travel through. They are strong enough to kill cancer cells or dangerous enough to cause illness or even death. Gamma rays can penetrate the body and damage its cells. In a nuclear disaster, damage to the land and all living organisms is inevitable.

Logging also has a negative impact on the environment. Clear-cutting forests leaves the soil unprotected and can cause disasters such as mudslides. Also, the quality of soil in that area diminishes the chances of successful re-growth of living organisms.

There are some benefits of human activities in the environment. The populations of many animal species that were endangered have risen because of protection laws and studying the animals and their habitats.

With the increasing development of new technology come other benefits to the environment. The recycling process has prevented the unnecessary waste of plastics, glass, and paper by reusing the products to create new ones.

COMPETENCY 20.0

LIFE SCIENCE

In seed time learn, in harvest teach, in winter enjoy.

William Blake

COMPETENCY 20.0   UNDERSTAND THE PRINCIPLES OF LIFE SCIENCE

SKILL 20.1   Identify variations in life forms resulting in adaptation to the environment

The debate over evolution or creationism causes a hotbed of reactions. Where once evolution was strongly taught as a singular response now, Ohio in 2002 like many other states is mandating that opposing viewpoints are presented in the classroom. Textbooks that mention God and creationism are no longer banned as a breach of separation of church and state but rather introduced so that students can be exposed to varied ideology. Freedom of speech is the law.

Darwin defined the theory of Natural Selection in the mid-1800's. Through the study of finches on the Galapagos Islands, Darwin theorized that nature selects the traits that are advantageous to the organism. Those that do not possess the desirable trait die and do not pass on their genes. Those more fit to survive reproduce, thus increasing that gene in the population. Darwin listed four principles to define natural selection:

1. The individuals in a certain species vary from generation to generation.

2. Some of the variations are determined by the genetic makeup of the species.

3. More individuals are produced than will survive.

4. Some genes allow for better survival of an animal.

Causes of evolution - certain factors increase the chances of variability in a population, thus leading to evolution. Items that increase variability include mutations, sexual reproduction, immigration, large population, and variation in geographic local. Items that decrease variation would be natural selection, emigration, small population, and random mating.

Sexual selection - obviously the genes that happen to come together determine the makeup of the gene pool. Animals that use mating behaviors may be successful or unsuccessful. An animal that lacks attractive plumage or has a weak mating call will not attract the female, thereby eventually limiting that gene in the gene pool. Mechanical isolation, where sex organs do not fit the female, has an obvious disadvantage.

SKILL 20.2   Knowledge of ecology

Ecology is the study of organisms, where they live and their interactions with the environment. A population is a group of the same species in a specific area. A community is a group of populations residing in the same area. Communities that are ecologically similar in regards to temperature, rainfall and the species that live there are called biomes. Specific biomes include:

Marine - covers 75% of the earth. This biome is organized by the depth of the water. The intertidal zone is from the tide line to the edge of the water. The littoral zone is from the waters edge to the open sea. It includes coral reef habitats and is the most densely populated area of the marine biome. The open sea zone is divided into the epipelagic zone and the pelagic zone. The epipelagic zone receives more sunlight and has a larger number of species. The ocean floor is called the benthic zone and is populated with bottom feeders.

Tropical Rain Forest - temperature is constant (25 degrees C), rainfall exceeds 200 cm. per year. Located around the area of the equator, the rain forest has abundant, diverse species of plants and animals.

Savanna - temperatures range from 0 - 25 degrees C depending on the location. Rainfall is from 90 to 150 cm per year. Plants include shrubs and grasses. The savanna is a transitional biome between the rain forest and the desert.

Desert - temperatures range from 10 - 38 degrees C. Rainfall is under 25 cm per year. Plant species include xerophytes and succulents. Lizards, snakes and small mammals are common animals

Temperate Deciduous Forest - temperature ranges from -24 to 38 degrees C. Rainfall is between 65 to 150 cm per year. Deciduous trees are common, as well as deer, bear and squirrels.

Taiga - temperatures range from -24 to 22 degrees C. Rainfall is between 35 to 40 cm per year. Taiga is located very north and very south of the equator, getting close to the poles. Plant life includes conifers and plants that can withstand harsh winters. Animals include weasels, mink, and moose.

Tundra - temperatures range from -28 to 15 degrees C. Rainfall is limited, ranging from 10 to 15 cm per year. The tundra is located even further north and south of the taiga. Common plants include lichens and mosses. Animals include polar bears and musk ox.

Polar or Permafrost - temperature ranges from -40 to 0 degrees C. It rarely gets above freezing. Rainfall is below 10 cm per year. Most water is bound up as ice. Life is limited.

Succession - Succession is an orderly process of replacing a community that has been damaged or has begun where no life previously existed. Primary succession occurs after a community has been totally wiped out by a natural disaster or where life never existed before, as in a flooded area. Secondary succession takes place in communities that were once flourishing but disturbed by some source, either man or nature, but not totally stripped. A climax community is a community that is established and flourishing.

Definitions of feeding relationships

Parasitism - two species that occupy a similar place; the parasite benefits from the relationship, the host is harmed.

Commensalism - two species that occupy a similar place; neither species is harmed or benefits from the relationship.

Mutualism - two species that occupy a similar place; both species benefit from the relationship.

Competition - two species that occupy the same habitat or eat the same food are said to be in competition with each other.

Predation - animals that eat other animals are called predators. They animals they feed on are called the prey. Population growth depends upon competition for food, water, shelter and space. The amount of predators determines the amount of prey, which in turn affects the number of predators.

Carrying Capacity - this is the total amount of life a habitat can support. Once the habitat runs out of food, water, shelter or space, the carrying capacity decreases, and then stabilizes.

Biotic factors - living things in an ecosystem; plants, animals, bacteria, fungi, etc.

Abiotic factors - non-living aspects of an ecosystem; soil quality, rainfall, temperature.

Biogeochemical cycles - essential elements are recycled through an ecosystem. At times, the element needs to be "fixed" in a useable form. Some cycles are dependent on plants, algae and bacteria to fix nutrients for use by animals.

Water cycle - 2% of all the available water is fixed and unavailable in ice or the bodies of organisms. Available water includes surface water (lakes, ocean, rivers) and ground water (aquifers, wells) 96% of all available water is from ground water. Water is recycled through the processes of evaporation and precipitation. The water present now is the water that has been here since our atmosphere formed.

ELEMENTARY EDUCATION 121

Carbon cycle - Ten percent of all available carbon in the air (from carbon dioxide gas) is fixed by photosynthesis. Plants fix carbon in the form of glucose, animals eat the plants and are able to obtain their source of carbon. When animals release carbon dioxide through respiration, the plants again have a source of carbon to fix again.

Nitrogen cycle - Eighty percent of the atmosphere is in the form of nitrogen gas. Nitrogen must be fixed and taken out of the gaseous form to be incorporated into an organism. Only a few genera of bacteria have the correct enzymes to break the triple bond between nitrogen atoms. These bacteria live within the roots of legumes (peas, beans, alfalfa) and add bacteria to the soil so it may be taken up by the plant. Nitrogen is necessary to make amino acids and the nitrogenous bases of DNA.

Phosphorus cycle - Phosphorus exists as a mineral and is not found in the atmosphere. Fungi and plant roots have a structure called mycorrhizae that are able to fix insoluble phosphates into useable phosphorus. Urine and decayed matter returns phosphorus to the earth where it can be fixed in the plant. Phosphorus is needed for the backbone of DNA and for ATP manufacture.

Ecological Problems - nonrenewable resources are fragile and must be conserved for use in the future. Man's impact and knowledge of conservation will control our future.

Biological magnification - chemicals and pesticides accumulate along the food chain. Tertiary consumers have more accumulated toxins than animals at the bottom of the food chain.

Simplification of the food web - Three major crops feed the world (rice, corn, wheat). The planting of these foods wipe out other habitats and push those animals into other habitats causing overpopulation or extinction.

Fuel sources - strip mining and the overuse of oil reserves have depleted these resources. At the current rate of consumption, conservation or alternate fuel sources will guarantee our future as a species.

Pollution - although technology gives us many advances, pollution is a side effect of production. Waste disposal and the burning of fossil fuels has polluted our land, water and air. Global warming and acid rain are two results of the burning of hydrocarbons and sulfur.

Global warming - rain forest depletion, the use of fossil fuels and aerosols has caused an increase in carbon dioxide production. This leads to a decrease in the amount of oxygen, which is directly proportional to the amount of ozone. As the ozone layer depletes, more heat enters our atmosphere and is trapped. This causes an overall warming effect that may eventually melt polar ice caps, causing a rise in water levels and changes in climate, which will affect weather systems.

Endangered species - construction to house our overpopulated world has caused a destruction of habitat for other animals leading to extinction.

Overpopulation - the human race is still growing at an exponential rate. Carrying capacity has not been met due to our ability to use technology to produce more food

COMPETENCY 21.0

PHYSICAL SCIENCE

What people need and what they want may be very
different...Teachers are those who educate the people
to appreciate the things they need.

Elbert Hubbard

COMPETENCY 21.0   UNDERSTAND THE PRINCIPLES OF PHYSICAL SCIENCE

SKILL 21.1   Analyzing celestial and atmospheric phenomena

The **sun** is considered the nearest star to earth that produces solar energy by the process of nuclear fusion, hydrogen gas is converted to helium gas. Energy flows out of the core to the surface, radiation then escapes into space.

Parts of the sun include: (1) **core**, the inner portion of the sun where fusion takes place, (2) **photosphere**, considered the surface of the sun which produces **sunspots** (cool, dark areas that can be seen on its surface), (3) **chromosphere**, hydrogen gas causes this portion to be red in color, **solar flares** (sudden brightness of the chromosphere) and **solar prominences** (gases that shoot outward from the chromosphere) is found in the chromosphere, and (4) **corona**, the transparent area of sun visible only during a total eclipse.

Solar radiation is energy traveling from the sun that radiates into space. **Solar flares** produce excited protons and electrons that shoot outward from the chromosphere at great speeds reaching earth. These particles disturb radio reception and also effect the magnetic field on earth.

Earth's orbit around the sun and the Earth's axis of rotation determine the seasons of the year. When the northern and southern hemispheres of Earth are pointed towards the sun, it is summer and when it is pointed away from the sun it is winter. Because of the axis of rotation, both hemispheres cannot be in the same season. The two hemispheres are in opposite seasons at all times.

The **moon** is a sphere which is always half illuminated by the sun. The moon phase we see is dependent of the position of the moon to the earth. During each lunar orbit (a lunar month), we see the Moon's appearance change from not visibly illuminated through partially illuminated to fully illuminated, then back through partially illuminated to not illuminated again. Although this cycle is a continuous process, there are eight distinct, traditionally recognized stages, called phases. The phases designate both the degree to which the Moon is illuminated and the geometric appearance of the illuminated part.

New Moon - The Moon's unilluminated side is facing the Earth. The Moon is not visible (except during a solar eclipse).

Waxing Crescent - The Moon appears to be partly but less than one-half illuminated by direct sunlight. The fraction of the Moon's disk that is illuminated is increasing.

First Quarter - One-half of the Moon appears to be illuminated by direct sunlight. The fraction of the Moon's disk that is illuminated is increasing.

Waxing Gibbous - The Moon appears to be more than one-half but not fully illuminated by direct sunlight. The fraction of the Moon's disk that is illuminated is increasing.

Full Moon - The Moon's illuminated side is facing the Earth. The Moon appears to be completely illuminated by direct sunlight.

Waning Gibbous - The Moon appears to be more than one-half but not fully illuminated by direct sunlight. The fraction of the Moon's disk that is illuminated is decreasing.

Last Quarter - One-half of the Moon appears to be illuminated by direct sunlight. The fraction of the Moon's disk that is illuminated is decreasing.

Waning Crescent - The Moon appears to be partly but less than one-half illuminated by direct sunlight. The fraction of the Moon's disk that is illuminated is decreasing.

The moon, the earth, and the sun affect ocean tides. Along the west coast of the United States we experience 4 different tides per day: 2 highs and 2 lows. When the moon, the earth, and the sun are in a line *Spring Tides* are formed. During these tides you may observe higher and lower than normal tides. In other words, there will be very high tides and very low tides. When the moon, the earth, and sun are at right angles to each other *Neap Tides* are formed. During these tides you will not be able to observe a great deal of difference in the heights of the high and low tides.

SKILL 21.2   Forces that shape the earth's surface

Orogeny is the term given to natural mountain building.

A mountain is terrain that has been raised high above the surrounding landscape by volcanic action, or some form of tectonic plate collisions. The plate collisions could be intercontinental or ocean floor collisions with a continental crust (subduction). The physical composition of mountains would include igneous, metamorphic, or sedimentary rocks; some may have rock layers that are tilted or distorted by plate collision forces.

There are many different types of mountains. The physical attributes of a mountain range depends upon the angle at which plate movement thrust layers of rock to the surface. Many mountains (Adirondacs, Southern Rockies) were formed along high angle faults.

Folded mountains (Alps, Himalayas) are produced by the folding of rock layers during their formation. The Himalayas are the highest mountains in the world and contains Mount Everest which rises almost 9 km above sea level. The Himalayas were formed when India collided with Asia. The movement which created this collision is still in process at the rate of a few centimeters per year.

Fault-block mountains (Utah, Arizona, New Mexico) are created when plate movement produces tension forces instead of compression forces. The area under tension produces normal faults and rock along these faults is displaced upward. Dome mountains are formed as magma tries to push up through the crust but fails to break the surface. Dome mountains resemble a huge blister on the earth's surface.

Upwarped mountains (Black Hills of S.D.) are created in association with a broad arching of the crust. They can also be formed by rock thrust upward along high angle faults.

Volcanic mountains are built up by successive deposits of volcanic materials.

Volcanism is the term given to the movement of magma through the crust and its emergence as lava onto the earth's surface.

An active volcano is one that is presently erupting or building to an eruption. A dormant volcano is one that is between eruptions but still shows signs of internal activity that might lead to an eruption in the future. An extinct volcano is said to be no longer capable of erupting. Most of the world's active volcanoes are found along the rim of the Pacific Ocean, which is also a major earthquake zone. This curving belt of active faults and volcanoes is often called the Ring of Fire.

The world's best known volcanic mountains include: Mount Etna in Sicily and Mount Kilimanjaro in Africa. The Hawaiian islands are actually the tops of a chain of volcanic mountains that rise from the ocean floor.

There are three types of volcanic mountains: shield volcanoes, cinder cones and composite volcanoes.

Shield Volcanoes are associated with quiet eruptions. Lava emerges from the vent or opening in the crater and flows freely out over the Earth's surface until it cools and hardens into a layer of igneous rock. Repeated lava flows builds this type of volcano into the largest volcanic mountain. Mauna Loa found in Hawaii, is the largest volcano on Earth.

Cinder Cone Volcanoes associated with explosive eruptions as lava is hurled high into the air in a spray of droplets of various sizes. These droplets cool and harden into cinders and particles of ash before falling to the ground. The ash and cinder pile up around the vent to form a steep, cone-shaped hill called the cinder cone. Cinder cone volcanoes are relatively small but may form quite rapidly.

Composite Volcanoes are described as being built by both lava flows and layers of ash and cinders. Mount Fuji in Japan, Mount St. Helens in Washington, USA and Mount Vesuvius in Italy are all famous Composite Volcanoes.

Mechanisms of producing mountains

Mountains are produced by different types of mountain-building processes. Most major mountain ranges are formed by the processes of folding and faulting.

Folded Mountains are produced by folding of rock layers. Crustal movements may press horizontal layers of sedimentary rock together from the sides, squeezing them into wavelike folds. Up-folded sections of rock are called anticlines; down-folded sections of rock are called synclines. The Appalachian Mountains are an example of folded mountains with long ridges and valleys in a series of anticlines and synclines formed by folded rock layers.

Faults are fractures in the earth's crust which have been created by either tension or compression forces transmitted through the crust. These forces are produced by the movement of separate blocks of crust.

Faultings are categorized on the basis of the relative movement between the blocks on both sides of the fault plane. The movement can be horizontal, vertical or oblique.

A dip-slip fault occurs when the movement of the plates is vertical and opposite. The displacement is in the direction of the inclination, or dip, of the fault. Dip-slip faults are classified as normal faults when the rock above the fault plane moves down relative to the rock below.

Reverse faults are created when the rock above the fault plane moves up relative to the rock below. Reverse faults having a very low angle to the horizontal are also referred to as thrust faults.

Faults in which the dominant displacement horizontal movement along the trend or strike (length) of the fault, are called strike-slip faults. When a large strike-slip fault is associated with plate boundaries it is called a transform fault. The San Andreas Fault in California is a well-known transform fault. Faults that have both vertical and horizontal movement are called oblique-slip faults.

When lava cools, igneous rock is formed. This formation can occur either above ground or below ground.

Intrusive rock includes any igneous rock that was formed below the earth's surface. Batholiths are the largest structures of intrusive type rock and are composed of near granite materials; they are the core of the Sierra Nevada Mountains.
Extrusive rock includes any igneous rock that was formed at the earth's surface

Dikes are old lava tubes formed when magma entered a vertical fracture and hardened. Sometimes magma squeezes between two rock layers and hardens into a thin horizontal sheet called a sill. A **laccolith** is formed in much the same way as a sill, but the magma that creates a **laccolith** is very thick and does not flow easily. It pools and forces the overlying strait creating an obvious surface dome.

A **caldera** is normally formed by the collapse of the top of a volcano. This collapse can be caused by a massive explosion that destroys the cone and empties most if not all of the magma chamber below the volcano. The cone collapses into the empty magma chamber forming a caldera.

An inactive volcano may have magma solidified in its pipe. This structure, called a volcanic neck, is resistant to erosion and today may be the only visible evidence of the past presence of an active volcano.

When lava cools, igneous rock is formed. This formation can occur either above ground or below ground.

Glaciation

A continental glacier covered a large part of North America during the most recent ice age. Evidence of this glacial coverage remains as abrasive grooves, large boulders from northern environments dropped in southerly locations, glacial troughs created by the rounding out of steep valleys by glacial scouring, and the remains of glacial sources called cirques that were created by frost wedging the rock at the bottom of the glacier. Remains of plants and animals found in warm climate have been discovered in the moraines and out wash plains help to support the theory of periods of warmth during the past ice ages.

The Ice Age began about 2 -3 million years ago. This age saw the advancement and retreat of glacial ice over millions of years. Theories relating to the origin of glacial activity include Plate Tectonics where it can be demonstrated that some continental masses, now in temperate climates, were at one time blanketed by ice and snow. Another theory involves changes in the earth's orbit around the sun, changes in the angle of the earth's axis, and the wobbling of the earth's axis. Support for the validity of this theory has come from deep ocean research that indicates a correlation between climatic sensitive micro-organisms and the changes in the earth's orbital status.

About 12,000 years ago, a vast sheet of ice covered a large part of the northern United States. This huge, frozen mass had moved southward from the northern regions of Canada as several large bodies of slow-moving ice, or glaciers. A time period in which glaciers advance over a large portion of a continent is called an ice age. A glacier is a large mass of ice that moves or flows over the land in response to gravity. Glaciers form among high mountains and in other cold regions.

There are two main types of glaciers: valley glaciers and continental glaciers. Erosion by valley glaciers are characteristic of U-shaped erosion. They produce sharp peaked mountains such as the Matterhorn in Switzerland. Erosion by continental glaciers often ride over mountains in their paths leaving smoothed, rounded mountains and ridges.

SKILL 21.3   Distinguish between physical and chemical properties of matter

Everything in our world is made up of **matter**, whether it is a rock, a building, an animal, or a person. Matter is defined by its characteristics: *It takes up space and it has mass.*

Mass is a *measure of the amount of matter in an object*. Two objects of equal mass will balance each other on a simple balance scale no matter where the scale is located. For instance, two rocks with the same amount of mass that are in balance on earth will also be in balance on the moon. They will feel *heavier* on earth than on the moon because of the gravitational pull of the earth. So , although the two rocks have the same mass, they will have different weight.

Weight is the *measure of the earth's pull of gravity on an object*. It can also be defined as the pull of gravity between other bodies. The units of weight measure that we commonly use are the pound in English measure and the **kilogram** in metric measure.

In addition to mass, matter also has the property of volume. **Volume** is the amount of cubic space that an object occupies. Volume and mass together give a more exact description of the object. Two objects may have the same volume, but different mass, the same mass but different volumes, etc. For instance, consider two cubes that are each one cubic centimeter, one made from plastic, one from lead. They have the same volume, but the lead cube has more mass. The measure that we use to describe the cubes takes into consideration both the mass and the volume. **Density** *is the mass of a substance contained per unit of volume.* If the density of an object is less than the density of a liquid, the object will float in the liquid. If the object is more dense than the liquid, then the object will sink.

Density is stated in grams per cubic centimeter (g / cm^3) where the gram is the *standard unit of mass.* To find an object's density, you must measure its mass and its volume. Then divide the mass by the volume (**D = m / V**).

To find an object's density, first use a balance to find its mass. Then calculate its volume. If the object is a regular shape, you can find the volume by multiplying the length, width, and height together. However, if it is an irregular shape, you can find the volume by seeing how much water it displaces. Measure the water in the container before and after the object is submerged. The difference will be the volume of the object.

Specific gravity *is the ratio of the density of a substance to the density of water.* For instance, the specific density of one liter of turpentine is calculated by comparing it's mass (0.81 kg) to the mass of one liter of water (1 kg):

$$\frac{\text{mass of 1 L alcohol}}{\text{mass of 1 L water}} = \frac{0.81\ kg}{1.00\ kg} = 0.81$$

Physical properties and chemical properties of matter describe the appearance or behavior of a substance. A **physical property** *can be observed without changing the identity of a substance.* For instance, you can describe the color, mass, shape, and volume of a book. **Chemical properties** *describe the ability of a substance to be changed into new substances.* Baking powder goes through a chemical change as it changes into carbon dioxide gas during the baking process.

Matter constantly changes. A **physical change** *is a change that does not produce a new substance.* The freezing and melting of water is an example of physical change. a **chemical change (or chemical reaction)** *is any change of a substance into one or more other substances.* Burning materials turn into smoke, a seltzer tablet fizzes into gas bubbles.

The **phase of matter** (solid, liquid, or gas) *is identified by its* **shape** *and* **volume**. A **solid** has a definite shape and volume. A **liquid** has a definite volume, but no shape. A **gas** has no shape or volume because it will spread out to occupy the entire space of whatever container it is in.

Energy *is the ability to cause change in matter*. Applying heat to a frozen liquid changes it from solid back to liquid. Continue heating it and it will boil and give off steam, a gas.

Evaporation *is the change in phase from liquid to gas*. **Condensation** *is the change in phase from gas to liquid*.

SKILL 21.4 The physical science principle

Dynamics *is the study of the relationship between motion and the forces affecting motion*. **Force** causes **motion.**

Mass and **weight** are not the same quantities. An object's **mass** gives it a reluctance to change its current state of motion. It is also the measure of an object's resistance to acceleration. The force that the earth's gravity exerts on an object with a specific mass is called the objects weight on earth. Weight is a force that is measured in newtons. Weight (W) = mass times acceleration due to gravity. (**W = mg**). To illustrate the difference between mass and weight, picture two rocks of equal mass on a balance scale. If the scale is balanced in one place, it will be balanced everywhere, regardless of the gravitational field. However, the weight of the stones would vary on a spring scale, depending upon the gravitational field. In other words, the stones would be balanced both on earth and on the moon. However, the weight of the stones would be greater on earth than on the moon.

Newton's laws of motion:

Newton's first law of motion *is also called the law of inertia*. It states that an object at rest will remain at rest and an object in motion will remain in motion at a constant velocity unless acted upon by an external force.

Newton's second law of motion *states that if a net force acts on an object, it will cause the acceleration of the object*. The relationship between force and motion is Force equals mass times acceleration. (**F = ma**)

Newton's third law *states that for every action there is an equal and opposite reaction*. Therefore, if an object exerts a force on another object, that second object exerts an equal and opposite force on the first.

Surfaces that touch each other have a certain resistance to motion. This resistance is **friction.**

1. The materials that make up the surfaces will determine the magnitude of the frictional force.

2. The frictional force is independent of the area of contact between the two surfaces.

3. The direction of the frictional force is opposite to the direction of motion.

4. The frictional force is proportional to the normal force between the two surfaces in contact.

Static friction describes the force of friction of two surfaces that are in contact but do not have any motion relative to each other, such as a block sitting on an inclined plane. **Kinetic friction** describes the force of friction of two surfaces in contact with each other when there is relative motion between the surfaces

When an object moves in a circular path, *a force must be directed toward the center of the circle in order to keep the motion going*. This constraining force is called **centripetal force**. Gravity is the centripetal force that keeps a satellite circling the earth.

COMPETENCY 22.0

INQUIRY SKILLS

Learning is by nature curiosity.

Plato

COMPETENCY 22.0   **APPLY INQUIRY SKILLS AND PROCESSES TO DEVELOP EXPLANATIONS OF NATURAL PHENOMENA**

SKILL 22.1   Classifying information and interpreting data presented in graphs, charts, or tables

Science may be defined as a body of knowledge that is systematically derived from study, observations and experimentation. Its goal is to identify and establish principles and theories which may be applied to solve problems. Pseudoscience, on the other hand, is a belief that is not warranted. There is no scientific methodology or application. Some of the more classic examples of pseudoscience includes witchcraft, alien encounters, or any topics that are explained by hearsay.

Science uses the metric system as it is accepted worldwide and allows easier comparison among experiments done by scientists around the world. Learn the following basic units and prefixes:

meter - measure of length
liter - measure of volume
gram - measure of mass

deca-(meter, liter, gram)= 10X the base unit   **deci** = 1/10 the base unit
hecto-(meter, liter, gram)= 100X the base unit   **centi** = 1/100 the base unit
kilo-(meter, liter, gram) = 1000X the base unit   **milli** = 1/1000 the base unit

Graphing is an important skill to visually display collected data for analysis. The two types of graphs most commonly used are the *line graph* and the *bar graph* (histogram). Line graphs are set up to show two variables represented by one point on the graph. The X axis is the horizontal axis and represents the dependent variable. Dependent variables are those that would be present independently of the experiment. A common example of a dependent variable is time. Time proceeds regardless of anything else going on. The Y axis is the vertical axis and represents the independent variable. Independent variables are manipulated by the experiment, such as the amount of light, or the height of a plant. Graphs should be calibrated at equal intervals. If one space represents one day, the next space may not represent ten days. A "best fit" line is drawn to join the points and may not include all the points in the data. Axes must always be labeled, or the graph means nothing. A good title will describe both the dependent and the independent variable. Bar graphs are set up similarly in regards to axes, but points are not plotted. Instead, the dependent variable is set up as a bar where the X axis intersects with the Y axis. Each bar is a separate item of data and are not joined by a continuous line.

ELEMENTARY EDUCATION   135

Classifying is grouping items according to their similarities. It is important for students to realize relationships and similarity as well as differences to reach a reasonable conclusion in a lab experience.

SKILL 22.2   Applying mathematical rules or formulas to analyze data

Moles = mass X 1 mole/molecular weight

For example, to determine the moles of 20 grams of water, you would take the mass of the water (20 g) and multiply it by 1 mole of water divided by the molecular weight of a molecule of water (18 g).

Percent solution and *proportions* are basically the same thing. Then to find percent volume, divide the grams of the substance by the amount of the solvent. For example, 20 grams of salt divided by 100 ml of water would result in a 20% solution of saltwater. To determine % mass, divide the ml of substance being mixed by the amount of solvent. Percent mass is not used as often as percent volume.

Rate is determined by dividing the *change in distance* (or the independent variable) by the *change in time*. If a plant grew four inches in two days, the rate of growth would be two inches per day.

COMPETENCY 23.0

SCIENCE
INVESTIGATION

It is the supreme art of the teacher to awaken joy in creative expression and knowledge.

Albert Einstein

COMPETENCY 23.0   UNDERSTAND PRINCIPLES AND PROCEDURES RELATED TO THE DESIGN OF SCIENTIFIC INVESTIGATIONS

SKILL 23.1   Features of a given experimental design

The **independent variable** is controlled by the experimenter. It is the variable in your experiment that you would change to get different outcomes of your experiment. The **dependent variable** is the outcome of your experiment that the experimenter does not control. The dependent variable is an outcome of the independent variable.

An independent variable might be the temperature in an experiment to determine at what temperature plants grow best at. The dependent variable would be the difference in height amongst the plants in the experiment.

The **controlled variable** is the variable(s) which remains constant. For the example above, the controlled variables would be using the same plant and using the same amounts of water and sun.

SKILL 23.2   Formulating hypotheses and evaluating the conclusion

Normally, knowledge is integrated in the form of a lab report. It should include a specific title and tell exactly what is being studied. The purpose should always be defined and will state the problem. The purpose should include the **hypothesis** (educated guess) of what is expected from the outcome of the experiment. The entire experiment should relate to this problem. It is important to describe exactly what was done to prove or disprove a hypothesis. A **control** is necessary to prove that the results occurred from the changed conditions and would not just happen normally. Only one variable should be manipulated at one time. **Observations** and results of the experiment should be recorded including all data that resulted. Drawings, graphs and illustrations should be included to support information. Observations are objective, whereas analysis and interpretation is subjective. A **conclusion** should explain why the results of the experiment either proved or disproved the hypothesis.

The specific steps are as follows:

Posing a question
Although many discoveries happen by chance the standard thought process of a scientist begins with forming a question to research. The more limited the question, the easier it is to set up an experiment to answer it.

ELEMENTARY EDUCATION

Form a hypothesis.
Once the question is formulated take an educated guess about the answer to the problem or question.

Doing the test
To make a test fair data from an experiment must have a **variable** or any condition that can be changed such as temperature or mass. A good test will try to manipulate as few variables as possible so as to see which variable is responsible for the result. This requires a second example of a **control**. A control is an extra setup in which all the conditions are the same except for the variable being tested.

Observe and record the data
Reporting of the data should state specifics of how the measurements were calculated. A graduated cylinder needs to be read with proper procedures (see next page). As beginning students technique must be part of the instructional process so as to give validity to the data.

Drawing a conclusion
After you take your data you compare it with that from the other groups. A **conclusion** is the judgment derived from the data results.

Graphing data
Graphing takes numbers and demonstrates patterns that might otherwise be harder to make conclusions from.

Laws and Theories
A scientific law is a statement that describes how something behaves. A law does not explain why things happen. Theories are explanations for the way something behaves. Most scientific theories are changed, replaced, or refined with extensive testing.

SKILL 23.3 Care and humane treatment of animals and safe and appropriate use of laboratory equipment

Dissections - Animals which are not obtained from recognized sources should not be used. Decaying animals or those of unknown origin may harbor pathogens and/or parasites. Specimens should be rinsed before handling. Latex gloves are desirable. If not available, students with sores or scratches should be excused from the activity. Formaldehyde is carcinogenic and should be avoided or disposed of according to district regulations. Students objecting to dissections for moral reasons should be given an alternative assignment.

Live specimens - No dissections may be performed on living mammalian vertebrates or birds. Lower order life and invertebrates may be used. Biological experiments may be done with all animals except mammalian vertebrates or birds. No physiological harm may result to the animal. All animals housed and cared for in the school must be handled in a safe and humane manner. Animals are not to remain on school premises during extended vacations unless adequate care is provided.

Microbiology - Pathogenic organisms must never be used for experimentation. Students should adhere to the following rules at all times when working with microorganisms to avoid accidental contamination:

    1. Treat all microorganisms as if they were pathogenic.
    2. Maintain sterile conditions at all times

Instructions on the use of some laboratory equipment:

Bunsen burners - Hot plates should be used whenever possible to avoid the risk of burns or fire. If Bunsen burners are used, the following precautions should be followed:

    1. Know the location of fire extinguishers and safety blankets and train students in their use. Long hair and long sleeves should be secured and out of the way.

    2. Turn the gas all the way on and make a spark with the striker.

    3. Adjust the air valve at the bottom of the Bunsen burner until the flame shows an inner cone.

    4. Adjust the flow of gas to the desired flame height by using the adjustment valve.

    5. Do not touch the barrel of the burner as it is hot.

Graduated Cylinder - These are used for precise measurements. They should always be placed on a flat surface. The surface of the liquid will form a meniscus (a lens-shaped curve). The measurement is read at the bottom of this curve.

Balance - Electronic balances are easier to use, but more expensive. An electronic balance should always be zeroed before measuring and used on a flat surface. Substances should always be placed on a piece of paper, or another device, to avoid messes and damage to the instrument. Triple beam balances must be used on a level surface. There are screws located at the bottom of the balance to make any adjustments. Start with the largest counterweight first to the last notch that does not tip the balance. Do the same with the next largest, etc until the pointer remains at zero. The total mass is the total of all the readings on the beams. Again, use paper under the substance to protect the equipment.

Light microscopes are commonly used in laboratory experiments. Several procedures should be followed to properly care for this equipment.
- Clean all lenses with lens paper only.
- Carry microscopes with two hands; one on the arm and one on the base.
- Always begin focusing on low power, then switch to high power.
- Store microscopes with the low power objective down.
- Always use a coverslip when viewing wet mount slides.
- Bring the objective down to its lowest position then focus moving up to avoid breaking the slide or scratching the lens.

Wet mount slides should be made by placing a drop of water on the specimen and then putting a glass coverslip on top of the drop of water. Dropping the coverslip at a forty-five degree angle will help in avoiding air bubbles
Total magnification is determined by multiplying the ocular (usually 10X) and the objective (usually 10X on low, 40X on high).

All science labs should contain the following items of safety equipment. The following are requirements by law.

- Fire blanket which is visible and accessible
- Ground Fault Circuit Interrupters (GCFI) within two feet of water supplies signs designating room exits
- Emergency shower providing a continuous flow of water
- Emergency eye wash station which can be activated by the foot or forearm
- Eye protection for every student and a means of sanitizing equipment
- Emergency exhaust fans providing ventilation to the outside of the building
- Master cut-off switches for gas, electric and compressed air. Switches must have permanently attached handles. Cut-off switches must be clearly labeled.
- An ABC fire extinguisher

ELEMENTARY EDUCATION   141

- Storage cabinets for flammable material

Also recommended, but not required by law:
- Chemical spill control kit
- Fume hood with a motor which is spark proof
- Protective laboratory aprons made of flame retardant material
- Signs which will alert potential hazardous conditions
- Containers for broken glassware, flammables, corrosives and waste.
- Containers should be labeled.

It is the responsibility of teachers to provide a safe environment for their students. Proper supervision greatly reduces the risk of injury and a teacher should never leave a class for any reason without providing alternate supervision. After an accident, two factors are considered; foreseeability and negligence. *Foreseeability is the anticipation that an event may occur under certain circumstances.* **Negligence** *is the failure to exercise ordinary or reasonable care.* Safety procedures should be a part of the science curriculum and a well managed classroom is important to avoid potential lawsuits

The *"Right to Know Law"* statutes covers science teachers who work with potentially hazardous chemicals. Briefly, the law states that employees must be informed of potentially toxic chemicals. An inventory must be made available if requested. The inventory must contain information about the hazards and properties of the chemicals. Training must be provided in the safe handling and interpretation of the Material Safety Data Sheet.

The following chemicals are a partial listing potential carcinogens and not allowed in school facilities:

Acrylonitriel, Arsenic compounds, Asbestos, Bensidine, Benzene, Cadmium compounds, Chloroform, Chromium compounds, Ethylene oxide, Ortho-toluidine, Nickle powder, Mercury.

The accepted procedures for **safe use**, **storage**, and **disposal of chemicals**:

All laboratory solutions should be prepared as directed in the lab manual. Care should be taken to avoid contamination. All glassware should be rinsed thoroughly with distilled water before using, and cleaned well after use. All solutions should be made with distilled water as tap water contains dissolved particles which may affect the results of an experiment. Chemical storage should be located in a secured, dry area. Chemicals should be stored in accordance with reactability. Acids are to be locked in a separate area. Used solutions should be disposed of according to local disposal procedures. Any questions regarding safe disposal or chemical safety may be directed to the local fire department.

COMPETENCY 24.0

SOCIAL SCIENCES

Education has for its object the formation of character.

Herbert Spencer

COMPETENCY 24.0   SOCIAL SCIENCES

SKILL 24.1   Be able to describe each of the social science disciplines and explain each one's methods of study and tools for research.

The disciplines within the social sciences, sometimes referred to as social studies, include anthropology, geography, history, sociology, economics, and political science. Some programs include psychology, archaeology, philosophy, religion, law, and criminology. Also, the subjects of civics and government may be a part of an educational curriculum as separate from political science.

ANTHROPOLOGY - is the scientific study of human culture and humanity, the relationship between man and his culture. Anthropologists study different groups, how they relate to other cultures, patterns of behavior, similarities and differences. Their research is two-fold: cross-cultural and comparative. The major method of study is referred to as "participant observation". The anthropologist studies and learns about the people being studied by living among them and participating with them in their daily lives. Other methods may be used but this is the most characteristic method used.

ARCHAEOLOGY - is the scientific study of past human cultures by studying the remains they left behind - objects such as pottery, bones, buildings, tools, and artwork. Archaeologists locate and examine any evidence to help explain the way people lived in past times. They use   special equipment and techniques to gather the evidence and make special effort to keep detailed records of their findings because a lot of their research results in destruction of the remains being studied. The first step is to locate an archaeological site using various methods. Next, surveying the site takes place starting with a detailed description of the site with notes, maps, photographs, and collecting artifacts from the surface. Excavating follows, either by digging for buried objects or by diving and working in submersible decompression chambers, when underwater. They record and preserve the evidence for eventual classification, dating, and evaluating their find.

CIVICS - is the study of the responsibilities and rights of citizens with emphasis on such subjects as freedom, democracy, and individual rights. Students study local, state, national, and international governments' structures, functions, and problems. Related to this are other social, political, and economic institutions. As a method of study, students gain experience and understanding through direct participation in student government, school publications, and other organizations. They also participate in community activities such as conservation projects and voter registration drives.

ECONOMICS - generally is the study of the ways goods and services are produced and the ways they are distributed. It also includes the ways people and nations choose what they buy from what they want. Some of the methods of study include research, case studies, analysis, statistics, and mathematics.

GEOGRAPHY - involves studying location and how living things and earth's features are distributed throughout the earth. It includes where animals, people, and plants live and the effects of their relationship with earth's physical features. Geographers also explore the locations of earth's features, how they got there, and why it is so important. What geographers study can be broken down into four areas:

(1) Location - being able to find the exact site of anything on the earth; (2) Spatial relations - the relationships of earth's features, places, and groups of people with one another due to their location; (3) Regional characteristics - characteristics of a place such as landform and climate, types of plants and animals, kinds of people who live there, and how they use the land; and (4) Forces that change the earth - such as human activities and natural forces.

Geographical studies are divided into: (1) Regional - elements and characteristics of a place or region; (2) Topical - one earth feature or one human activity occurring throughout the entire world; (3) Physical - earth's physical features, what creates and changes them, their relationships to each other as well as human activities; and (4) Human - human activity patterns and how they relate to the environment, including political, cultural, historical, urban, and social geographical fields of study. Special research methods used by geographers include mapping, interviewing, field studies, mathematics and statistics, and scientific instruments.

HISTORY - is the study of the past, especially the aspects of the human past, political and economic events as well as cultural and social conditions. Students study history through textbooks, research, field trips to museums and historical sights, and other methods. Most nations set the requirement in history to study the country's heritage, usually to develop an awareness and feeling of loyalty and patriotism. History is generally divided into the three main divisions based on (a) time periods, (b) nations, and (c) specialized topics. Study is accomplished through research, reading, and writing about it.

POLITICAL SCIENCE - is the study of political life, different forms of government including elections, political parties, and public administration. Also political science studies include values such as justice, freedom, power, and equality. There are six main fields of political study in the United States: (1) political theory and philosophy; (2) comparative governments; (3) international relations; (4) political behavior; (5) public administration; and (6) American government and politics.

PSYCHOLOGY - involves scientifically studying behavior and mental processes. The ways people and animals relate to each other are observed and recorded. Psychologists scrutinize specific patterns which will enable them to discern and predict certain behaviors, using scientific methods to verify their ideas. In this way they have been able to learn how to help people fulfill their individual human potential and strengthen understanding between individuals as well as groups and in nations and cultures. The results of the research of psychologists have deepened our understanding of the reasons for people's behavior.

Psychology is not only closely connected to the natural science of biology and the medical field of psychiatry but it is also connected to the social science areas of anthropology and sociology which have to do with people in society. Along with the sociologists and anthropologists, psychologists also study humans in their social settings, analyzing their attitudes and relationships. The disciplines of anthropology, psychology, and sociology often research the same kinds of problems but from different points of view, with the emphasis in psychology on individual behavior, how an individual's actions are influenced by feelings and beliefs.

In their research, psychologists develop hypotheses, then test them using the scientific method. These methods used in psychological research include: (1) naturalistic observation which includes observing the behavior of animals and humans in their natural surroundings or environment; (2) systematic assessment which describes assorted ways to measure the feelings, thoughts, and personality traits of people using case histories, public opinion polls or surveys, and standardized tests. These three types of assessments enable psychologists to acquire information not available through naturalistic observations. (3) Experimentation enables psychologists to find and corroborate the cause-and-effect relationships in behavior, usually by randomly dividing the subjects into two groups: experimental group and control group.

SOCIOLOGY - is the study of human society - the individuals, groups, and institutions making up human society. It includes every feature of human social conditions. It deals with the predominant behaviors, attitudes, and types of relationships within a society, which is defined as a group of people with a similar cultural background living in a specific geographical area. Sociology is divided into five major areas of study: (1) population studies - general social patterns of groups of people living in a certain geographical area; (2) social behaviors - such as changes in attitudes, morale, leadership, conformity, and others; (3) social institutions - organized groups of people performing specific functions within a society such as churches, schools, hospitals, business organizations, and governments; (4) cultural influences - including customs, knowledge, arts, religious beliefs, and language; and (5) social change - such as wars, revolutions, inventions, fashions, and any other events or activities. Sociologists use three major methods to test and verify theories: (1) surveys; (2) controlled experiments; and (3) field observation.

COMPETENCY 25.0

GEOGRAPHY

Teachers and learners are correlates; one of which
was never intended to be without the other.

Jonathan Edwards

COMPETENCY 25.0 **GEOGRAPHY**

SKILL 25.1 **Know the earth's physical features and be able to give examples and their locations**

The earth's surface is made up of 70% water and 30% land. Physical features of the land surface include mountains, hills, plateaus, valleys, and plains. Other minor landforms include deserts, deltas, canyons, mesas, basins, foothills, marshes and swamps. Earth's water features include oceans, seas, lakes, rivers, and canals.

Mountains are landforms with rather steep slopes at least 2,000 feet or more above sea level. Mountains are found in groups called mountain chains or mountain ranges. At least one range can be found on six of the earth's seven continents. North America has the Appalachian and Rocky Mountains; South America the Andes; Asia the Himalayas; Australia the Great Dividing Range; Europe the Alps; and Africa the Atlas, Ahaggar, and Drakensburg Mountains.

Hills are elevated landforms rising to an elevation of about 500 to 2000 feet. They are found everywhere on earth including Antarctica where they are covered by ice.

Plateaus are elevated landforms usually level on top. Depending on location, they range from being an area that is very cold to one that is cool and healthful. Some are dry because of being surrounded by mountains that keep out any moisture. Some examples include the Kenya Plateau in East Africa which is very cool. The plateaus extending north from the Himalayas are extremely dry while those in Antarctica and Greenland are covered with ice and snow.

Plains are described as areas of flat or slightly rolling land, usually lower than the landforms next to them. Sometimes called lowlands (and sometimes located along seacoasts) they support the majority of the world's people. Some are found inland and many have been formed by large rivers. This resulted in extremely fertile soil for successful cultivation of crops and numerous large settlements of people. In North America, the vast plains areas extend from the Gulf of Mexico north to the Arctic Ocean and between the Appalachian and Rocky Mountains. In Europe rich plains extend east from Great Britain into central Europe on into the Siberian region of Russia. Plains in river valleys are found in China (the Yangtze River valley), India (the Ganges River valley), and Southeast Asia (the Mekong River valley).

Valleys are land areas that are found between hills and mountains. Some have gentle slopes containing trees and plants; others have very steep walls and are referred to as canyons. One famous example is Arizona's Grand Canyon of the Colorado River.

Deserts are large dry areas of land receiving 10 inches or less of rainfall each year. Among the more well-known deserts are Africa's large Sahara Desert, the Arabian

Desert on the Arabian Peninsula, and the desert Outback covering roughly one third of Australia.

Deltas are areas of lowlands formed by soil and sediment deposited at the mouths of rivers. The soil is generally very fertile and most fertile river deltas are important crop-growing areas. One well-known example if the delta of Egypt's Nile River, known for its production of cotton.

Mesas are the flat tops of hills or mountains usually with steep sides. Sometimes plateaus are also called mesas. Basins are considered to be low areas drained by rivers or low spots in mountains. Foothills are generally considered a low series of hills found between a plain and a mountain range. Marshes and swamps are wet lowlands providing growth of such plants as rushes and reeds.

Oceans are the largest bodies of water on the planet. The four oceans of the earth are the Atlantic Ocean, one-half the size of the Pacific and separating North and South America from Africa and Europe; the Pacific Ocean, covering almost one-third of the entire surface of the earth and separating North and South America from Asia and Australia; the Indian Ocean, touching Africa, Asia, and Australia; and the ice-filled Arctic Ocean, extending from North America and Europe to the North Pole. The waters of the Atlantic, Pacific, and Indian Oceans also touch the shores of Antarctica.

Seas are smaller than oceans and are almost completely surrounded by land. Some examples include the Mediterranean Sea found between Europe, Asia, and Africa; and the Caribbean Sea, touching the West Indies, South and Central America. A lake is a body of water completely surrounded by land. The Great Lakes in North America are a good example.

Rivers, considered a nation's lifeblood, usually begin as very small streams, formed by melting snow and rainfall, flowing from higher to lower land, emptying into a larger body of water, usually a sea or an ocean. Examples of important rivers for the people and countries affected by and/or dependent on them include the Nile, Niger, and Zaire Rivers of Africa; the Rhine, Danube, and Thames Rivers of Europe; the Yangtze, Ganges, Mekong, Hwang He, and Irrawaddy Rivers of Asia; the Murray-Darling in Australia; and the Orinoco in South America. River systems are made up of large rivers and numerous smaller rivers or tributaries flowing into them. Examples include the vast Amazon Rivers system in South America and the Mississippi River system in the United States.

Canals are man-made water passages constructed to connect two larger bodies of water. Famous examples include the Panama Canal across Panama's isthmus connecting the Atlantic and Pacific Oceans and the Suez Canal in the Middle East.

SKILL 25.2   Know the difference between climate and weather and the descriptions and locations of the different types of climates

Weather is the condition of the air which surrounds, the day-to-day atmospheric conditions including temperature, air pressure, wind and moisture or precipitation which includes rain, snow, hail or sleet.

Climate is average weather or daily weather conditions for a specific region or location over a long or extended period of time. Studying the climate of an area includes information gathered on the area's monthly and yearly temperatures and its monthly and yearly amounts of precipitation. Also a part of an area's climate is the length of its growing season. Four reasons for the different climate regions on the earth are differences in (1) latitude, (2) the amount of moisture, (3) temperatures in land and water, and (4) the earth's land surface.

There are many different climates throughout the earth. It is most unusual if one single country contains just one kind of climate. Regions of climates are divided according to latitudes:

> 23 1/2 degrees are the "low latitudes"; 23 1/2 - 66 1/2 degrees are the "middle latitudes"; and 66 1/2 degrees to the Poles are the "high latitudes".

In the low latitudes are the rainforest, savanna, and desert climates. The tropical rainforest climate is found in equatorial lowlands and is hot and wet. There is sun overhead, extreme heat and rain - everyday. Even though daily temperatures rarely rise above 90 degrees F., the daily humidity is always high, leaving everything sticky and damp. North and south of the tropical rainforests are located the tropical grasslands called "savannas", the "lands of two seasons" - a winter dry season and a summer wet season. Further north and south of the tropical grasslands or savannas are the deserts. These areas are the hottest and driest parts of the earth receiving less than 10 inches of rain a year. These areas have extreme temperatures between night and day. After the sun sets, the land cools quickly dropping the temperature as much as 50 degrees.

The middle latitudes contain the Mediterranean, humid-subtropical, humid continental, marine, steppe, and desert climates. Lands containing the Mediterranean climate are considered "sunny" lands found in six areas of the world: lands bordering the Mediterranean Sea, a small portion of southwestern Africa, areas in southern and southwestern Australia, a small part of the Ukraine near the Black Sea, central Chile, and southern California. Summers are hot and dry with mild winters. The growing season usually lasts all year and what little rain falls is usually during the winter months. What is rather unusual is that the Mediterranean climate is located between 30 and 40 degrees north and south latitude on the western coasts of countries.

The humid subtropical climate is found north and south of the tropics and is moist indeed. The areas having this type of climate are found on the eastern side of their continents and include Japan, mainland China, Australia, Africa, South America, and the United States - the southeastern coasts of these areas. An interesting feature of their locations is that warm ocean currents are found there. The winds that blow across these currents bring in warm moist air all year round. Long, warm summers; short, mild winters; a long growing season allowing for different crops to be grown several times a year all contribute to the productivity of this type of climate which supports more people than any of the others.

The marine climate is found in Western Europe, the British Isles, the U.S. Pacific Northwest, the western coast of Canada and southern Chile, along with southern New Zealand and southeastern Australia. A common characteristic of these lands are that they are either near water or surrounded by it. The ocean winds are wet and warm bringing a mild, rainy climate to these areas. In the summer, the daily temperatures average at or below 70 degrees F. During the winter, because of the warming effect of the ocean waters, the temperatures rarely fall below freezing.

In northern and central United States, northern China, south-central and southeastern Canada, and the western and southeastern parts of the former Soviet Union is found the "climate of four seasons", the humid continental climate - spring, summer, fall, and winter. Cold winters, hot summers, and enough rainfall to grow a variety of crops are the major characteristics of this climate. In areas where the humid continental climate is found are some of the world's best farmlands as well as important activities such as trading and mining. Differences in temperatures throughout the year are determined by the distance a place is inland away from the coasts.

The steppe or prairie climate is located in the interiors of the large continents like Asia and North America. These dry flatlands are far from ocean breezes and are called prairies or the Great Plains in Canada and the United States and steppes in Asia. Even though the summers are hot and the winters are cold as in the humid continental climate, the big difference is rainfall. In the steppe climate, rainfall is light and uncertain, ten to 20 inches a year mainly in spring and summer and is considered normal. Where rain is more plentiful, grass grows; in areas of less, the steppes or prairies gradually become deserts. These are found in the Gobi Desert of Asia, central and western Australia, southwestern United States, and in the smaller deserts found in Pakistan, Argentina, and Africa south of the Equator.

The two major climates found in the high latitudes are "tundra" and "taiga". The word "tundra" meaning "marshy plain" is a Russian word and aptly describes the climatic conditions in the northern areas of Russia, Europe, and Canada. Winters are extremely cold and very long. Most of the year the ground is frozen but becomes rather mushy during the very short summer months. Surprisingly less snow falls in the area of the tundra than in the eastern part of the United States. However, due to the harshness of the extreme cold, very few people live there and no crops can be raised. Despite having a small human population, many plants and animals are found there.

The "taiga" is the northern forest region and is located south of the tundra. In fact, the Russian word "taiga" means "forest". The world's largest forest lands are found here along with vast mineral wealth and furbearing animals. The climate is so extreme that very few people live here, not being able to raise crops due to the extremely short growing season. The winter temperatures are colder and the summer temperatures are hotter than those in the tundra due to the the fact that the taiga climate region is farther from the waters of the Arctic Ocean. The taiga is found in the northern parts of Russia, Sweden, Norway, Finland, Canada, and Alaska with most of their lands covered with marshes and swamps.

In certain areas of the earth exists a type of climate unique to areas with high mountains, usually different from their surroundings. This type of climate is called "vertical climate" because the temperatures, crops, vegetation, and human activities change and become different as one ascends the different levels of elevation. At the foot of the mountain a hot and rainy climate is found with the cultivation of many lowland crops. As one climbs higher, the air becomes cooler, the climate changes sharply and different economic activities change, such as grazing sheep and growing corn. At the top of many mountains, snow is found all year round.

SKILL 25.3   Be able to explain how physical and political locations are determined and give examples

Physical locations of the earth's surface features include the four major hemispheres and the parts of the earth's continents in them. Political locations are basically the political divisions, if any, within each continent. Both physical and political locations are precisely determined in two ways: (1) Surveying is done to determine boundary lines and distance from other features. (2) Exact locations are precisely determined by imaginary lines of latitude (parallels) and longitude(meridians). The intersection of these lines at right angles forms a grid, making it possible to pinpoint an exact location of any place using any two grip coordinates.

The Eastern Hemisphere, located between the North and South Poles and between the Prime Meridian (0 degrees longitude) east to the International Date Line at 180 degrees longitude, consists of most of Europe, all of Australia, most of Africa, and all of Asia, except for a tiny piece of the eastern-most part of Russia that extends east of 180 degrees longitude.

The Western Hemisphere, located between the North and South Poles and between the Prime Meridian (0 degrees longitude) west to the International Date Line at 180 degrees longitude, consists of all of North and South America, a tiny part of the easternmost part of Russia that extends east of 180 degrees longitude, and a part of Europe that extends west of the Prime Meridian (0 degrees longitude).

The Northern Hemisphere, located between the North Pole and the Equator, contains all of the continents of Europe and North America and parts of South America, Africa, and most of Asia. The Southern Hemisphere, located between the South Pole and the Equator, contains all of Australia, a small part of Asia, about one-third of Africa, most of South America, and all of Antarctica.

Of the seven continents, only one contains just one entire country and also is the only island continent, Australia. Its political divisions consist of six states and one territory: Western Australia, South Australia, Tasmania, Victoria, New South Wales, Queensland, and Northern Territory.

Africa is made up of 54 separate countries, the major ones being Egypt, Nigeria, South Africa, Zaire, Kenya, Algeria, Morocco, and the large island of Madagascar.

Asia consists of 49 separate countries, some of which include China, Japan, India, Turkey, Israel, Iraq, Iran, Indonesia, Jordan, Vietnam, Thailand, and the Philippines. Europe's 43 separate nations include France, Russia, Malta, Denmark, Hungary, Greece, Bosnia and Herzegovina.

North American consists of not only Canada and the United States of America but also the island nations of the West Indies and the "land bridge" of Middle America, including Cuba, Jamaica, Mexico, Panama, and others.

Thirteen separate nations together occupy the continent of South America, among them such nations as Brazil, Paraguay, Ecuador, and Suriname.

The continent of Antarctica has no political boundaries or divisions but is the location of a number of science and research stations managed by nations such as Russia, Japan, France, Australia, and India.

SKILL 25.4   Be able to show an understanding of the relationship of geography to culture

Social scientists use the term culture to describe the way of life of a group of people. This would include not only art, music, and literature but also beliefs, customs, languages, traditions, inventions - in short, any way of life whether complex or simple. The term geography is defined as the study of earth's features and living things as to their location, relationship with each other, how they came to be there, and why so important.

Physical geography is concerned with the locations of such earth features as climate, water, and land; how these relate to and affect each other and human activities; and what forces shaped and changed them. All three of these earth features affect the lives of all humans having a direct influence on what is made and produced, where it occurs, how it occurs, and what makes it possible. The combination of the different climate conditions and types of landforms and other surface features works together all around the earth to give the many varied cultures their unique characteristics and distinctions.

Cultural geography studies the location, characteristics, and influence of the physical environment on different cultures around the earth. Also included in these studies are comparisons and influences of the many varied cultures. Ease of travel and up-to-the-minute state-of-the-art communication techniques ease the difficulties of understanding cultural differences making it easier to come in contact with them.

COMPETENCY 26.0

ECONOMICS

The average teacher makes $43,350.00. a year. Are they overpaid, underpaid, or fairly paid?

AOL question Aug. 3, 2003

COMPETENCY 26.0   ECONOMICS

SKILL 26.1   Be able to apply the principles of consumer economics

A **consumer** is a person who uses goods and services and, in a capitalist or free enterprise economy, decides with other consumers what is produced by what they choose to buy. The terms **"supply and demand"** are used to explain the influence of consumers on production. This law or principle of supply and demand means that prices of goods rise due to an increased demand and fall when there is an increase in the supply of goods.

Due to unstable economies, inflation, job insecurity due to downsizing, bankruptcy and other factors, having cash on hand while buying is less prevalent than having a credit card. These are frequently referred to as "plastic money" but in reality is not money. They are a convenient tool for receiving a short-term loan from whatever financial institutions issued the cards. These popular pieces of plastic aid consumers in such economic activities as purchasing items on "installment plans". Financial institutions are not the only ones issuing credit cards. Oil companies, airlines, national automobile manufacturers, large corporations are just some of the backers of credit cards. Department store charge cards do not enable the holder to obtain money from an ATM but do enable one to buy on credit or on the installment plan. Automobile dealerships, banks, credit unions, loan companies all, in similar ways, make it possible for just about anyone to purchase on installment and drive a car. Mortgages allow people to pay for their own home or condominium.

SKILL 26.2   Give descriptions and comparisons of various economic systems

Capitalism (or Free Enterprise)

This economic system provides for individual ownership of land and capital allowing individuals to pursue their economic activities with as little government control or interference as possible. The individuals are the consumers, owners, managers, workers, producers, and make their own economic decisions. The vast majority of the means of production are owned by individuals, not the government. This type of economic system is used and practiced in such countries as the United States and Canada. However, Canada tends to be more socialistic as exemplified by their national health care system. It is not as capitalistic as the United States.

Socialism

This economic system has more control and planning by the government than in capitalist economies. The government owns and operates key industries such as the railroads, steel mills, and coal mines. Individuals are allowed to own most of the other industries. The main type of a mixed economy is "socialism". Proponents of socialism feel that the capitalistic free enterprise system is wasteful, inefficient, and leads to serious economic problems such as poverty, unemployment, cycles in business, and conflicts between management and labor. One variety of socialism favors basic industries owned by the government, private ownership of other businesses, and government regulation of privately-owned businesses.

In non-Communist lands, some countries with a socialist economy provide for democratic ways to decide what goods will be produced. The people choose the government, casting votes on some of the economic policies. Sometimes they also vote on how much control over the economy the government has, increasing or reducing it whenever adjustments need to be made. This type of economic system is sometimes called "democratic socialism" and is practiced in such countries as Sweden and Great Britain.

Communism

This economic system is based on the theory that the government not only owns all productive resources but also directs all of the important economic activities, deciding what is produced, how much to produce, prices, workers' wages, and even the rate of economic growth.

The only exception would be the private land plots for personal use and production. Choice of products to buy is left up to the consumers but quantity, quality, and choice are limited. The people have no control over the government's economic policies. This type of economic system is practiced in the few remaining "Communist" nations, such as China, North Korea, and Cuba.

SKILL 26.3   Show an understanding of the role of markets

A *market* is an economic term to describe the places and situations in which goods and services are bought and sold. In a capitalistic free enterprise economy, the market prices of goods and services rise and fall according to decreases and increases in the supply and demand and the degree of competition.

In an economic system, there is also a "market" for land, capital, and labor. The labor market, for example, is studied by economists in order to better understand trends in jobs, productivity of workers, activities of labor unions, and patterns of employment. Potential customers for a product or service are also called a market and are the subject of market research to determine who would possibly make use of whatever is offered to customers.

Other types of markets part of countries' economic systems include the following:

Stock Market

This is part of a capitalistic free enterprise system and is one of significant investment and speculation. Any changes in the prices of stocks are seriously affected by those who buy stocks when their prices are rising and sell them when their prices are start to fall. Business planners quite often regard the stock market as a barometer of the degree of confidence investors have in the conditions of businesses in the future. When the stock market is a rising "bull" market, economists and investors see it as the public showing confidence in the future of business. At the same time, when the market is a falling "bear" market, it is an indication of a lack of confidence. In unstable economic conditions, one or more of a number of conditions and situations can seriously affect the stock market's rise and fall. The "bottom line" is that these fluctuations are directly tied to and directly affected by investment changes.

"Black" Market

This illegal market has in the past and even today exists in countries where wage and price controls are in place and enforced by law. In these markets, goods and products are priced and sold above legal limits, especially if the maximum legal price is much less than free-market price, if certain products are unavailable in the regulated market, or if wage and price controls are in place for an extended period of time.

Common Market

This market, also called the European Economic Community (EEC), began in 1958 and is made up of several European nations. Its major purpose was to remove all restrictive tariffs and import quotas in order to encourage and facilitate free trade amongmember nations. Included also were efforts to move workers and services without restrictions.

SKILL 26.4   Be able to understand and illustrate global economic concepts

Globalism is defined as the principle of the interdependence of all the world's nations and their peoples. Within this global community, every nation, in some way to a certain degree, is dependent on other nations. Since no one nation has all of the resources needed for production, trade with other nations is required to obtain what is needed for production, to sell what is   produced or to buy finished products, to earn money - in other words, to maintain and strengthen the nation's economic system.

Developing nations receive technical assistance and financial aid from developed nations. Many international organizations have been set up to promote and encourage cooperation and economic progress among member nations. Through the elimination of such barriers to trade as tariffs, trade is stimulated resulting in increased productivity, economic progress, increased cooperation and understanding on the diplomatic levels.

Those nations not part of an international trade organization not only must make those economic decisions of what to produce, how and for whom, but must also deal with the problem of tariffs and quotas on imports. Regardless of international trade memberships, economic growth and development are vital and affect all trading nations. Businesses, labor, and governments share common interests and goals in a nation's economic status. International systems of banking and finance have been devised to assist governments and businesses in setting the policy and guidelines for the exchange of currencies.

COMPETENCY 27.0

POLITICAL SCIENCE

The true teacher defends his pupils against his own personal influence. He inspires self trust. He guides their eyes from himself to the spirit that quickens him. He will have no disciple.

Amos Bronson Alcott

COMPETENCY 27.0   THE AMERICAN POLITICAL SYSTEM

SKILL 27.1   Be able to show knowledge of the American political and governmental systems, including the national, state, and local levels

The American governmental system is a federal system - fifty individual states federated or forming or uniting as one nation. The national and state governments share the powers of government. This federal system required decentralization which makes it impossible to coexist with totalitarianism. Both national and state governments exist and govern by the will of the people who are the source of their authority. Local governmental systems operate under the same guidelines.

The American political system is a two-party system, consisting of the Democratic and Republican parties. Political parties in America have approximately five major functions: (1) They choose candidates who will run for public office. (2) They assist in organizing the government. (3) They oppose the political party in power. (4) They obtain the funds needed to conduct election campaigns. (5) They take the initiative to make sure voters are aware of issues, problems to be solved, and any other information about public affairs. The two-party system in America operates at the national, state, and local levels.

SKILL 27.2   Know and understand the major principles of the U.S. Constitution

The U.S. Constitution set up a federal system of government, dividing powers between the national and state governments. The national government is balanced by having its authority divided among the three branches.

The **legislative branch** includes Congress and eight administrative agencies. Congress is made up of the House of Representatives and the Senate. It is the responsibility of the U.S. Congress to make, repeal, and amend all federal laws as well as levying federal taxes and distributing funds for the government.

The U.S. Senate consists of 100 members, two from each state regardless of size or population, who serve six-year terms. Its exclusive powers include approval of Presidential nominations for major federal offices, approval of any treaty made, and conducting impeachment cases of federal officials. Charges for impeachment include treason, bribes, high crimes and misdemeanors. The Vice-President presides at all impeachment proceedings except in the case of the President, when the Chief Justice of the Supreme Court presides. Two-thirds of the Senate must agree on the verdict.

The House of Representatives has 435 members who serve two-year terms. The number of representatives from each state is determined by population with a guarantee

ELEMENTARY EDUCATION   161

of at least one representative regardless. The number of representatives is set by law and is not subject to change. Its exclusive powers include initiating all money bills and bringing impeachment charges against high federal officials.

The **executive branch** includes the Executive Office of the President, various executive departments and independent agencies. The U.S. President is the nation's chief of state, chief executive, and the head of the government of the United States. He is responsible for enforcing federal laws, appointing and removing any high federal officials, commanding all the armed forces, conducting foreign affairs, and recommending laws to Congress.

He is responsible for appointing American representatives to carry out diplomatic missions in foreign lands and to serve in international organizations. The President is also required to perform many ceremonial duties. He is elected to a term of four years and is limited constitutionally to no more than two terms.

The **judicial branch** is made up of the Supreme Court and other lower federal courts. Consisting of a chief justice and eight associate justices, the Supreme Court is the highest court in the land. All nine justices are appointed by the president with Senate approval. The lower federal courts consist of district courts, courts of appeal, and a group of courts handling specialized cases. All federal courts hear cases involving the Constitution and federal laws. These judges are also appointed by the President with Senate approval and, along with the Supreme Court justices, hold office for life. Under the process called "judicial review" (as set forth in "Marbury vs Madison, 1803), the Supreme Court has the authority to declare unconstitutional any executive orders or any legislative acts of both federal and state governments, based on the statement in the U.S. Constitution stating that it and all treaties and federal laws are the supreme law of the land.

The U.S. Constitution created a federal government solidly based on four fundamental principles. The first principle is that of "federalism", a system of government in which powers are divided between the national and state governments. This, in turn, set up four types of govern-mental powers: (1) delegated or expressed - those listed directly; (2) implied powers - not stated directly but suggested; (3) reserved powers - not given to the national government but reserved for the people or for the states; and (4) concurrent powers - given to both national and state governments at the same time.

The second principle is the separation of powers with the system of checks and balances. The writers of the Constitution were greatly concerned about protecting the new nation from any form of tyranny, seizure of power by a military dictator, or any one branch of government becoming stronger and more powerful than the others. Therefore it was determined to keep the three branches separate and equal. Additionally a system of checks and balances was written into the Constitution. This gives each of the three branches some powers that affect the other two. Some examples include: Congress checks the President by having the authority to appropriate funds for running the government. Congress checks the judicial branch due to its power to provide for and set up the courts along with their rules of procedure. The President can check Congress with his power to veto bills it passes. The President checks the courts with his power to appoint judges and justices. The courts can check both Congress and the President by reviewing executive orders and legislative acts and declaring them unconstitutional.

A third principle provides for the protection of individual rights and liberties. These provisions include the following: The Constitution prohibits the passage of "ex post facto laws" (laws passed "after the deed" providing the penalty for an act that was not an illegal act at the time it was committed) and "bills of attainder" (laws that render punishment to someone through fines, imprisonment, and confiscation of property without a court trial first). Individual rights are also protected by granting one a "writ of habeas corpus" which is a legal document requiring release from jail or prison if an individual has not been formally charged with or convicted of a crime. Special protection is given to those accused of treason as well as their innocent relatives. The accused was entitled to a fair trial and due process of law and would be protected against being accused merely because of criticism against the government. Treason was defined by the Constitution as waging war against the United States or supporting enemies of the U.S. giving them assistance. It would require at least two witnesses testifying for conviction. Only the guilty would be convicted and punished; no punishment or penalty is allowed against that one's family or relatives.

The first ten amendments to the Constitution, known as the **Bill of Rights**, guaranteed protection for individuals against any action by the federal government which would threaten the loss of their life, liberty, or property without proper legal procedure. These laws guaranteed freedoms such as speech, press, assembly, religion, petition, unreasonable searches and seizures, and protection against arbitrary arrest and punishment.

The fourth principle is the fact that for over 200 years the Constitution has adapted to changing times and circumstances. One important process is the ability to meet needed changes through amendments. The other great reason for its flexibility is the inclusion of what is known as the "elastic clause". In addition to its specific powers, the writers granted to Congress the power to make any additional laws needed and appropriate in order to implement other powers.

The U.S. Constitution is a most unique document among human governments today. It has stood the test of time for two reasons: (1) It has set out procedural rules that must be followed, even in extreme and critical circumstances; and (2) due to amending along with customs and practices, it is flexible and adaptable making it possible to meet the demands and changes of a growing nation.

SKILL 27.3   Recognize the rights and responsibilities of U.S. citizens

Citizens' rights vary from nation to nation. The U.S. Constitution and Congressional laws provide basic as well as additional rights to American citizens. These civil rights include such rights as freedom of religion, assembly, speech, voting, holding public office, and traveling throughout the country. U.S. citizens have the right to live in America and cannot be forced to leave. American citizenship is guaranteed and will not be taken away for any reason, unless one commits certain serious actions. Civil rights have limitations such as minimum age for voting and limited free speech, forbidding the damage to someone's reputation by slander and lying.

Citizens' duties also vary from nation to nation. Duties demanded by law (also considered civic responsibilities) include paying taxes, obeying the laws, and defending the country. Although some governments require jury duty, in the United States this would be a duty not required by law along with voting, doing volunteer work to help others, and becoming aware of public problems.

Citizenship is granted one of two ways: either by birth or by naturalization. Some hold citizenship in two nations the same two ways.

SKILL 27.4 **Be able to recognize and understand the main features of international relations**

The governments of all independent states are considered "sovereign", meaning that each national government does not recognize any authority higher than its own. Governments of all countries seek benefits for their citizens which result in cooperating with each other if this is in the best interests of their nation. Peaceful relations between countries are maintained by four methods:

(1) Diplomacy

The day-to-day relations between governments are carried out by ambassadors and other diplomats. They arrange treaties; work to get political advantages for their government; protect the interests of their fellow citizens who are traveling abroad; and make every effort to settle any disputes through negotiations.

(2) International Conferences and Organizations

If many countries have an international problem or if several disagreements must be settled, an international conference may be convened. Some international or multi-national organizations, the United Nations for example, may become involved.

(3) Treaties

These are considered formal agreements, used by national governments for various reasons such as: providing for military protection, ending military conflict, promoting economic interests, establishing important agencies and organizations, and drawing and limiting borders.

(4) International law

This area develops and sets up, either in treaties or through custom, rules and guidelines for governments to observe in pursuing their relations with one another.

SKILL 27.5   Be able to understand and to compare different political theories and systems

A political system can be explained or defined as the unique way a nation governs itself. There are several different political systems in existence:

(1) Monarchy - a government ruled by a king or queen. Most monarchies are considered constitutional or limited, meaning that the king or queen does not have sole, absolute authority but that executive power is usually carried out through a prime minister and cabinet and laws are made in a legislative body, such as a parliament.

(2) Oligarchy - a type of modern government in which a small group of people control the government. Some examples are a republic, an aristocracy, even some dictatorships, especially if based on wealth or military authority.

(3) Democracy - means "rule by the people". There are two types of democracy: (a) pure or direct democracy - when the citizens themselves meet in one place and make laws for themselves and their community. A familiar example of this form was in ancient Greece practiced by the citizens of Athens. The other type is (b) representative democracy - practiced by most modern democracies. Usually it is impossible or most inconvenient for all the people to meet in one place to make laws. So they choose or elect representatives to meet and make laws for them. This form of government is also sometimes referred to as republican government or a democratic republic.

(4) Despotism and Dictatorships - a form of government and any ruler where there is unlimited power over the people and no legislative body to limit rulership. This is similar to the definitions for tyranny, autocracy, and totalitarianism.

(5) Parliamentary system - a government made up of a legislative body, called a parliament, and a cabinet with a premier or prime minister heading the cabinet. The cabinet is chosen and supported by the majority political party in parliament and stays in power as long as it has this support.

(6) Presidential system - a government of separate executive and legislative branches. The executive branch is headed by a president, elected for a fixed term.

(7) Federalism - a single government of limited powers under which two or more sovereign political units, such as states or provinces, are united.

(8) Constitutionalism - a political system in which laws and traditions limit the powers of government.

ELEMENTARY EDUCATION   166

COMPETENCY 28.0

WORLD HISTORY

Learning without thought is labor lost; thought without learning is learning is perilous.

Confucius

COMPETENCY 28.0   WORLD HISTORY

SKILL 28.1   Establish an understanding of prehistory and the ancient civilizations, including the non-Western world

Prehistory is defined as the period of man's achievements before the development of writing. In the Stone Age cultures the three different periods with their accomplishments include the Lower Paleolithic period with the use of crude tools; the Upper Paleolithic period exhibiting a greater variety of better-made tools and implements, the wearing of clothing, highly organized group life, and skills in art; and the Neolithic period which showed domesticated animals, food production, the arts of knitting, spinning and weaving cloth, starting fires through friction, building houses rather than living in caves, the development of institutions including the family, religion, and a form of government or the origin of the state.

Ancient civilizations were those cultures which developed to a greater degree and were considered advanced. These included the following eleven with their major accomplishments:

Egypt made numerous significant contributions including construction of the great pyramids; development of hieroglyphic writing; preservation of bodies after death; making paper from papyrus; contributing to developments in arithmetic and geometry; the invention of the method of counting in groups of 10 (the decimal system) but had nothing to denote or represent zero; completion of a solar calendar; and laying the foundation for science and astronomy.

The ancient civilization of the Sumerians invented the wheel; developed irrigation through use of canals, dikes, and devices for raising water; devised the system of cuneiform writing; learned to divide time; and built large boats for trade. The Babylonians devised the famous Code of Hammurabi, a code of laws.

The ancient Assyrians were warlike and aggressive due to a highly organized military and used chariots drawn by horses. The Hebrews/ancient Israelites instituted "monotheism", which is the worship of one God, Yahweh, and combined the 66 books of the Hebrew and Christian Greek scriptures into the Bible we have today.

The Minoans had a system of writing using symbols to represent syllables in words; built palaces with multiple levels containing many rooms, water and sewage systems with flush toilets, bathtubs, hot and cold running water, and bright paintings on the walls.

The Mycenaeans changed the Minoan writing system to aid their own language and also used symbols to represent syllables.

The Phoenicians were sea traders well-known for their manufacturing skills in glass and metals; the development of their famous purple dye; became so very proficient in the skill of navigation that they were able to sail by the stars at night; devised an alphabet using symbols to represent single sounds, which was an improved extension of the Egyptian principle and writing system.

In India, the caste system was developed, the principle of zero in mathematics was discovered, and the major religion of Hinduism was begun.

China began building the Great Wall; practiced crop rotation and terrace farming; increased the silk industry in importance; developed caravan routes across Central Asia for extensive trade; increased proficiency in rice cultivation; developed a written language based on drawings or pictographs (no alphabet symbolizing sounds as each word or character had a form different from all others).

The ancient Persians developed an alphabet; contributed the religions/philosophies of Zoroastrianism, Mithraism, and Gnosticism; allowed conquered peoples to retain their own customs, laws, and religions.

SKILL 28.2   Understand the important contributions of classical civilizations, including the non-Western world

The classical civilization of Greece reached the highest levels in man's achievements based on the foundations already laid by such ancient groups as the Egyptians, Phoenicians, Minoans, and Mycenaeans. Among the more important contributions of Greece were: from the Phoenicians the letters for the Greek alphabet forming the basis for the Roman and our present-day alphabets; extensive trading and colonization resulting in the spread of the Greek civilization; the love of sports with emphasis on a sound body, leading to the tradition of the Olympic games; the rise of independent, strong city-states; the complete contrast between independent, freedom-loving Athens with its practice of pure democracy (direct, personal, active participation in government by qualified citizens) and rigid, totalitarian, militaristic Sparta; important accomplishments in drama, epic and lyric poetry, fables, myths centered around the many gods and goddesses, science, astronomy, medicine, mathematics, philosophy, art, architecture, writing about and recording historical events; the conquests of Alexander the Great spreading Greek ideas to the areas he conquered and bringing to the Greek world many ideas from Asia; and above all, the value of ideas, wisdom, curiosity, and the desire to learn as much about the world as was possible.

The ancient civilization of Rome lasted approximately 1,000 years including the periods of republic and empire, although its lasting influence on Europe and its history was for a much longer period of time. There was a very sharp contrast between the curious, imaginative, inquisitive Greeks and the practical, simple, down-to-earth, no-nonsense Romans who spread and preserved the ideas of ancient Greece and other culture groups. The contributions and accomplishments of the Romans are numerous but their greatest include language, engineering and building, law, government, roads, trade, and the "Pax Romana" - the long period of peace enabling free travel and trade, spreading people, cultures, goods, and ideas all over a vast area of the known world.

A most interesting and significant characteristic of the Greek, Hellenic, and Roman civilizations was "secularism" where emphasis shifted away from religion to the state. Men were not absorbed in or dominated by religion as had been the case in Egypt and the nations located in Mesopotamia. Religion and its leaders did not dominate the state and its authority was greatly diminished.

In India Hinduism was a continuing influence along with the rise of Buddhism. Industry and commerce developed along with extensive trading with the Near East. Outstanding advances in the fields of science and medicine were made along with being one of the first to be active in navigation and maritime enterprises during this time period.

China is considered by some historians as the oldest, uninterrupted civilization in the world and was in existence around the same time as the ancient civilizations found in Egypt, Mesopotamia, and the Indus Valley. The Chinese studied nature and weather; stressed the importance of education, family, and a strong central government; followed the religions of Buddhism, Confucianism, and Taoism; and invented such things as gunpowder, paper, printing, and the magnetic compass.

The civilization in Japan appeared in this time period having borrowed much of their culture from China. It was the last of these classical civilizations to develop and although they used, accepted, and copied Chinese art, law, architecture, dress, writing, and others, the Japanese refined these into their own unique way of life, including incorporating the religion of Buddhism into their culture.

The civilizations in Africa south of the Sahara were developing the refining and use of iron, especially for farm implements and later for weapons. Trading was overland using camels and at important seaports. The Arab influence was extremely important as was their later contact with Indians, Christian Nubians, and Persians. In fact, their trading activities were probably the most important factor in the spread of and assimilation of different ideas and stimulation of cultural growth.

SKILL 28.3   Show an understanding of the period known as the Middle Ages

The official end of the Roman Empire came when Germanic tribes took over and controlled most of Europe. The five major ones were the Visigoths, Ostrogoths, Vandals, Saxons, and the Franks. In later years, the Franks successfully stopped the invasion of southern Europe by Muslims by soundly defeating them, under the leadership of Charles Martel, at the Battle of Tours in 732 A.D. Thirty-six years later in 768 A.D. the grandson of Charles Martel became King of the Franks and is known in history as Charlemagne. Charlemagne was a man of war but was unique in his respect for and encouragement of learning. He made great efforts to rule fairly and ensure just treatment for his people.

The Vikings had a lot of influence at this time with their spreading ideas and their knowledge of trade routes and sailing, accomplished first through their conquests and later through trade.

The purpose of the Crusades was to rid Jerusalem of Muslim control and these series of violent, bloody conflicts did affect trade and stimulated later explorations seeking the new, exotic products such as silks and spices. The Crusaders came into contact with other religions and cultures and spread and received many new ideas.

During this time period, the system of feudalism became the dominant feature. It was a system of loyalty and protection. The strong protected the weak who returned the service with farm labor, military service, and loyalty. Life was lived out on a vast estate, owned by a nobleman and his family, called a "manor". It was in actuality a complete village supporting a few hundred people, mostly peasants. Improved tools and farming methods made life more bearable although most never left the manor or traveled from their village their entire lifetime.

Also coming into importance at this time were the era of knighthood and its code of chivalry as well as the tremendous influence of the Church (Roman Catholic). Until the period of the Renaissance, the Church was the only place where people could be educated. The Bible and other books were hand-copied by monks in the monasteries. Cathedrals were built and were decorated with art depicting religious subjects.

With the increase in trade and travel, cities sprang up and began to grow. Craft workers in the cities developed their skills to a high degree, eventually organizing guilds to protect the quality of the work and to regulate the buying and selling of their products. City government developed and flourished, centered on strong town councils. Active in city government and the town councils were the wealthy businessmen who made up the rising middle class.

The end of the feudal manorial system was sealed by the outbreak and spread of the infamous Black Death which killed over one-third of the total population of Europe. Those who survived and were skilled in any job or occupation were in demand and many serfs or peasants found freedom and, for that time period, a decidedly improved standard of living. Strong nation-states became powerful and people developed a renewed interest in life and learning.

In other parts of the world were the Byzantine and Saracenic (or Islamic) civilizations, both dominated by religion. The major contributions of the Saracens were in the areas of science and philosophy. Included were accomplishments in astronomy, mathematics, physics, chemistry, medicine, literature, art, trade and manufacturing, agriculture, and a marked influence on the Renaissance period of history.

The Byzantines (Christians) made important contributions in art and the preservation of Greek and Roman achievements including architecture (especially in eastern Europe and Russia), the Code of Justinian and Roman law.

SKILL 28.4   Show an understanding of the importance and accomplishments of the Renaissance and Reformation periods

The word "Renaissance" literally means "rebirth" and signaled the rekindling of interest in the glory and learning of ancient classical Greece and Rome. It was the period of time in human history marking the start of many ideas and innovations leading to our modern age.

The **Renaissance** began in Italy with many of its ideas starting in Florence, controlled by the infamous Medici family. Education, especially for some of the merchants, required reading, writing, math, the study of law, and the writings of classical Greece and Rome. Contributions of the Italian Renaissance period were in: (1) art - the more important artists were Giotto and his development of perspective in paintings; Leonardo da Vinci who was not only an artist but also a scientist and inventor; Michelangelo who was a sculptor, painter, and architect; others included Raphael, Donatello, Titian, and Tintoretto; (2) political philosophy - the writings of Machiavelli; (3) literature - the writings of Petrarch and Boccaccio; (4) science - Galileo; and (5) medicine - the work of Brussels-born Andrea Vesalius earned him the title of "father of anatomy" and had a profound influence on the Spaniard Michael Servetus and the Englishman William Harvey.

In Germany, Gutenberg's invention of the printing press with movable type facilitated the rapid spread of Renaissance ideas, writings and innovations, thus insuring the enlightenment of most of Western Europe. Also in Germany, contributions were made by Durer and Holbein in art and by Paracelsus in science and medicine.

The effects of the Renaissance in the Low Countries can be seen in the literature and philosophy of Erasmus and the art of van Eyck and Breughel the Elder. Rabelais and de Montaigne in France also made contributions in literature and philosophy. In Spain the art of El Greco and de Morales fluorished as did the writings of Cervantes and de Vega. In England Sir Thomas More and Sir Francis Bacon wrote and taught philosophy and inspired by Vesalius, William Harvey made important contributions in medicine. The greatest talent was found in literature and drama given to mankind by Chaucer, Spenser, Marlowe, Jonson, and the incomparable Shakespeare.

The **Reformation** period consisted of two phases: the Protestant Revolution and the Catholic Reformation. The Protestant Revolution came about because of religious, political, and economic reasons. The religious reasons stemmed from abuses in the Catholic Church including fraudulent clergy with their scandalous immoral lifestyles; the sale of religious offices, indulgences, and dispensations; different theologies within the Church; and frauds involving sacred relics.

The political reasons for the Protestant Revolution involved the increase in the power of rulers who were considered "absolute monarchs" wanting all power and control, especially over the Church; and the growth of "nationalism" or patriotic pride in one's own country.

Economic reasons included the greedy desire of ruling monarchs to possess and control all lands and wealth of the Church; deep animosity against the burdensome papal taxation; the rise of the affluent middle class and its clash with medieval Church ideals; and the increase of an active system of "intense" capitalism.

The **Protestant Revolution** began in Germany with the revolt of Martin Luther against Church abuses. It spread to Switzerland where it was led by Calvin. It began in England with the efforts of King Henry VIII to have his marriage to Catherine of Aragon annulled so he could wed another and have a male heir. The results were the increasing support given not only by the people but also by nobles and some rulers and of course the attempts of the Church to stop it.

The **Catholic Reformation** was undertaken by the Church to "clean up its act" and to slow down or stop the Protestant Revolution. The major efforts to this end were supplied by the Council of Trent and the Jesuits. Six major results of the Reformation include: religious freedom and tolerance; more opportunities for education; power and control of rulers limited; increase in religious wars; and an increase in fanaticism and persecution.

SKILL 28.5   Understand the importance and results of the Age of Exploration

A number of different individuals and events led to the time period of exploration and discoveries. The Vivaldo brothers and Marco Polo wrote of their travels and experiences which signaled the early beginnings. The survivors of the Crusades made their way home to different places in Europe bringing with them fascinating, new information about exotic lands, people, customs, and desired foods and goods such as spices and silks.

The Renaissance ushered in a time of curiosity, learning, and incredible energy sparking the desire for trade to procure these new, exotic products and to find better, faster, cheaper trade routes to get to them. The work of geographers, astronomers and map-makers made important contributions and many studied and applied the work of such men as Hipparchus of Greece, Ptolemy of Egypt, Tycho Brahe of Denmark, and Fra Mauro of Italy.

Portugal made the start under the encouragement, support, and financing of Prince Henry the Navigator. The more well-known explorers who sailed under the flag of Portugal included Cabral, Diaz, and Vasco da Gama, who successfully sailed all the way from Portugal, around the southern tip of Africa, to Calcutta, India.

Christopher Columbus, sailing for Spain, is credited with the discovery of America although he never set foot on its soil. Magellan is credited with the first circumnavigation of the earth. Other Spanish explorers made their marks in parts of what are now the United States, Mexico, and South America.

For France, claims to various parts of North America were the result of the efforts of such men as Verrazano, Champlain, Cartier, LaSalle, Father Marquette and Joliet. Dutch claims were based on the work of one Henry Hudson. John Cabot gave England its stake in North America along with John Hawkins, Sir Francis Drake, and the half-brothers Sir Walter Raleigh and Sir Humphrey Gilbert.

Actually the first Europeans in the New World were Norsemen led by Eric the Red and later, his son Leif the Lucky. But before any of these, the ancestors of today's Native Americans and Latin American Indians crossed the Bering Strait from Asia to Alaska, eventually settling in all parts of the Americas.

SKILL 28.6 Understand the significance of revolutionary movements

The time period of the 1700's and 1800's was characterized in Western countries by the opposing political ideas of democracy and nationalism, resulting in strong nationalistic feelings and people of common cultures asserting their belief in the right to have a part in their government.

The American Revolution resulted in the successful efforts of the English colonies in America, experienced in over one hundred years of mostly self-government and resentful of increased British meddling and ever-increasing control, in declaring their freedom, winning a war with aid from France, and forming a new independent nation.

The French Revolution was the revolt of the middle and lower classes against the gross political and economic excesses of the rulers and the supporting nobility. It ended with the establishment of the First in a series of French Republics. Conditions leading to revolt included extreme taxation, inflation, lack of food, and the total ignoring and disregard for the impossible, degrading, unacceptable condition of the people on the part of the rulers, nobility, and the Church.

The Industrial Revolution, which began in Great Britain and spread elsewhere, was the development of power-driven machinery (fueled by coal and steam) leading to the accelerated growth of industry with large factories replacing homes and small workshops as work centers. The lives of people changed drastically and a largely agricultural society changed to an industrial one. In Western Europe, the period of empire and colonialism began as the industrial nations seized and claimed parts of Africa and Asia in an effort to control and provide the raw materials needed to feed the industries and machines in the "mother country". Later developments included power based on electricity and internal combustion, replacing coal and steam.

The Russian Revolution occurred first in March (or February on the old calendar) 1917 with the abdication of Tsar Nicholas II and the establishment of a democratic government. But the strength of the Bolsheviks, those who were the extreme Marxists and had a majority in Russia's socialist party, overcame opposition and in November (October on the old calendar) did away with the provisional democratic government and set up the world's first Marxist state. The conditions in Russia in previous centuries led up to this. Russia's harsh climate, tremendous size, and physical isolation from the rest of Europe, along with the brutal despotic rule and control of the tsars over enslaved peasants, contributed to the final conditions leading to revolution. Despite the tremendous efforts of Peter the Great to bring his country up to the social, cultural, and economic standards of the rest of Europe, Russia always remained a hundred years or more behind. Autocratic rule, the existence of the system of serfdom or slavery of the peasants, lack of money, defeats in wars, lack of enough food and food production, little, if any, industrialization - all of these contributed to conditions ripe for revolt.

By 1914 Russia's industrial growth was even faster than Germany's and agricultural production was improving, along with better transportation. But the conditions of poverty were horrendous; the Orthodox Church was steeped in and mixed in the political activities; and the absolute rule of the tsar was the order of the day. By the time the nation entered World War I, conditions were just right for revolution. Marxist socialism seemed to be the solution or answer to all the problems. Russia had to stop participation in the war, even though winning a big battle. Industry could not meet the military's needs, transportation by rail was severely disrupted, and it was most difficult to procure supplies from the Allies. The people had had enough of war, injustice, starvation, poverty, slavery, and cruelty. The support for and strength of the Bolsheviks were mainly in the cities. After two or three years of civil war, fighting foreign invasions, and opposing other revolutionary groups, the Bolsheviks were finally successful in making possible a type of "pre-Utopia" for the workers and the people.

As succeeding Marxist or Communist leaders came to power, the effects of this violent revolution were felt all around the earth and until 1989-1991, when Communism eventually gave way to various forms of democracies and free enterprise societies in Eastern Europe and the former Soviet Union, the foreign policies of all free Western nations were directly, immensely affected by the Marxist-Communist ideology. It effect on Eastern Europe and the former Soviet Union was felt politically, economically, socially, culturally, geographically. The people of ancient Russia simply exchanged one autocratic dictatorial system for another and its impact on all of the people on the earth is still being felt to this day.

SKILL 28.7   Understand the importance of the growth of nationalism

The time period from 1830 to 1914 is characterized by the extraordinary growth and spread of patriotic pride in a nation along with intense, wide-spread imperialism. Loyalty to one's nation included national pride, extension and maintenance of sovereign political boundaries, unification of smaller states with common language, history, and culture into a more powerful nation, or smaller national groups who, as part of a larger multi-cultural empire, wished to separate into smaller, political, cultural nations. Examples of major events of this time period resulting from the insurgence of nationalism include:

> In the United States, territorial expansion occurred in the expansion westward under the banner of "Manifest Destiny". Also the U.S. was involved in the War with Mexico, the Spanish-American War, and support of the Latin American colonies of Spain in their revolt for independence. In Latin America, the Spanish colonies were successful in their fight for independence and self-government.

In Europe, Italy and Germany were each totally united into one nation from many smaller states. There were revolutions in Austria and Hungary, the Franco-Prussian War, the dividing of Africa among the strong European nations, interference and intervention of Western nations in Asia, and the breakup of Turkish dominance in the Balkans.

In Africa, France, Great Britain, Italy, Portugal, Spain, Germany, and Belgium controlled all of the continent except Liberia and Ethiopia. In Asia and the Pacific Islands, only China, Japan, and present-day Thailand (Siam) kept their independence. The others were controlled by the strong European nations.

An additional reason for European imperialism was the harsh, urgent demand for the raw materials needed to fuel and feed the great Industrial Revolution. These resources were not available in the huge quantity so desperately needed which necessitated (and rationalized) the partitioning of the continent of Africa and parts of Asia. In turn, these colonial areas would purchase the finished manufactured goods.

SKILL 28.8   Understand the causes and results of the wars of the 20th century

World War I - 1914 to 1918

Causes were (a) the surge of nationalism; (b) the increasing strength of military capabilities; (c) massive colonization for raw materials needed for industrialization and manufacturing; and (d) military and diplomatic alliances. The initial spark which started the conflagration was the assassination of Austrian Archduke Francis Ferdinand and his wife in Sarajevo.

There were a total of 28 nations involved in the war, not including colonies and territories. It began July 28, 1914 and ended November 11, 1918 with the signing of the Treaty of Versailles. Economically, the war cost a total of $337 billion, increased inflation and huge war debts, and caused a loss of markets, goods, jobs, and factories. Politically, old empires collapsed, many monarchies disappeared, smaller countries gained temporary independence, Communists seized power in Russia, and, in some cases, nationalism increased. Socially, total populations decreased because of war deaths and low birth rates, there were millions of displaced persons, villages and farms were destroyed, cities grew, women made significant gains in the work force and the ballot box; there was less social distinction and classes, attitudes completely changed and old beliefs and values were questioned. The peace settlement established the League of Nations to ensure peace, but it failed to do so.

World War II - 1939 to 1945

Causes were (a) ironically, the Treaty of Paris, the peace treaty ending World War I, ultimately led to the second World War. Countries that fought in the first war were either dissatisfied over the "spoils" of war, or were punished so harshly that resentment continued building to an eruption twenty years later. (b) The economic problems of both winners and losers of the first war were never resolved and the world-wide Great Depression of the 1930s dealt the final blow to any immediate rapid recovery. Democratic governments in Europe were severely strained and weakened which in turn gave strength and encouragement to those political movements that were extreme and made promises to end the economic chaos in their countries. (c) Nationalism, which was a major cause of World War I, grew even stronger and seemed to feed the feelings of discontent which became more and more rampant. (d) Because of unstable economic conditions and political unrest, harsh dictatorships arose in several of the countries, especially where there was no history of experience in democratic government. (e) Countries such as Germany, Japan, and Italy began to aggressively expand their borders and acquire additional territory.

In all, a total of 59 nations became embroiled in World War II which began September 1, 1939 and ended September 2, 1945. These dates include both the European and Pacific Theaters of war. The horrible tragic results of this second global conflagration were more deaths and more destruction than in any other armed conflict. It completely uprooted and displaced millions of people. The end of the war brought renewed power struggles, especially in Europe and China, with many Eastern European nations as well as China coming under complete control and domination of the Communists, supported and backed by the Soviet Union. With the development of and two-time deployment of an atomic bomb against two Japanese cities, the world found itself in the nuclear age. The peace settlement established the United Nations Organization, still existing and operating today.

Korean War - 1950 to 1953

Causes: Korea was under control of Japan from 1895 to the end of the Second World War in 1945. At war's end, the Soviet and U.S. military troops moved into Korea with the U.S. troops in the southern half and the Soviet troops in the northern half with the 38 degree North Latitude line as the boundary. The General Assembly of the U.N. in 1947 ordered elections throughout all of Korea to select one government for the entire country. The Soviet Union would not allow the North Koreans to vote, so they set up a Communist government there. The South Koreans set up a democratic government but both claimed the entire country. At times there were clashes between the troops from 1948 to 1950. After the U.S. removed its remaining troops in 1949 and announced in early 1950 that Korea was not part of its defense line in Asia, the Communists decided to take action and invaded the south.

Participants were: North and South Korea, United States of America, Australia, New Zealand, China, Canada. France, Great Britain, Turkey, Belgium, Ethiopia, Colombia, Greece, South Africa, Luxembourg, Thailand, the Netherlands, and the Philippines. It was the first war in which a world organization played a major military role and it presented quite a challenge to the U.N. which had only been in existence five years.

The war began June 25, 1950 and ended July 27, 1953. A truce was drawn up and an armistice agreement was signed ending the fighting. A permanent treaty of peace has never been signed and the country remains divided between the Communist North and the Democratic South. It was a very costly and bloody war destroying villages and homes, displacing and killing millions of people.

The Vietnam War - U.S. Involvement - 1957 to 1973

Causes: U.S. involvement was the second phase of three in Vietnam's history. The first phase began in 1946 when the Vietnamese fought French troops for control of the country. Vietnam prior to 1946 had been part of the French colony of Indochina (since 1861 along with Laos and Kampuchea or Cambodia). In 1954 the defeated French left and the country became divided into Communist North and Democratic South. U.S. aid and influence continues as part of U.S. "Cold War" foreign policy to help any nation threatened by Communism.

The second phase involved the U.S. commitment. The Communist Vietnamese considered the war one of national liberation, a struggle to avoid continual dominance and influence of a foreign power. A cease-fire was arranged in January 1973 and a few months later U.S. troops left for good. The third and final phase consisted of fighting between the Vietnamese but ended April 30, 1975 with the surrender of South Vietnam, the entire country being united under Communist ruler.

Participants were the United States of America, Australia, New Zealand, South and North Vietnam, South Korea, Thailand, and the Philippines. With active U.S. involvement from 1957 to 1973, it was the longest war participated in by the U.S.; was tremendously destructive and completely divided the American public in their opinions and feelings about the war. Many were frustrated and angered by the fact that it was the first war fought on foreign soil in which U.S. combat forces were totally unable to achieve their goals and objectives. Returning veterans faced not only readjustment to normal civilian life but also faced bitterness, anger, rejection, and no heroes' welcomes. Many suffered severe physical and deep psychological problems. The war set a precedent with Congress and the American people actively challenging U.S. military and foreign policy. The conflict, though tempered markedly by time, still exists and still has a definite effect on people.

SKILL 28.9 Show understanding of major contemporary world issues and trends

The struggle between the Communist world under Soviet Union leadership and the non-Communist world under Anglo-American leadership resulted in what became known as the Cold War. Communism crept into the Western Hemisphere with Cuban leader Fidel Castro and his regime. Most colonies in Africa, Asia, and the Middle East gained independence from European and Western influence and control. In South Africa in the early 1990s, the system of racial segregation, called "apartheid", was abolished.

The Soviet Union was the first industrialized nation to successfully begin a program of space flight and exploration, launching Sputnik and putting the first man in space. The United States also experienced success in its space program successfully landing space crews on the moon. In the late 1980s and early 1990s, the Berlin Wall was torn down and Communism fell in the Soviet Union and Eastern Europe. The 15 republics of the former U.S.S.R. became independent nations with varying degrees of freedom an d democracy in government and together formed the Common-wealth of Independent States (CIS). The former Communist nations of Eastern Europe also emphasized their independence with democratic forms of government.

Tremendous progress in communication and transportation has tied all parts of the earth and drawn them closer. There are still vast areas of unproductive land, extreme poverty, food shortages, rampant diseases, violent friction between cultures, the ever-present nuclear threat, environmental pollution, rapid reduction of natural resources, urban over-crowding, acceleration in global terrorism and violent crimes, and a diminishing middle class.

SKILL 28.10 Know the differences between the world's major religions

Eight major religions practiced today are:

(1) Judaism - the oldest of the eight and was the first to teach and practice the belief in one God, Yahweh.

(2) Christianity - came from Judaism, grew and spread in the First Century throughout the Roman Empire, despite persecution. A later schism resulted in the Western (Roman Catholic) and Eastern (Orthodox) parts. Protestant sects developed as part of the Protestant Revolution. The name "Christian" means one who is a follower of Jesus Christ who started Christianity. Christians follow his teachings and examples, living by the laws and principles of the Bible.

3) Islam - founded in Arabia by Mohammed who preached on God, Allah. Islam spread through trade, travel, and conquest and followers of it fought in the Crusades and other wars against Christians and today against the Jewish nation of Israel. Practicers of Islam, called Muslims, live by the teachings of the Koran, their holy book, and of their prophets.

(4) Hinduism - begun by people called Aryans around 1500 B.C. and spread into India. The Aryans blended their culture with the culture of the Dravidians, natives they conquered. Today it has many sects, promotes worship of hundreds of gods and goddesses and belief in reincarnation. Though forbidden today by law, a prominent feature of Hinduism in the past was a rigid adherence to and practice of the infamous caste system.

(5) Buddhism - developed in India from the teachings of Prince Gautama and spread to most of Asia. Its beliefs opposed the worship of numerous deities, the Hindu caste system and the supernatural. Worshippers must be free of attachment to all things worldly and devote themselves to finding release from life's suffering.

(6) Confucianism is a Chinese religion based on the teachings of the Chinese philosopher Confucius. There is no clergy, no organization, no belief in a deity nor in life after death. It emphasizes political and moral ideas with respect for authority and ancestors. Rulers were expected to govern according to high moral standards.

(7) Taoism - a native Chinese religion with worship of more deities than almost any other religion. It teaches all followers to make the effort to achieve the two goals of happiness and immortality. Practices and ceremonies include meditation, prayer, magic, reciting scriptures, special diets, breath control, beliefs in witchcraft, fortune-telling, astrology, and communicating with the spirits of the dead.

(8) Shinto - the native religion of Japan developed from native folk beliefs worshipping spirits and demons in animals, trees, and mountains. According to its mythology, deities created Japan and its people which resulted in worshipping the emperor as a god. Shinto was strongly influenced by Buddhism and Confucianism but never had strong doctrines on salvation or life after death.

Interestingly, all of these eight major religions have divisions or smaller sects within them.

COMPETENCY 29.0

AMERICAN HISTORY

It is a general insight, which merits more attention than it receives, that teaching should not be compared to filling a bottle with water but rather to helping a flower to grow in its own way. As any good teacher knows, the methods of instruction and the rang of material covered are matters of small importance as compared with the success in arousing the natural curiosity of the students and instilling their interest in exploring on their own.

Chomsky

COMPETENCY 29.0   AMERICAN HISTORY

SKILL 29.1   Understand the importance of the Age of Exploration

The Age of Exploration actually had its beginnings centuries before exploration actually took place. The rise and spread of Islam in the seventh century and its subsequent control over the holy city of Jerusalem led to the European so-called holy wars, the Crusades, to free Jerusalem and the Holy Land from this control. Even though, as a whole, the Crusades were not a success, those who survived and returned to their homes and countries in Western Europe brought back with them new products such as silks, spices, perfumes, new and different foods - luxuries unheard of that gave new meaning to colorless, drab, dull lives.

New ideas, new inventions, and new methods also went to Western Europe with the returning Crusaders and from these new influences was the intellectual stimulation which led to the period known as the Renaissance. Revival of interest in classical Greece led to increased interest in art, architecture, literature, science, astronomy, medicine and increased trade between Europe and Asia plus the invention of the printing press to give the spread of knowledge a big push was all that was needed to start exploring.

For many centuries, various map-makers made many maps and charts which in turn stimulated curiosity and the seeking of more knowledge. At the same time, the Chinese were using the magnetic compass in their sailings. Pacific islanders were going from island to island, covering thousands of miles in open canoes navigating by sun and stars. Arab traders were sailing all over the Indian Ocean. The trade routes between Europe and Asia were slow, difficult, dangerous, and very expensive. Between sea voyages on the Indian Ocean and Mediterranean Sea and the camel caravans in central Asia and the Arabian Desert, the trade was still controlled by the Italian merchants in Genoa and Venice. It would take months and even years for the exotic luxuries of Asia to reach the markets of Western Europe. There had to be found a faster cheaper way. And a way had to be found which would by-pass and end the control of the Italian merchants.

Prince Henry of Portugal (also called the Navigator) encouraged, supported, and financed the Portuguese seamen who led in the search for an all-water route to Asia. A shipyard was built along with a school teaching navigation. New types of sailing ships were built which would carry the seamen safely through the ocean waters. Experiments were conducted in newer maps, newer navigational methods, and newer instruments. These included the astrolabe and the compass enabling sailors to determine direction as well as latitude and longitude for exact location. Even though Prince Henry died in 1460, the Portuguese kept on, sailing along and exploring Africa's west coastline.

ELEMENTARY EDUCATION   183

In 1488, Bartholomew Diaz and his men sailed around Africa's southern tip and were headed toward Asia. Diaz discouraged and weary from the long months at sea, extremely fearful of the unknown, and just refusing to travel any further. But the Portuguese were finally successful ten years later in 1498 when Vasco da Gama and his men, continuing the route of Diaz, rounded Africa's Cape of Good Hope, sailing across the Indian Ocean, reaching India's port of Calicut (Calcutta). Even though, six years earlier, Columbus had reached the New World and an entire hemisphere, da Gama had proved Asia could be reached from Europe by sea.

Of course, everyone knows that Columbus' first trans-Atlantic voyage was to try to prove his theory or idea that Asia could be reached by sailing west. And to a certain extent his idea was true. It could be done but only after figuring how to go around or across or through the land mass in between. Long after Spain dispatched explorers and her famed conquistadores to gather the wealth for the Spanish monarchs and their coffers, the British were searching valiantly for the "Northwest Passage", a land-sea route across North America and the eventual open sea to the wealth of Asia. It wasn't until after the Lewis and Clark Expedition when Captains Meriwether Lewis and William Clark proved conclusively that there simply was no Northwest Passage. It did not exist.

But this did not deter exploration and settlement. Spain, France, and England along with some participation by the Dutch, led the way with expanding Western European civilization in the New World. These three nations had strong monarchial governments and were struggling for dominance and power in Europe. With the defeat of Spain's mighty Armada in 1588, England became undisputed mistress of the seas. Spain lost its power and influence in Europe and it was left to France and England to carry on the rivalry, leading to eventual British control in Asia as well.

Spain's influence was in Florida, the Gulf Coast from Texas all the west to California and south to the tip of South America and some of the islands of the West Indies. French control centered from New Orleans north to what is now northern Canada including the entire Mississippi Valley, the St. Lawrence Valley, the Great Lakes, and the land that was part of the Louisiana Territory. There were some West Indies islands as part of France's empire also. England settled the eastern seaboard of North America, including parts of Canada and from Maine to Georgia. Some West Indies islands also came under British control. The Dutch had New Amsterdam for a period of time but later ceded it into British hands. Of course, one interesting aspect of all of this was that in each of these three nations, especially in England, the land claims extended partly or all the way across the continent, regardless of the fact that the others claimed the same land. The wars for dominance and control of power and influence in Europe would undoubtedly and eventually extend to the Americas, especially North America, which is exactly what happened.

Importance of the Age of Exploration was not only the discovery and colonization of the New World, but also better maps and charts, new accurate navigational instruments, increased knowledge, great wealth, new and different foods and items not known in Europe, a new hemisphere as a refuge from poverty, persecution, a place to start a new and better life, and proof that Asia could be reached by sea and that the earth was round, ships and sailors would not sail off the edge of a flat earth and disappear forever into nothingness.

SKILL 29.2   Know the significance of the Colonial Period

The part of North America claimed by France was called New France and consisted of the land west of the Appalachian Mountains. This area of claims and settlement included the St. Lawrence Valley, the Great Lakes, the Mississippi Valley, and the entire region of land westward to the Rockies. They established the permanent settlements of Montreal and New Orleans, thus giving them control of the two major gateways into the heart of North America, the vast, rich interior. The St. Lawrence River, the Great Lakes, and the Mississippi River along with its tributaries made it possible for the French explorers and traders to roam at will, virtually unhindered in exploring, trapping, trading, and furthering the interests of France.

Spanish settlement had its beginnings in the Caribbean with the establishment of colonies on Hispaniola (at Santo Domingo which became the capital of the West Indies), Puerto Rico, and Cuba. There were a number of reasons for Spanish involvement in the Americas: the spirit of adventure: the desire for land, extension of Spanish power, influence, and empire, the desire for great wealth, expansion of Roman Catholic influence and conversion of native peoples - to name just a few. The first permanent settlement in what is now the United States was in 1565 at St. Augustine, Florida. A later permanent settlement in the southwestern United States was in 1609 at Santa Fe, New Mexico. At the peak of Spanish power, the area in the United States claimed, settled, and controlled by Spain included Florida and all land west of the Mississippi River - quite a piece of choice real estate. Of course, France and England also lay claim to the same areas. Nonetheless, ranches and missions were built and the Indians who came in contact with the Spaniards were introduced to animals, plants, and seeds from the Old World that they had never seen before. Animals brought in included horses, cattle, donkeys, pigs, sheep, goats, and poultry. Barrels were cut in half and filled with earth to transport and transplant trees bearing apples, olives, oranges, lemons, limes, figs, cherries, apricots, pears, almonds, and walnuts. Even sugar cane and flowers made it to America along with bags bringing seeds of wheat, barley, rye, flax, lentils, rice, and peas.

For the needed labor in the mines and on the plantations, Native Americans were used first as slaves. But they either rapidly died out due to a lack of immunity from European

ELEMENTARY EDUCATION   185

diseases or escaped into nearby jungles or mountains. As a result, African slaves were brought in, especially to the islands of the West Indies. Some historians state that Latin American slavery was less harsh than in the later English colonies in North America. Three reasons are given: (a) the following of a slave code based on ancient Roman laws; (b) the efforts of the Roman Catholic Church to protect and defend slaves because of efforts to convert them; and (c) supposedly the existence of less prejudice because of racial mixtures in parts of Spain controlled at one time by dark-skinned Moors from North Africa. Regardless, slavery was still slavery and was very harsh - cruelly denying dignity and human worth and leading to desperate resistance.

It's interesting that before 1763, when England was rapidly on the way to becoming the most powerful of the three major Western European powers, its thirteen colonies, located between the Atlantic and the Appalachians, physically occupied the least amount of land. And it is also interesting that even before the Spanish Armada was defeated, two Englishmen, Sir Humphrey Gilbert and his half-brother Sir Walter Raleigh, were unsuccessful in their attempts to build successful permanent colonies in the New World. Nonetheless, the thirteen English colonies were successful and, by the time they had gained their independence from Britain, were more than able to govern themselves. They had a rich historical heritage of law, tradition, and documents leading the way to constitutional government conducted according to laws and customs. The settlers in the British colonies highly valued individual freedom, democratic government, and getting ahead through hard work. The English colonies, with only a few exceptions, were considered commercial ventures to make a profit for the crown or the company or whoever financed its beginnings. One was strictly a philanthropic enterprise and three others were primarily for religious reasons but the other nine were started for economic reasons. Settlers in these unique colonies came for different reasons: religious freedom, political freedom, economic prosperity, and land ownership.

The colonies were divided generally into the three regions of New England, Middle Atlantic, and Southern. The culture of each was distinct and affected attitudes, ideas towards politics, religion, and economic activities. The geography of each region also contributed to its unique characteristics.

The New England colonies consisted of Massachusetts, Rhode Island, Connecticut, and New Hampshire. Life in these colonies was centered on the towns. Farming was done by each family on its own plot of land but a short summer growing seas on and limited amount of good soil gave rise to other economic activities such as manufacturing, fishing, shipbuilding, and trade. The vast majority of the settlers shared similar origins, coming from England and Scotland. Towns were carefully planned and laid out the same way. The form of government was the town meeting where all adult males met to make the laws. The legislative body, the General Court, consisted of an upper and lower house.

The Middle or Middle Atlantic colonies included New York, New Jersey, Pennsylvania, Delaware, and Maryland. New York and New Jersey were at one time the Dutch colony of New Netherlands and Delaware at one time was New Sweden. These five colonies, from their beginnings were considered "melting pots" with settlers from many different nations and backgrounds. The main economic activity was farming with the settlers scattered over the countryside cultivating rather large farms. The Indians were not as much of a threat as in New England so they did not have to settle in small farming villages. The soil was very fertile, the land was gently rolling, and a milder climate provided a longer growing season. These farms produced a large surplus of food, not only for the colonists themselves but also for sale. This colonial region became known as the "breadbasket" of the New World and the New York and Philadelphia seaports were constantly filled with ships being loaded with meat, flour, and other foodstuffs for the West Indies and England. There were other economic activities such as shipbuilding, iron mines, and factories producing paper, glass, and textiles. The legislative body in Pennsylvania was unicameral or consisted of one house. In the other four, the legislative body had two houses. Also units of local government were in counties and towns.

The Southern colonies were Virginia, North and South Carolina, and Georgia. Virginia was the first permanent successful English colony and Georgia was the last. The year 1619 was a very important year in the history of Virginia and the United States with three very significant events. First, sixty women were sent to Virginia to marry and establish families; second, twenty Africans, the first of thousands, arrived; third, most importantly, the Virginia colonists were granted the right to self-government and they began by electing their own representatives to the House of Burgesses, their own legislative body. The major economic activity in this region was farming. Here too the soil was very fertile and the climate was very mild with an even longer growing season. The large plantations eventually requiring large numbers of slaves were found in the coastal or tidewater areas. Even though the wealthy slave-owning planters set the pattern of life in this region, most of the people lived inland away from coastal areas. They were small farmers and very few, or any, owned slaves.

The settlers in these four colonies came from diverse backgrounds and cultures. Virginia was colonized mostly by people from England while Georgia was started as a haven for debtors from English prisons. Pioneers from Virginia settled in North Carolina while South Carolina welcomed people from England and Scotland, French Protestants, Germans, and emigrants from islands in the West Indies. Products from farms and plantations included rice, tobacco, indigo, cotton, some corn and wheat. Other economic activities included lumber and naval stores (tar, pitch, rosin, and turpentine) from the pine forests and fur trade on the frontier. Cities such as Savannah and Charleston were important seaports and trading centers.

SKILL 29.3   Explain the crucial effects of the period of the American Revolution

By the 1750's in Europe, Spain was "out of the picture", no longer the most powerful nation and not even a contender. The remaining rivalry was between Britain and France. For nearly 25 years, between 1689 and 1748, a series of "armed conflicts" involving these two powers had been taking place. These conflicts had spilled over into North America. The War of the League of Augsburg in Europe, 1689 to 1697, had been King William's War. The War of the Spanish Succession, 1702 to 1713, had been Queen Anne's War. The War of the Austrian Succession, 1740 to 1748, was called King George's War in the colonies. The two nations fought for possession of colonies, especially in Asia and North America, and for control of the seas, but none of these conflicts were decisive.

The final conflict, which decided once and for all who was the most powerful, began in North America in 1754, in the Ohio River Valley. It was known in America as the French and Indian War and in Europe as the Seven Years War, since it began there in 1756. In America, both sides had advantages and disadvantages. The British colonies were well-established and consolidated in a smaller area. British colonists outnumbered French colonists 23 to 1. Except for a small area in Canada, French settlements were scattered over a much larger area (roughly half of the continent) and were smaller. However, the French settlements were united under one government and were quick to act and cooperate together when necessary. Also the French had many more Indian allies than the British. The British colonies had separate, individual governments and very seldom cooperated together, even when needed. Too, in Europe, at that time, France was the more powerful of the two nations.

The war for independence occurred due to a number of changes, the two most important ones being economic and political. The British Parliament implemented new laws and taxes that made the colonist furious. In 1765 the Quartering Act was passed requiring the colonists to provide supplies and living quarters for the British troops.   The colonists were taxed on newspapers, legal documents, and other printed matter under the Stamp Act of 1765. The Townshend Acts passed in 1767 taxing lead, paint, paper, and tea brought into the colonies. This really increased anger and tension resulting in the British sending troops to New York City and Boston. In Boston, mob violence provoked retaliation by the troops thus bringing about the deaths of five people and the wounding of eight others. The so-called Boston Massacre shocked Americans and British alike so in 1770, Parliament voted to repeal all of the provisions of the Townshend Acts except the tax on tea. In 1773, the tax on tea sold by the British East India Company was substantially reduced, fueling colonial anger once more. This gave the company an unfair trade advantage and forcibly reminded the colonists of the British right to tax them. Merchants refused to sell the tea; colonists refused to buy and drink it; and a shipload of it was dumped into Boston harbor - a most violent Tea Party.

The Americans equated ownership of land or property with the right to vote. Property was considered the foundation of life and liberty and, in the colonial mind and tradition, these went together. Therefore when an indirect tax on tea was made, the British felt that since it wasn't a direct tax, there should be no objection to it. The colonists viewed any tax, direct or indirect, as an attack on their property. They felt that as a representative body, the British Parliament should protect British citizens, including the colonists, from arbitrary taxation. But since they felt they were not represented, Parliament, in their eyes, gave them no protection. So - war began.

August 23, 1775, George III declared that the colonies were in rebellion and warned them to stop or else. By 1776 the colonists and their representatives in the Second Continental Congress realized that things were past the point of no return. The Declaration of Independence was drafted and declared July 4, 1776. George Washington labored against tremendous odds to wage a victorious war. The turning point in the Americans' favor occurred in 1777 with the American victory at Saratoga. This decided the French to align themselves with the Americans against the British. With the aid of Admiral de Grasse and French warships blocking the entrance to Chesapeake Bay, British General Cornwallis trapped at Yorktown, Virginia, surrendered in 1781 and the war was over. The Treaty of Paris officially ending the war was signed in 1783.

On November 15, 1777, the Articles of Confederation were adopted, creating a league of free and independent states. The central government of the new United States of America consisted of a Congress of two to seven delegates from each state with each state having just one vote. The government under the Articles solved some of the postwar problems but had serious weaknesses. Some of its powers included: borrowing and coining money, directing foreign affairs, declaring war and making peace, building and equipping a Navy, regulating weights and measures, asking the states to supply men and money for an army. The delegates to Congress had no real authority as each state carefully and jealously guarded its own interests and limited powers under the Articles. Also, the delegates to Congress were paid by their states and had to vote as directed by their state legislatures. The serious weaknesses were the lack of power to regulate finances, over interstate trade, over foreign trade, to enforce treaties, and military power. Something better and more efficient was needed. In May of 1787, delegates from all states except Rhode Island began meeting in Philadelphia. At first they met to revise the Articles of Confederation as instructed by Congress; but they soon realized that much more was needed. Abandoning the instructions, they set out to write a new Constitution, a new document, the foundation of all government in the United States and a model for representative government throughout the world.

The separation of powers of the three branches of government and the built-in system of checks and balances to keep power balanced was a stroke of genius. It provided for the individuals and the states as well as an organized central authority to keep a new inexperienced young nation on track. They created a system of government so flexible that it had continued in its basic form to this day. In 1789 the Electoral College unanimously elected George Washington as the first President and the new nation was on its way.

SKILL 29.4   Understand how the new nation developed from 1791 to 1860

Beginning with Washington's election to the Presidency in 1791 to the election of Abraham Lincoln in 1860, the United States had expanded to the boundaries of today's 48 conterminous states. During that 69-year period, four wars were fought: the War of 1812 with Great Britain, the war with the Barbary pirates in the Mediterranean, the war with Mexico, and the Seminole wars in Florida. Domestically, by 1860, the nation had had 15 presidents (Lincoln was the 16th), had greatly increased its area, established and strengthened the federal court system, saw the beginnings of and increased influence of political parties, the first and second U.S. banks, economic "panics" or depressions, the abolition movement, the controversies and turmoil leading to the Civil War. There were 33 states in the Union by 1860.

The Industrial Revolution had spread from Great Britain to the United States. Before 1800, most manufacturing activities were done in small shops or in homes. But starting in the early 1800s, factories with modern machines were built making it easier to produce goods faster. The eastern part of the country became a major industrial area although some developed in the West. At about the same time, improvements began to be made in building roads, railroads, canals, and steamboats. The increased ease of travel facilitated the westward movement as well as boosted the economy with faster and cheaper shipment of goods and products, covering larger and larger areas. Some of the innovations include the Erie Canal connecting the interior and Great Lakes with the Hudson River and the coastal port of New York. Many other natural waterways were connected by canals.

Robert Fulton's "Clermont", the first commercially successful steamboat, led the way in the fastest way to ship goods, making it the most important way to do so. Later, steam-powered railroads soon became the biggest rival of the steamboat as a means of shipping, eventually being the most important transportation method opening up the West. The expansion into the interior of the country allowed the United States became the leading agricultural nation in the world. The hardy pioneer farmers produced a vast surplus and emphasis went to producing products with a high-sale value. Such implements as the cotton gin and reaper aided in this. Travel and shipping were greatly assisted in areas not yet touched by railroad or, by improved or new roads, such as the National Road in the East and in the West the Oregon and Santa Fe Trails. People were exposed to works of literature, art, newspapers, drama, live entertainments, and political rallies. With better communication and travel, more information was desired about previously unknown areas of the country, especially the West. The discovery of gold and other mineral wealth resulted in a literal surge of settlers and even more interest.

Public schools were established in many of the states with more and more children being educated. With more literacy and more participation in literature and the arts, the young nation was developing its own unique culture becoming less and less influenced by and dependent on that of Europe.

More industries and factories required more and more labor. Women, children, and, at times, entire families worked the long hours and days, until the 1830s. By that time, the factories were getting even larger and employers began hiring immigrants who were coming to America in huge numbers. Before then, efforts were made to organize a labor movement to improve working conditions and increase wages. It never really caught on until after the Civil War, but the seed had been sown.

Following is just a partial list of well-known Americans who contributed their leadership and talents in various fields and reforms: Lucretia Mott and Elizabeth Cady Stanton for women's rights; Emma Hart Willard, Catharine Esther Beecher, and Mary Lyon for education for women; Dr. Elizabeth Blackwell, the first woman doctor; Antoinette Louisa Blackwell, the first female minister; Dorothea Lynde Dix for reforms in prisons and insane asylums; Elihu Burritt and William Ladd for peace movements; Robert Owen for a Utopian society; Horace Mann, Henry Barmard, Calvin E. Stowe, Caleb Mills, and John Swett for public education; Benjamin Lundy, David Walker, William Lloyd Garrison, Isaac Hooper, Arthur and Lewis Tappan, Theodore Weld, Frederick Douglass, Harriet Tubman, James G. Birney, Henry Highland Garnet, James Forten, Robert Purvis, Harriet Beecher Stowe, Wendell Phillips, and John Brown for abolition of slavery and the Underground Railroad; Louisa Mae Alcott, James Fenimore Cooper, Washington Irving, Walt Whitman, Henry David Thoreau, Ralph Waldo Emerson, Herman Melville, Richard Henry Dana, Nathaniel Hawthorne, Henry Wadsworth Longfellow, John Greenleaf Whittier, Edgar Allan Poe, Oliver Wendell Holmes, famous writers; John C. Fremont, Zebulon Pike, Kit Carson, explorers; Henry Clay, Daniel Webster, Stephen Douglas, John C. Calhoun, American statesmen; Robert Fulton, Cyrus McCormick, Eli Whitney, inventors; Noah Webster, American dictionary and spellers. The list could go on and on but the contributions of these and many, many others greatly enhanced the unique American culture.

SKILL 29.5   Know the effects of westward expansion

Westward expansion occurred for a number of reasons, one important one being economic. Cotton had become most important to most of the people who lived in the southern states. The effects of the Industrial Revolution, which began in England, were now being felt in the United States. With the invention of power-driven machines, the demand for cotton fiber greatly increased for the yarn needed in spinning and weaving. Eli Whitney's cotton gin made the separation of the seeds from the cotton much more efficient and faster. This, in turn, increased the demand and more and more farmers became involved in the raising and selling of cotton. The California gold rush also had a very large influence on the movement west. There were also religious reasons for westward expansion. Increased settlement was encouraged by missionaries who traveled west with the fur traders. They sent word back East for more settlers and the results were tremendous. By the 1840s the population increases in the Oregon country alone were at a rate of about a thousand people a year. People of many different religions and cultures as well as Southerners with black slaves made their way west which leads to a third reason: political.

It was the belief of many that the United States was destined to control all of the land between the two oceans or as one newspaper editor termed it, "Manifest Destiny". This mass migration westward put the U.S. government on a collision course with the Native Americans, Great Britain, Spain, and Mexico. The fur traders and missionaries ran up against the Indians in the northwest and the claims of Great Britain for the Oregon country. The U.S. and Britain had shared the Oregon country but by the 1840's, with the increases in the free and slave populations and the demand of the settlers for control and government by the U.S., the conflict had to be resolved. In a treaty, signed in 1846, by both nations, a peaceful resolution occurred with Britain giving up its claims south of the 49th parallel.

In the American southwest, the results were exactly the opposite. Spain had claimed this area since the 1540's, had spread northward from Mexico City, and, in the 1700's, had established missions, forts, villages and towns, and very large ranches. After the purchase of the Louisiana Territory in 1803, Americans began moving into Spanish territory. A few hundred American families in what is now Texas were allowed to live there but had to agree to become loyal subjects to Spain. In 1821 Mexico successfully revolted against Spanish rule, won independence, and chose to be more tolerant towards the American settlers and traders. The Mexican government encouraged and allowed extensive trade and settlement, especially in Texas. Many of the new settlers were southerners and brought with them their slaves. Slavery was outlawed in Mexico and technically illegal in Texas, although the Mexican looked the other way.

SKILL 29.6 Make comparisons of the political, economic, and social characteristics of both North and South from 1800 to 1860

Slavery in the English colonies began in 1619 when 20 Africans arrived in the colony of Virginia at Jamestown. From then on, slavery had a foothold, especially in the agricultural South, where a large amount of slave labor was needed for the extensive plantations. Free men refused to work for wages on the plantations when land was available for settling on the frontier. So slave labor was the only recourse left. If it had been profitable to use slaves in New England and the Middle Colonies, then without a doubt slavery would have been more widespread. But it came down to whether or not slavery was profitable. It was in the South, but not in the other two colonial regions. It is interesting that the West was involved in the controversy as well as the North and South. By 1860, the country was made up of these three major regions. The people in all three sections or regions had a number of beliefs and institutions in common. Of course there were major differences with each region having its own unique characteristics. But the basic problem was their development along very different lines.

The Supreme Court in 1857 handed down a decision guaranteed to cause explosions throughout the country. Dred Scott was a slave whose owner had taken him from slave state Missouri, then to free state Illinois, into Minnesota Territory, free under the provisions of the Missouri Compromise, then finally back to slave state Missouri. Abolitionists pursued the dilemma by presenting a court case, stating that since Scott had lived in a free state and free territory, he was in actuality a free man. Two lower courts had ruled before the Supreme Court became involved, one ruling in favor and one against. The Supreme Court decided that residing in a free state and free territory did not make Scott a free man because Scott (and all other slaves) were not U.S. citizens or state citizens of Missouri. Therefore, he did not have the right to sue in state or federal courts. The Court went a step further and ruled that the old Missouri Compromise was now unconstitutional due to the fact that Congress did not have the power to prohibit slavery in the Territories.

Anti-slavery supporters were stunned. They had just recently formed the new Republican Party and one of its platforms was keeping slavery out of the Territories. Now, according to the decision in the Dred Scott case, this basic party principle was unconstitutional. The only way to ban slavery in new areas was by a Constitutional amendment, requiring ratification by three-fourths of all states. At this time, this was out of the question because the supporters would be unable to get a majority due to Southern opposition.

In 1858 Abraham Lincoln and Stephen A. Douglas were running for the office of U.S. Senator from Illinois and participated in a series of debates which directly affected the outcome of the 1860 Presidential election. Douglas, a Democrat, was up for re-election and knew that if he won this race, he had a good chance of becoming President in

ELEMENTARY EDUCATION   193

1860. Lincoln, a Republican, was not an abolitionist but he believed that slavery was wrong morally and he firmly believed in and supported the Republican party principle that slavery must not be allowed to be extended any further. Douglas, on the other hand, originated the doctrine of "popular sovereignty" and was responsible for supporting and getting through Congress the inflammatory Kansas-Nebraska Act. In the course of the debates, Lincoln challenged Douglas to show that popular sovereignty reconciled with the Dred Scott decision. Either way he answered Lincoln, Douglas would lose crucial support from one group or the other. If he supported the Dred Scott decision, southerners would support him but he would lose northern support. If he stayed with popular sovereignty, northern support would be his but southern support would be lost. His reply to Lincoln, stating that Territorial legislatures could exclude slavery by refusing to pass laws supporting it, gave him enough support and approval to be re-elected to the Senate, but it cost him the Democratic nomination for President in 1860. Southerners came to the realization that Douglas may support and be devoted to popular sovereignty but not necessarily to the expansion of slavery. On the other hand, two years later, Lincoln received the nomination of the Republican Party for President.

The final straw came with the election of Lincoln to the Presidency the next year. Due to a split in the Democratic Party, there were a total of four candidates from four political parties. With Lincoln receiving a minority of the popular vote and a majority of electoral votes, the Southern states, one by one, voted to secede from the Union as they had promised they would do if Lincoln and the Republicans were victorious. The die was cast.

SKILL 29.7   Be knowledgeable about the Civil War and Reconstruction from 1860 to 1877

It is ironic that South Carolina was the first state to secede from the Union and the first shots of the war were fired on Fort Sumter in Charleston Harbor. Both sides quickly made preparations for war. The North had more in its favor: a larger population; superiority in finances and transportation facilities; manufacturing, agricultural, and natural resources. The North possessed most of the nation's gold, had about 92% of all industries, and almost all known supplies of copper, coal, iron, and various other minerals. Since most of the nation's railroads were in the North and mid-West, men and supplies could be moved wherever needed; food could be transported from the farms of the mid-West to workers in the East and to soldiers on the battlefields. Trade with nations overseas could go on as usual due to control of the navy and the merchant fleet. The Northern states numbered 24 and included western (California and Oregon) and border (Mary-land, Delaware, Kentucky, Missouri, and West Virginia) states.

The Southern states numbered 11 and included South Carolina, Georgia, Florida, Alabama, Mississippi, Louisiana, Texas, Virginia, North Carolina, Tennessee, and Arkansas, making up the Confederacy. Even though outnumbered in population, the South was completely confident of victory. They knew that all they had to do was fight a defensive war, protecting their own territory until the North, who had to invade and defeat an area almost the size of Western Europe, tired of the struggle and gave up. Another advantage of the South was that a number of its best officers had graduated from the U.S. Military Academy at West Point and had had long years of army experience, some even exercising varying degrees of command in the Indian wars and the war with Mexico. Men from the South were conditioned to living outdoors and were more familiar with horses and firearms than many men from Northeastern cities. Since cotton was such an important crop, Southerners felt that British and French textile mills were so dependent on raw cotton that they would be forced to help the Confederacy in the war. The South had specific reasons and goals for fighting the war, more so than the North. The major aim of the Confederacy never wavered: to win independence, the right to govern themselves as they wished, and to preserve slavery. The Northerners were not as clear in their reasons for conducting war. At the beginning, most believed, along with Lincoln, that preservation of the Union was paramount. Only a few extremely fanatical abolitionists looked on the war as a way to end slavery once and for all. However, by war's end, more and more northerners had come to believe that freeing the slaves was just as important as restoring the Union.

The Union won the Battles of Gettysburg in Mobile Bay and in May 1864, William Tecumseh Sherman began his march to successfully demolish Atlanta, then on to Savannah. He and his troops turned northward through the Carolinas to Grant in Virginia. On April 9, 1865, General Lee of the Confederacy formally surrendered to Grant at Appamattox Courthouse, Virginia.

The Civil War took more American lives than any other war in history, the South losing one-third of its soldiers in battle compared to about one-sixth for the North. More than half of the total deaths were caused by disease and the horrendous conditions of field hospitals. Both sections paid a tremendous economic price but the South suffered more severely from direct damages. Destruction was pervasive with towns, farms, trade, industry, lives and homes of men, women, children all destroyed and an entire Southern way of life was lost. The deep resentment, bitterness, and hatred that remained for generations gradually lessened as the years went by but legacies of it surface and remain to this day. The South had no voice in the political, social, and cultural affairs of the nation, lessening to a great degree the influence of the more traditional Southern ideals. The Northern Yankee Protestant ideals of hard work, education, and economic freedom became the standard of the United States and helped influence the development of the nation into a modern, industrial power.

The effects of the Civil War were tremendous. It changed the methods of waging war and has been called the first modern war. It introduced weapons and tactics that, when improved later, were used extensively in wars of the late 1800's and 1900's. Civil War soldiers were the first to fight in trenches, first to fight under a unified command, first to wage a defense called "major cordon defense", a strategy of advance on all fronts. They were also the first to use repeating and breech loading weapons. Observation balloons were first used during the war along with submarines, ironclad ships, and mines. Telegraphy and railroads were put to use first in the Civil War. It was considered a modern war because of the vast destruction and was "total war", involving the use of all resources of the opposing sides. There was probably no way it could have ended other than total defeat and unconditional surrender of one side or the other.

By executive proclamation and constitutional amendment, slavery was officially and finally ended, although there remained deep prejudice and racism, still raising its ugly head today. But also, the Union was preserved and the states were finally truly united. Sectionalism, especially in the area of politics, remained strong for another 100 years but not to the degree and with the violence as existed before 1861. It has been noted that the Civil War may have been American democracy's greatest failure for, from 1861 to 1865, calm reason, basic to democracy, fell to human passion. Yet, democracy did survive. The victory of the North established once and for all that no state has the right to end or leave the Union. As a result of unity, the U.S. became a major global power.

As the war dragged on to its bloody, destructive conclusion, Lincoln was very concerned and anxious to get the states restored to the Union and showed flexibility in his thinking as he made changes to his Reconstruction program to make it as easy and painless as possible. Of course, Congress had final approval of many actions and it would be interesting to know how differently things might have turned out if Lincoln had lived to see some or all of his kind policies, supported by fellow moderates, put into action. But, unfortunately, it didn't turn out that way. After Andrew Johnson became President and the radical Republicans gained control of Congress, the harsh measures of radical Reconstruction were implemented.

Congress drafted its own program of Reconstruction, including laws that would protect and further the rights of blacks. Three amendments were added to the Constitution: the 13th Amendment of 1865 outlawed slavery throughout the entire United States. The 14th Amendment of 1868 made blacks American citizens. The 15th Amendment of 1870 gave black Americans the right to vote and made it illegal to deny anyone the right to vote on the basis of race. Reconstruction officially ended when the last Federal troops left the South in 1877. It can be said that Reconstruction had a limited success as it set up public school systems and expanded legal rights of black Americans. But white supremacy came to be in control once again and its bitter fruitage is still with us today.

SKILL 29.8   Understand the significance of post-Reconstruction industrialization and reform

There was a marked degree of industrialization before and during the Civil War, but at war's end, industry in America was small. After the war, dramatic changes took place: machines replacing hand labor, extensive nationwide railroad service making possible the wider distribution of goods, invention of new products made available in large quantities, large amounts of money from bankers and investors for expansion of business operations. American life was definitely affected by this phenomenal industrial growth. Cities became the centers of this new business activity resulting in mass population movements there and tremendous growth. This new boom in business resulted in huge fortunes for some Americans and extreme poverty for many others. The discontent this caused resulted in a number of new reform movements from which came measures controlling the power and size of big business and helping the poor. Of course, industry before, during, and after the Civil War was centered mainly in the North, especially the tremendous industrial growth after. The late 1800s and early 1900s saw the increasing buildup of military strength and the U.S. becoming a world power.

Between 1870 and 1916, more than 25 million immigrants came into the United States adding to the phenomenal population growth taking place. This tremendous growth aided business and industry in two ways: (1) The number of consumers increased creating a greater demand for products thus enlarging the markets for the products. And (2) with increased production and expanding business, more workers were available for newly created jobs. The completion of the nation's transcontinental railroad in 1869 contributed greatly to the nation's economic and industrial growth. Some examples of the benefits of using the railroads include: raw materials were shipped quickly by the mining companies and finished products were sent to all parts of the country. Many wealthy industrialists and railroad owners saw tremendous profits steadily increasing due to this improved method of transportation.

American women began actively campaigning for the right to vote. Elizabeth Cady Stanton and Susan B. Anthony in 1869 founded the organization called National Women Suffrage Association, the same year the Wyoming Territory gave women the right to vote. Soon after, a few states followed by giving women the right to vote, limited to local elections only.

SKILL 29.9   Understand the importance and impact of events, issues, and effects of the period of World War I

In Europe, war broke out in 1914 and ended in 1918, eventually involving nearly 30 nations. One of the major causes of the war was the tremendous surge of nationalism during the 1800's and early 1900's. People of the same nationality or ethnic group sharing a common history, language or culture began uniting or demanding the right of unification, especially in the empires of Eastern Europe, such as Russia, Ottoman and Austrian-Hungarian Empires. Getting stronger and more intense were the beliefs of these peoples in loyalty to common political, social, and economic goals, considered to be before any loyalty to the controlling nation or empire. Emotions ran high and minor disputes magnified into major ones and sometimes quickly led to threats of war. Especially sensitive to these conditions was the area of the states on the Balkan Peninsula. Along with the imperialistic colonization for industrial raw materials, military build-up (especially by Germany), and diplomatic and military alliances, the conditions for one tiny spark to set off the explosion were in place. In July 1914, a Serbian national assassinated the Austrian heir to the throne and his wife and war began a few weeks later. There were a few attempts to keep war from starting, but these efforts were futile.

World War I saw the introduction of such warfare as use of tanks, airplanes, machine guns, submarines, poison gas, and flame throwers. Fighting on the Western front was characterized by a series of trenches which were used throughout the war until 1918. U.S. involvement in the war did not occur until 1916. When it began in 1914, President Woodrow Wilson declared that the U.S. was neutral and most Americans were opposed to any involvement anyway. In 1916, Wilson was reelected to a second term on the basis of the slogan proclaiming his efforts at keeping America out of the war. For a few months after, he put forth most of his efforts to stopping the war but German submarines began unlimited warfare against American merchant shipping. At the same time, Great Britain intercepted and decoded a secret message from Germany to Mexico urging Mexico to go to war against the U.S. The publishing of this information along with continued German destruction of American ships resulted in the eventual entry of the U.S. into the conflict, the first time the country prepared to fight in a conflict not on American soil. Though unprepared for war, governmental efforts and activities resulted in massive defense mobilization with America's economy directed to the war effort. Though America made important contributions of war materials, its greatest contribution to the war was manpower - soldiers desperately needed by the Allies.

Some ten months before the war ended, President Wilson had proposed a program called the Fourteen Points as a method of bringing the war to an end with an equitable peace settlement. In these Points he had five points setting out general ideals, there were eight pertaining to immediately working to resolve territorial and political problems, and the fourteenth point counseled establishing an organization of nations to help keep world peace. When Germany agreed in 1918 to an armistice, it assumed that the peace settlement would be drawn up on the basis of these Fourteen Points. But the peace conference in Paris basically ignored these points and Wilson had to be content with efforts at establishing the League of Nations. Italy, France, and Great Britain, having suffered and sacrificed far more in the war than America, wanted retribution. The treaties punished severely the Central Powers, taking away arms and territories and requiring payment of reparations. Germany was punished more than the others and, according to one clause in the treaty, was forced to assume the responsibility for causing the war.

Pre-war empires lost tremendous amounts of territories as well as the wealth of natural resources in them. New, independent nations were formed and some predominately ethnic areas came under control of nations of different cultural backgrounds. Some national boundary changes overlapped and created tensions and hard feelings as well as political and economic confusion. The wishes and desires of every national or cultural group could not possibly be realized and satisfied, resulting in disappointments for both those who were victorious and those who were defeated. Germany received harsher terms than expected from the treaty which weakened its post-war government and, along with the world-wide depression of the 1930s, set the stage for the rise of Adolf Hitler and his Nationalist Socialist Party and World War II.

SKILL 29.10 Understand the importance and impact of events, issues, and effects of the period of World War II

The end of World War I and the decade of the 1920's saw tremendous changes in the United States, signifying the beginning of its development into its modern society today. The shift from farm to city life was occurring in tremendous numbers. Social changes and problems were occurring at such a fast pace that it was extremely difficult and perplexing for many Americans to adjust to them. Politically the 18th Amendment to the Constitution, the so-called prohibition amendment, prohibited selling alcoholic beverages throughout the U.S. resulting in problems affecting all aspects of society. The passage of the 19th Amendment gave to women the right to vote in all elections. The decade of the 1920's also showed a marked change in roles and opportunities for women with more and more of them seeking and finding careers outside the home. They began to think of themselves as the equal of men and not as much as housewives and mothers.

The influence of the automobile, the entertainment industry, and the rejection of the morals and values of pre-World War I life, resulting in the fast-paced "Roaring Twenties", had significant effects on events leading to the depression-era 1930s and another world war. Many Americans greatly desired the pre-war life and supported political policies and candidates in favor of the return to what was considered to be normal. It was desired to end government's strong role and adopt a policy of isolating the country from world affairs, a result of the war.

Prohibition of the sale of alcohol had caused the increased activities of bootlegging and the rise of underworld gangs and the illegal speakeasies, the jazz music and dances they promoted. The customers of these clubs were considered "modern", reflected by extremes in clothing, hair styles, and attitudes towards authority and life. Movies and, to a certain degree, other types of entertainment, along with increased interest in sports figures and the accomplishments of national heroes, such as Lindbergh, influenced Americans to admire, emulate, and support individual accomplishments. As wild and uninhibited modern behavior became, this decade witnessed an increase in a religious tradition known as "revivalism", emotional preaching. Even though law and order were demanded by many Americans, the administration of President Warren G. Harding was marked by widespread corruption and scandal, not unlike the administration of Ulysses S. Grant, except Grant was honest and innocent. The decade of the 20s also saw the resurgence of such racist organizations as the Ku Klux Klan.

Germany, Italy, and Japan initiated a policy of aggressive territorial expansion with Japan being the first to conquer. In 1931 the Japanese forces seized control of Manchuria, a part of China containing rich natural resources, and in 1937 began an attack on China, occupying most of its eastern part by 1938. Italy invaded Ethiopia in Africa in 1935, having it totally under its control by 1936. The Soviet Union did not invade or take over any territory but along with Italy and Germany, actively participated in the Spanish Civil War, using it as a proving ground to test tactics and weapons setting the stage for World War II.

In Germany, almost immediately after taking power, in direct violation of the World War I peace treaty, Hitler began the buildup of the armed forces. He sent troops into the Rhineland in 1936, invaded Austria in 1938 and united it with Germany, seized control of the Sudetenland in 1938 (part of western Czechoslovakia and containing mostly Germans), the rest of Czechoslovakia in March 1939, and, on September 1, 1939, began World War II in Europe by invading Poland. In 1940 Germany invaded and controlled Norway, Denmark, Belgium, Luxembourg, the Netherlands, and France.

After the war began in Europe, U.S. President Franklin D. Roosevelt announced that the United States was neutral. Most Americans, although hoping for an Allied victory, wanted the U.S. to stay out of the war.

In Asia, the U.S. had opposed Japan's invasion of Southeast Asia, an effort to gain Japanese control of that region's rich resources. As a result, the U.S. stopped all important exports to Japan, whose industries depended heavily on petroleum, scrap metal, and other raw materials. Later Roosevelt refused the Japanese withdrawal of its funds from American banks. General Tojo became the Japanese premier in October 1941 and quickly realized that the U.S. Navy was powerful enough to block Japanese expansion into Asia. Deciding to cripple the Pacific Fleet, the Japanese aircraft, without warning, bombed the Fleet December 7, 1941, while at anchor in Pearl Harbor in

Hawaii. Temporarily it was a success. It destroyed many aircraft and disabled much of the U.S. Pacific Fleet. But, in the end, it was a costly mistake as it quickly motivated the Americans to prepare for and wage war.

The liberation of Italy began in July 1943 and ended May 2, 1945. The third part of the strategy was D-Day, June 6, 1944, with the Allied invasion of France at Normandy. At the same time, starting in January 1943, the Soviets began pushing the German troops back into Europe and they were greatly assisted by supplies from Britain and the United States. By April 1945, Allies occupied positions beyond the Rhine and the Soviets moved on to Berlin, surrounding it by April 25th. Germany surrendered May 7th and the war in Europe was finally over.

Meanwhile, in the Pacific, in the six months after the attack on Pearl Harbor, Japanese forces moved across Southeast Asia and the western Pacific Ocean. By August 1942, the Japanese Empire was at its largest size and stretched northeast to Alaska's Aleutian Islands, west to Burma, south to what is now Indonesia. Invaded and controlled areas included Hong Kong, Guam, Wake, Thailand, part of Malaysia, Singapore, the Philippines, and bombed Darwin on the north coast of Australia. The raid of General Doolittle's bombers on Japanese cities and the American naval victory at Midway along with the fighting in the Battle of the Coral Sea helped turn the tide against Japan. Island-hopping by U.S. Seabees and Marines and the grueling bloody battles fought resulted in gradually pushing the Japanese back towards Japan. After victory was attained in Europe, concentrated efforts were made to secure Japan's surrender, but it took dropping two atomic bombs on the cities of Hiroshima and Nagasaki to finally end the war in the Pacific. Japan formally surrendered on September 2, 1945, aboard the U.S. battleship Missouri, anchored in Tokyo Bay. The war was finally ended.

Major consequences of the war included horrendous death and destruction, millions of displaced persons, the gaining of strength and spread of Communism and Cold War tensions as a result of the beginning of the nuclear age. World War II ended more lives and caused more devastation than any other war. Besides the losses of millions of military personnel, the devastation and destruction directly affected civilians, reducing cities, houses, and factories to ruin and rubble and totally wrecking communication and transportation systems. Millions of civilian deaths, especially in China and the Soviet Union, were the results of famine.

More than 12 million people were uprooted by wars end having no place to live. Included were prisoners of war, those who survived Nazi concentration camps and slave labor camps, orphans, and people who escaped war-torn areas and invading armies. Changing national boundary lines also caused the mass movement of displaced persons. Germany and Japan were completely defeated; Great Britain and France were seriously weakened; and the Soviet Union and the United States became the world's leading powers.

Although allied during the war, the alliance fell apart as the Soviets pushed Communism in Europe and Asia. In spite of the tremendous destruction it suffered, the Soviet Union was stronger than ever. During the war, it took control of Lithuania, Estonia, and Latvia and by mid-1945 parts of Poland, Czechoslovakia, Finland, and Romania. It helped Communist governments gain power in Bulgaria, Romania, Hungary, Czechoslovakia, Poland, and North Korea. China fell to Mao Zedong's Communist forces in 1949. Until the fall of the Berlin Wall in 1989 and the dissolution of Communist governments in Eastern Europe and the Soviet Union, the United States and the Soviet Union faced off in what was called a Cold War, with the possibility of the terrifying destruction by nuclear weapons a likely deterrent to nuclear war.

SKILL 29.11 Know and understand the key events and issues pertaining to foreign affairs from post-World War II to the present

The first "hot war" in the post-World War II era was the Korean War, begun June 25, 1950 and ending July 27, 1953. Troops from Communist North Korea invaded democratic South Korea in an effort to unite both sections under Communist control. The United Nations organization asked its member nations to furnish troops to help restore peace. Many nations responded and President Truman sent American troops to help the South Koreans. The war dragged on for three years and ended with a truce, not a peace treaty. Like Germany then, Korea remained divided and does so to this day.

In 1954, the French were forced to give up their colonial claims in Indochina, the present-day countries of Vietnam, Laos, and Cambodia. Afterwards, the Communist northern part of Vietnam began battling with the democratic southern part over control of the entire country. In the late 1950s and early 1960s, U.S. Presidents Eisenhower and Kennedy sent to Vietnam a number of military advisers and military aid to assist and support South Vietnam's non-Communist government. During Lyndon Johnson's presidency, the war escalated with thousands of American troops being sent to participate in combat with the South Vietnamese. The war was extremely unpopular in America and caused such serious divisiveness among its citizens that Johnson decided not to seek reelection in 1968. It was in President Richard Nixon's second term in office that the U.S. signed an agreement ending war in Vietnam and restoring peace. This was done January 27, 1973, and by March 29th, the last American combat troops and American prisoners of war left Vietnam for home. It was the longest war in U.S. history and to this day carries the perception that it was a "lost war".

In 1962 during the administration of President John F. Kennedy, Premier Khrushchev and the Soviets decided, as a protective measure for Cuba against an American invasion, to install nuclear missiles on the island. In October, American U-2 spy planes photographed over Cuba what were identified as missile bases under construction. The dilemma in the White House was how to handle the situation without starting a war. The only recourse was removal of the missile sites and preventing more being set up.

Kennedy announced that the U.S. had set up a "quarantine" of Soviet ships heading to Cuba. It was in reality a blockade but the word itself could not be used publicly as a blockade was actually considered an act of war. A week of incredible tension and anxiety gripped the entire world until Khrushchev capitulated. Soviet ships carrying missiles for the Cuban bases turned back and the crisis eased. What precipitated the crisis was Khrushchev's under estimation of Kennedy. The President made no effort to prevent the erection of the Berlin Wall and was reluctant to commit American troops to invade Cuba and overthrow Fidel Castro. The Soviets assumed this was a weakness and decided they could install the missiles without any interference.

The Soviets were concerned about American missiles installed in Turkey aimed at the Soviet Union and about a possible invasion of Cuba. If successful, Khrushchev would demonstrate to the Russian and Chinese critics of his policy of peaceful coexistence, that he was tough and not to be intimidated. At the same time, the Americans feared that if Russian missiles were put in place and launched from Cuba to the U.S., the short distance of 90 miles would not give enough time for adequate warning and be coming from a direction radar systems didn't cover. Also, it was felt that if America gave in and allowed a Soviet presence practically at the back door that the effect on American security and morale would be devastating. As tensions eased in the aftermath of the crisis, several agreements were made. The missiles in Turkey were removed. A telephone "hot line" was set up between Moscow and Washington to make it possible for the two heads of government to have instant contact with each other. The U.S. agreed to sell its surplus wheat to the Soviets.

Probably the highlight of the foreign policy of President Richard Nixon, after the ending of the Vietnam War and withdrawal of troops, was his 1972 trip to China. Since 1949, when the Communists gained control of China, the policy of the U.S. government was refusal to recognize the Communist government but to regard as the legitimate government of China to be that of Chiang Kai-shek, exiled on the island of Taiwan. In 1971, Nixon sent Henry Kissinger on a secret trip to Peking to investigate whether or not it would be possible for America to give recognition to China. In February 1972 President and Mrs. Nixon spent a number of days in the country visiting well-known Chinese landmarks, dining with the two leaders, Mao Tse-tung and Chou En-lai. Agreements were made for cultural and scientific exchanges, eventual resumption of trade, and future unification of the mainland with Taiwan. In 1979 formal diplomatic recognition was achieved. The pattern of the Cold War was essentially shifted with this one visit.

In the administration of President Jimmy Carter, Egyptian President Anwar el-Sadat and Israeli Prime Minister Menachem Begin met at presidential retreat Camp David and agreed, after a series of meetings, to sign a formal treaty of peace between the two countries. In 1979, the Soviet invasion of Afghanistan was perceived by Carter and his advisers as a threat to the rich oil fields in the Persian Gulf but at the time, U.S. military capability to prevent further Soviet aggression in the Middle East was weak. The last year of Carter's presidential term was taken up with the 53 American hostages held in Iran. The shah had been deposed and control of the government and the country was in the hands of Muslim leader, Ayatollah Ruhollah Khomeini. Khomeini's extreme hatred for the U.S. was the result of the 1953 overthrow of Iran's Mossadegh government, sponsored by the CIA. To make matters worse, the CIA proceeded to train the shah's ruthless secret police force. So when the terminally ill exiled shah was allowed into the U.S. for medical treatment, a fanatical mob stormed into the American embassy taking the 53 Americans as prisoners, supported and encouraged by Khomeini. President Carter froze all Iranian assets in the U.S., set up trade restrictions, and approved a risky rescue attempt which failed. He had appealed to the UN for aid in gaining release for the hostages and to European allies to join the trade embargo on Iran. Khomeini ignored UN requests for releasing the Americans and Europeans refused to support the embargo so as not to risk losing access to Iran's oil. American prestige was damaged and Carter's chances for reelection were doomed. The hostages were released on the day of Ronald Reagan's inauguration as President when Carter released Iranian assets as ransom.

After President George Bush, Sr. took office, it appeared that the tensions and dangers of the post-World War II "Cold War" between the U.S. and Soviet-led Communism were over.

During the time of the American hostage crisis, Iraq and Iran fought a war in which the U.S. and most of Iraq's neighbors supported Iraq. In a five-year period, Saddam Hussein received $500 million worth of American technology, including lasers, advanced computers, and special machine tools used in missile development. The Iraq-Iran war was a bloody one resulting in a stalemate with a UN truce ending it. Neighboring Kuwait, in direct opposition to OPEC agreements, increased oil production. This caused oil prices to drop which upset Hussein, who was deeply in debt from the war and entirely dependent on oil revenues. After a short period of time, Saddam invaded and occupied Kuwait. The U.S. made extensive plans to successfully carry out Operation Desert Storm; the liberation of Kuwait. In four days, February 24-28, 1991, the war was over and Iraq had been defeated, its troops driven back into their country. Saddam remained in power even though Iraq's economy was seriously damaged.

President Bill Clinton sent U.S. troops to Haiti to protect the efforts of Jean-Bertrand Aristide to gain democratic power and to Bosnia to assist UN peacekeeping forces. He also inherited from the Bush administration the problem of Somalia in East Africa, where U.S. troops had been sent in December 1992 to support UN efforts to end the starvation of the Somalis and restore peace. The efforts were successful at first but eventually failed due to the severity of the intricate political problems within the country. After U.S. soldiers were killed in an ambush along with 300 Somalis, American troops were withdrawn and returned home.

The Gulf War victory was so quick and stunning that there was a sense of omnipotence among Americans. Shocked, awed, and stunned were words Americans would later use to describe fighting in the Middle East. But on 9/11/01, Americans were the ones who were shocked, awed, and stunned. Americans were not prepared for suicide bombers who would give their life for a religious jihad.

September 11, 2001, American Airlines flight 11 out of Boston, Massachusetts detoured, crashing into the north tower of the World Trade Center. Initially is was unclear if the crash was a plane out of control or a hijacker. It became clear in just 18 minutes later when a second hijacked airliner, Flight 175 from Boston crashed into the south tower of the World Trade Center. For the first time all flight operations at U.S. airports nationwide were halted. A third plane, American Airlines Flight 77 crashed into the Pentagon. The White House evacuated and Bush and other executives went in hiding. The Pentagon partially collapsed. The calamity continued when United Airlines Flight 93 was also hijacked and crashed in Somerset County, Pennsylvania, southeast of Pittsburgh. It was later thought to be destined for the White House. The nation watched on national television The World Trade Center's towers collapsed from the top down and people jumped from the highest floors to their death. The firefighters were branded as national heroes and the nation reacted with valor lining up to give blood as the nation came together to mourn what would be the worst disaster in American history.

Mayor Giuliani was asked how many people were killed, Giuliani said, "I don't think we want to speculate about that -- more than any of us can bear." The pictures went on every available wall clinging onto cell phone messages and voice mail messages describing their final moments but filled with love.

There were speeches naming the terrorist organization as Al Qaeda lead and funded by Osama bin Laden. There were news conferences using the phrase the "axis of evil" which left a very broad spectrum of possibilities of who American would hunt down and bring to justice.

The US did not have much time to grieve this tragedy because of the always present fear of more terrorist attacks against the United States. One of these fears came from Saddam Hussein and the rest of his Iraq regime. Many events led up to Operation Iraqi Freedom in 2003. In 1998, Operation Desert Fox came into effect. The months leading up to this had seen a mounting crisis between the UN weapons inspections body, Unscom, and the Iraqi regime. Iraq had denied access to the many presidential palaces for weapons inspection. This was not to be tolerated by the United States and Britain and dramatic action soon followed. In December of that year, UN staff were evacuated from Baghdad and airstrikes were launched on some 100 targets across Iraq.

The Operation Desert Fox bombing did not have the effect the United States and Britain wanted. Iraq said they would not let Unscom inspectors back into the country. With no inspectors in Iraq, the possibilities of the creation of weapons of mass destruction loomed over the United Nations.

Fearing that Iraq had a weapons program, the UN told Iraq to give up all weapons of mass destruction or suffer serious consequences. In November 2002, Iraq accepted the terms of the resolution and weapons inspections resumed.

It was not until February 2003 that any further dramatic action had taken place. US Secretary of State Colin Powell told the UN that inspections were not achieving the disarmament of Iraq. The United States and Britain wanted further action to be taken, but several other countries, France, Russia, and China, said they would veto any resolution that involved force.

The United States did not wait for a vote from the UN on the disarmament of Iraq. On March 19, 2003, the campaign to end the Iraqi regime began.

The first attack on Iraqi soil was much smaller than inspected. It mounted on short notice when the US thought they had the opportunity to target Saddam Hussein and his sons. It turned out the first bombing in Iraq was not where Saddam Hussein and his sons were hiding.

From that point on, US and British ground forces moved in from southern Iraq on their way up to Baghdad, capturing any towns on the way. On Friday, March 21, 2003, the US and British forces launched the "shock and awe" attack on Baghdad and a few other Iraqi cities. A barrage of missiles targeted major Iraqi cities and regime buildings in an attempt to "shock and awe" regime leaders and the Iraqi people. This did not have the dramatic effect the US was hoping for.

Thousands of Iraqi soldiers surrendered over the next two months, but there was no sign of Saddam Hussein. Baghdad and all other Iraqi cities were overtaken by US and British forces. Many key regime leaders were captured or surrendered. Saddam Husseins two sons, Uday and Qusay, were killed in late July 2003. But the Saddam himself has yet to be captured. The US believes he is on the move at least 3-4 times a day to avoid capture.

Efforts to rebuild Iraq have already begun, and President George W. Bush has promised that US forces will stay in Iraq until the country is secure and Saddam Hussein is captured.

SKILL 29.12 Recognize and be able to discuss the political, economic, and social issues of the 20th century

During the late 1800's and early 1900's, many Americans were concerned about and began actively campaigning for significant changes and reforms in the social, economic, and political systems in the country. Among their goals was ridding government of corruption, regulating big businesses, reducing poverty, improving the lives of the poor and their living conditions, and ensuring more government response to the needs of the people. Early efforts at reforms began with movements to organize farmers and laborers, the push to give women the right to vote, and the successful passage of Congressional legislation establishing merit as the basis for federal jobs rather than political favoritism. Other efforts were directed towards improvements in education, living conditions in city slums, breaking up trusts and monopolies in big businesses.

After World War I ended, the 18th Amendment to the U.S. Constitution was passed, forbidding the sale of alcoholic beverages. The violence and upheaval it caused was a major characteristic of the wild decade of the 1920's. The wild financial speculations came to an abrupt end with the stock market crash of October 1929 plunging the U.S. into the Great Depression.

The election of Franklin Roosevelt to the office of President in 1932 was the start of the social and economic recovery and reform legislative acts designed to gradually ease the country back to more prosperity. These acts included relief for the nation's farmers, regulation of banks, public works providing jobs for the unemployed, and giving aid to manufacturers. Some of the agencies set up to implement these measures included the Works Progress Administration (WPA), Civilian Conservation Camps (CCC), the Farm Credit Administration (FCA), and the Social Security Board. These last two agencies gave credit to farmers and set up the nation's social security system.

After World War II and the Korean War, efforts began to relieve the problems of millions of African-Americans, including ending discrimination in education, housing, and jobs and ending the grinding widespread poverty. The efforts of civil rights leaders found success in a number of Supreme Court decisions, the best-known case, "Brown vs. Board of Education of Topeka (1954)" ending compulsory segregation in public schools. In the 1960s, the black civil rights movement under the leadership of Dr. Martin Luther King Jr. really gained momentum and under President Lyndon B. Johnson, the Civil Rights Acts of 1964 and 1968 prohibited discrimination in housing sales and rentals, employment, public accommodations, and voter registration.
Poverty remained a serious problem in the central sections of large cities resulting in riots and soaring crime rates which ultimately found its way to the suburbs. The escalation of the war in Vietnam and the social conflict and upheaval of support vs opposition to U.S. involvement led to antiwar demonstrations, escalation of drug abuse,

weakening of the family unit, homelessness, poverty, mental illness, along with increasing social, mental, and physical problems experienced by the Vietnam veterans..

The Watergate scandal resulting in the first-ever resignation of a sitting American president was the most crucial domestic crisis of the 1970's. The population of the U.S. had greatly increased and along with it the nation's industries and the resulting harmful pollution of the environment. Factory smoke, automobile exhaust, waste from factories and other sources all combined to create hazardous air, water, and ground pollution which, if not brought under control and significantly diminished, would severely endanger all life on earth. The 1980's was the decade of the horrible Exxon Valdez oil spill off the Alaskan coast and the nuclear accident and melt-down at the Ukrainian nuclear power plant at Chernobyl. The U.S. had a close call with the near disaster at Three Mile Island Nuclear Plant in Pennsylvania.

Inflation increased in the late 1960's, and the 1970's witnessed a period of high unemployment, the result of a severe recession. The decision of the OPEC (Organization of Petroleum Exporting Countries) ministers to cut back on oil production thus raising the price of a barrel of oil created a fuel shortage. This made it clear that energy and fuel conservation was a must in the American economy, especially since fuel shortages created two energy crises in the decade of the nineteen-seventies. Americans experienced shortages of fuel oil for heating and gasoline for cars and other vehicles. The 1980's saw the ups and downs of rising inflation, recession, recovery, and the insecurity of long-term employment. Foreign competition and imports, the use of robots and other advanced technology in industries, the opening and operation of American companies and factories in other countries to lower labor costs all contributed to the economic and employment problems. The nation's farmers experienced economic hardships and October 1987 saw another one day significant drop in the Dow Jones on the New York Stock Exchange. January 28, 1986 was the day of the loss of the seven crew members of the NASA space shuttle "Challenger". The reliability and soundness of numerous savings and loans institutions were in serious jeopardy when hundreds of these failed and others went into bankruptcy due to customer default on loans and mismanagement. Congressional legislation helped rebuild the industry.

SKILL 29.13 Recognize the significant accomplishments made by immigrant, racial, ethnic, and gender groups

Most students of American history are aware of the tremendous influx of immigrants to America during the 19th century. It is also a known fact that the majority settled in the ethnic neighborhoods and communities of the large cities, close to friends, relatives, and the work they were able to find. But there is one interesting fact some are not aware of and that is, after the U.S. Congress passed the 1862 Homestead Act, when the Civil War ended and the West began to open up for settlement, more than half of the hardy pioneers who went to homestead and farm western lands were European immigrants: Swedes, Norwegians, Czechs, Germans, Danes, Finns, and Russians.

But, by far, the nation's immigrants were an important reason for America's phenomenal industrial growth from 1865 to 1900. They came seeking work and better opportunities for themselves and their families than what life in their native country could give them. What they found in America was suspicion and distrust because they were competitors with Americans for jobs, housing, and decent wages. Their languages, customs, and ways of living were different, especially between the different national and ethnic groups. Until the early 1880's most immigrants were from the parts of northwestern Europe such as Germany, Scandinavia, the Netherlands, Ireland, and Great Britain. After 1890 the new arrivals increasingly came from eastern and southern Europe. Chinese immigrants on the Pacific coast, so crucial to the construction of the western part of the first transcontinental railroad, were the first to experience this increasing distrust which eventually erupted into violence and bloodshed. From about 1879 to the present time, the U.S. Congress made, repealed, and amended numerous pieces of legislation concerning quotas, restrictions, and other requirements pertaining to immigrants. The immigrant laborers, both skilled and unskilled, were the foundation of the modern labor union movement as a means of gaining recognition, support, respect, rights, fair wages, and better working conditions.

The historical record of African-Americans is known to all. Sold into slavery by rival tribes, they were brought against their will to the West Indies and southern America to slave on the plantations in a life-long condition of servitude and bondage. The 13th Constitutional Amendment abolished slavery; the 14th gave them U.S. citizenship; and the 15th gave them the right to vote. Efforts of well-known African-Americans resulted in some improvements although the struggle was continuous without let-up. Many were outspoken and urged and led protests against the continuing onslaught of discrimination and inequality. The leading black spokesman from 1890 to 1915 was educator Booker T. Washington. He recognized the need of vocational education for African-Americans, educating them for skills and training for such areas as domestic service, farming, the skilled trades, and small business enterprises. He founded and built in Alabama the famous Tuskegee Institute.

W.E.B. DuBois, another outstanding African-American leader and spokesman, believed that only continuous and vigorous protests against injustices and inequalities coupled with appeals to black pride would effect changes. The results of his efforts was the formation of the Urban League and the NAACP (the National Association for the Advancement of Colored People) which today continue to eliminate discriminations and secure equality and equal rights. Others who made significant contributions were Dr. George Washington Carver's work improving agricultural techniques for both black and white farmers; the writers William Wells Brown, Paul L. Dunbar, Langston Hughes, and Charles W. Chesnutt; the music of Duke Ellington, W.C. Handy, Marion Anderson, Louis Armstrong, Leontyne Price, Jessye Norman, Ella Fitzgerald, and many, many others.

Students of American history are greatly familiar with the accomplishments and contributions of American women. Previous mention has been made of the accomplishments of such 19th century women as: writer Louisa Mae Alcott; abolitionist Harriet Beecher Stowe; women's rights activists Elizabeth Cady Stanton and Lucretia Mott; physician Dr. Elizabeth Blackwell; women's education activists Mary Lyon, Catharine Esther Beecher, and Emma Hart Willard; prison and asylum reform activist Dorothea Dix; social reformer, humanitarian, pursuer of peace Jane Addams; aviatrix Amelia Earhart; women's suffrage activists Susan B. Anthony, Carrie Chapman Catt, and Anna Howard Shaw; Supreme Court Associate Justices Sandra Day O'Connor and Ruth Bader Ginsberg; and many, many more who have made tremendous contributions in science, politics and government, music and the arts (such as Jane Alexander who is National Chairperson of the National Endowment for the Arts), education, athletics, law, etc.

COMPETENCY 30.0

PHYSICAL EDUCATION

It is that openness and awareness and innocence of sorts that I try to cultivate in my dancers. Although, as the Latin verb to educate, educere, indicates, it is not a question of putting something in but drawing it out, if it is there to begin with...I want all of my students and all of my dancers to be aware of the poignancy of life at that moment. I would like to feel that I had, in some way, given them the gift of themselves.

Martha Graham

SKILL 30.1 Identify and define locomotor skills.

Locomotor skills move an individual from one point to another.

1. Walking - with one foot contacting the surface at all times, walking shifts one's weight from one foot to the other while legs swing alternately in front of the body.

2. Running - an extension of walking that has a phase where the body is propelled with no base of support (speed is faster, stride is longer, and arms add power).

3. Jumping - projectile movements that momentarily suspend the body in midair.

4. Vaulting - coordinated movements that allow oneself to spring over an obstacle.

5. Leaping - similar to running but leaping has greater height, flight, and distance.

6. Hopping - using the same foot to take off from a surface and land.

7. Galloping - forward or backward advanced elongation of walking that is combined and coordinated with a leap.

8. Sliding - sideward stepping pattern that can be uneven, long or short.

9. Body Rolling - moving across a surface by rocking back and forth, by turning over and over or by shaping the body into a revolving mass.

10. Climbing - ascending or descending using the hands and feet with the upper body using the most control.

SKILL 30.2 Identify and define nonlocomotor skills.

Nonlocomotor skills are stability skills where there is movement with little or no movement of one's base of support.

1. <u>Bending</u> - movement around a joint where two body parts meet.

2. <u>Dodging</u> - sharp change of direction from original line of movement such as away from a person or object.

3. <u>Stretching</u> - extending/hyper extending joints to make body parts as straight or as long as possible.

4. <u>Twisting</u> - rotating body/body parts around an axis with a stationary base.

5. <u>Turning</u> - circular moving the body through space releasing the base of support.

6. <u>Swinging</u> - circular/pendular movements of the body/body parts below an axis.

7. <u>Swaying</u> - same as swinging but movement is above an axis.

8. <u>Pushing</u> - applying force against an object or person to move it away from one's body or to move one's body away from the object or person.

9. <u>Pulling</u> - executing force to cause objects/people to move toward one's body.

SKILL 30.3 Identify and define manipulative skills.

(Using body parts to propel or receive an object; controlling objects primarily with the hands and feet. Two types: receptive = catch + trap; propulsive = throw, strike; kick).

1. <u>Bouncing/Dribbling</u> - projecting a ball downwards.

2. <u>Catching</u> - stopping momentum of an object (for control) using the hands.

3. <u>Kicking</u> - striking an object with the foot.

4. <u>Rolling</u> - initiating force to an object to instill contact with a surface.

5. <u>Striking</u> - giving impetus to an object with the use of the hands or an object.

6. <u>Throwing</u> - using one or both arms to project an object into midair away from the body.

7. <u>Trapping</u> - without the use of the hands, receiving and controlling a ball

COMPETENCY 31.0

FITNESS

No pain, no gain.

Commonly quoted

Oddly, not the truth when applied to fitness

COMPETENCY 31.0   FITNESS, CONDITIONING, AND HEALTH

SKILL 31. 1 Apply concept of body awareness to physical education activities.

Body awareness can be assessed by playing and watching a game of "Simon Says" and asking the students to touch different body parts. Children can also be instructed to make their bodies into various shapes from straight to round to twisted varying sizes to fit into different sized spaces.

In addition, children can be instructed to touch one part of the body to another and to use various body parts to do something such: stamping their feet, twisting their neck, clapping their hands, nodding their heads, wiggling their noses, snapping their fingers, opening their mouths, shrugging their shoulders, bending their knees, closing their eyes, bending their elbows, and wiggling their toes.

SKILL 31.2 Apply the concept of spatial awareness to physical education activities.

Spatial awareness - making decisions of an object's positional changes in space (awareness of three dimensional space position changes).

Developing spatial awareness requires two sequential phases: the location of objects in relation to one's own body in space, and locating more than one object in relation to each object and independent of one's own body.

plan activities using different size balls or using boxes or hoops and have children move: near and away, under and over, in front and behind, and inside and outside and beside the objects.

SKILL 31.3 Apply the concept of effort qualities to physical education.

(Qualities of movement applying the mechanical principles of balance, time, and force).

- Balance - activities for balance include having children move on their hands and feet, leaning, movements on lines, and balancing and holding shapes while they are moving.

- Time - activities using the concept of time can involve having students move as fast as they can and as slow as they can in specified movement patterns that are timed.

- Force - activities using the concept of force can include having students use their bodies to produce enough force to move them through space. They can also paddle balls against walls, and jump over objects with various heights.

ELEMENTARY EDUCATION   215

SKILL 31.4 Identify the health-related components of physical fitness.

Many more children are obese today than ever before. The classroom teacher can oversee children that are not valuing exercise and encourage them to walk and experience the joy of movement. Each day they should set some goals to perhaps walk further, play longer. As k yourself as a teacher if you are using enough time to see that they stretch, run and just be kids! Use a large ball and have them roll into as many customized positions as they can. Stop kids that you see smoking and encourage them to preach that gospel to others. Drinking alcohol might be incorrectly assumed not to be a problem for elementary children.

There are five health related components of physical fitness: *cardio-respiratory or cardiovascular endurance, muscle strength, muscle endurance, flexibility, and body composition.*

SKILL 31.5 Identify the skill related components of physical fitness.

The skill related components of physical fitness are *agility, balance, coordination, power, reaction time, and speed.*

SKILL 31.6 Select valid physical fitness test items to measure health and skill related fitness components.

Cardio-respiratory fitness can be measured by the following tests: maximal stress test, sub maximal stress test, Bruce Protocol, Balke Protocol, Astrand and Rhyming Test, PWC Test, Bench Step Test, Rockport Walking Fitness Test; Cooper 1.5 Mile Run/Walk Fitness Test.

Muscle strength can be measured by the following: dynamometers (hand, back, and leg). The 1-RM Test (repetition maximum: bench press, standing press, arm curl, and leg press), Bench Squat Test, Sit-Up Test (one sit up holding a weight plate behind the neck); Lateral Pull-Down.

Muscle endurance can be assessed by the following: Squat Thrust Test, Pull-Ups Test, Sit-Ups Test, Lateral Pull-Down, Bench-Press Test, Arm Curl, push-ups; dips.

Flexibility can be measured by the following tests: sit and reach, Kraus-Webber Floor Touch Test, Trunk Extension, Forward Bend of Trunk Test, Leighton Flexometer, shoulder rotation/flexion test; goniometer.

Body Composition can be determined by the following: Hydrostatic Weighing, Skin fold Measurements, limb/girth circumference, and body mass index.

Agility can be assessed with The Illinois Agility Run.

Balance can be evaluated with the following: The Bass Test of Dynamic Balance (lengthwise and crosswise), the Johnson Modification of the Bass Test of Dynamic Balance, modified sideward leap; balance beam walk.

Coordination can be assessed by The Stick test of Coordination.

Power can be measured by the vertical jump.

Speed can be assessed with the 50-yard dash.

SKILL 31.7 Identify how the health-related components of physical fitness may be improved by implementing the principles of overload, progression, and specificity.

1. Cardio-respiratory Fitness:

   Overloading for cardio-respiratory fitness:

   - <u>Frequency</u> = minimum of 3 days/week

   - <u>Intensity</u> = exercising in target heart rate zone

   - <u>Time</u> = minimum of 15 minutes rate.

   Progression for cardiovascular fitness:

   - begin at a frequency of 3 days/week and work up to no more than 6 days/week

   - begin at an intensity near THR threshold and work up to 80% of THR

   - begin at 15 minutes and work up to 60 minutes

   Specificity for cardiovascular fitness:

   - To specifically develop cardiovascular fitness, aerobic (with oxygen) activities must be performed for at least fifteen minutes without developing an oxygen debt. Aerobic activities include, but are not limited to: brisk walking, jogging, bicycling, and swimming.

2. Muscle Strength:

Overloading for muscle strength:

- <u>Frequency</u> = every other day

- <u>Intensity</u> = 60% to 90% of assessed muscle strength

- <u>Time</u> = 3 sets of 3 - 8 reps (high resistance with a low number of repetitions)

Progression for muscle strength:

- begin 3/days week and work up to every other day

- begin near 60% of determined muscle strength and work up to no more than 90% of muscle strength

- begin with 1 set with 3 reps and work up to 3 sets with 8 reps

Specificity for muscle strength:

- to increase muscle strength for a specific part(s) of the body, that/those part(s) of the body must be targeted

3. Muscle endurance:

Overloading for muscle endurance:

- <u>Frequency</u> = every other day

- <u>Intensity</u> = 30% to 60% of assessed muscle strength

- <u>Time</u> = 3 sets of 12 - 20 reps (low resistance with a high number of repetitions)

Progression for muscle endurance:

- begin 3 days/week and work up to every other day

- begin at 20% to 30% of muscle strength and work up to no more than 60% of muscle strength

- begin with 1 set with 12 reps and work up to 3 sets with 20 reps

Specificity for muscle endurance:

- same as muscle strength.

4. Flexibility:

Overloading for flexibility:

- <u>Frequency</u>: 3 to 7 days/week

- <u>Intensity</u>: stretch muscle beyond its normal length

- <u>Time</u>: 3 sets of 3 reps holding stretch 15 to 60 seconds

*Progression for flexibility:*begin 3 days/week and work up to every day

- begin stretching with slow movement as far as possible without pain holding at the end of the range of motion (ROM) and work up to stretching no more than 10% beyond the normal ROM

- begin with 1set with 1 rep holding stretches 15 seconds and work up to 3 sets with 3 reps holding stretches for 60 seconds

Specificity for flexibility:

- ROM (range of movement) is joint specific

5. Body composition:

Overloading to improve body composition:

- <u>Frequency</u>: daily aerobic exercise

- <u>Intensity</u>: low

- <u>Time</u>: approximately one hour

Progression to improve body composition:

- begin daily

- begin a low aerobic intensity and work up to a longer duration (see cardio-respiratory progression)

- begin low intensity aerobic exercise for 30 minutes and work up to 60 minutes

Specificity to improve body composition:

- increase aerobic exercise and decrease caloric intake

SKILL 31.8 Identify the techniques and benefits of warming up and cooling down

Warming up is a gradual 5 to 10 minute aerobic warm-up utilizing the muscles that will be used in the activity to follow (similar movements at a lower activity). Include stretching of major muscle groups after the gradual warm-up.

The benefits of warming up are:

- preparing the body for physical activity

- reducing the risk of musculoskeletal injuries

- releasing oxygen from myoglobin

- warming the body's inner core

- increasing the reaction of muscles

- bringing the heart rate to an aerobic conditioning level

Cooling down is, basically, the same as warming up - a moderate to light tapering-off of vigorous activity at the end of an exercise session.

The benefits of cooling down are:

- redistributing circulation of the blood throughout the body to prevent pooling of blood

- preventing dizziness

- facilitating the removal of lactic acid

SKILL 31.9 Identify the health- and skill-related components of physical fitness developed by selected activities.

1. Aerobic Dance:
   Health related components of fitness = *cardio-respiratory; controls body composition.*
   Skill related components of fitness = *agility; coordination.*

2. Bicycling:
   Health related components of fitness = *cardio-respiratory, muscle strength, muscle endurance; controls body composition.*
   Skill related components of fitness = *balance.*

3. Calisthenics:
   Health related components of fitness = *cardio-respiratory, muscle strength, muscle endurance, flexibility; controls body fat.*
   Skill related components of fitness = *agility.*

4. Circuit Training:
   Health related components of fitness = *cardio-respiratory, muscle strength, muscle endurance; controls body composition.*
   Skill related components of fitness = *power.*

5. Cross Country Skiing:
   Health related component of fitness = *cardio-respiratory, muscle strength, muscle endurance; controls body composition.*
   Skill related components of fitness = *agility, coordination, power.*

6. Jogging/Running:
   Health related components of fitness = **cardio-respiratory; controls body fat.**

7. Rope Jumping:
   Health related components of fitness = *cardio-respiratory, controls body composition.*
   Skill related components of fitness = *agility, coordination, reaction time, speed.*

8. Rowing:
   Health related components of fitness = *cardio-respiratory, muscle strength, muscle endurance, controls body composition.*
   Skill related components of fitness = *agility, coordination, power.*

7. Skating:
   Health related components of fitness = *cardio-respiratory; controls body composition.* **Skill related components of fitness** = *agility, balance, coordination, speed.*

9. Swimming/Water Exercises:
   Health related components of fitness = *cardio-respiratory, muscle strength, muscle endurance, flexibility, controls body composition.*
   Skill related components of fitness = *agility, coordination.*

10. Walking (brisk):
    Health related components of fitness = *cardio-respiratory, controls body composition.*

SKILL 31.10 Interpret data from fitness assessments

Data from physical fitness assessments can diagnose an individual's level of fitness and identify the components of fitness requiring improvement. Data are compared to norms.

Cardio-respiratory data identifies an individual's functional aerobic capacity by the predicted maximum oxygen consumption. This can, partially, explain natural leanness, running ability, and motivation.

Muscle strength data identifies an individual's ability to execute some basic skills, an individual's potential of injury, an individual's potential to develop musculoskeletal problems, and an individual's potential to cope with life threatening situations.

Muscle strength data identifies an individual's ability to exercise, continually, for an extended period of time and an individual's potential to develop musculoskeletal problems.

Flexibility data identifies an individual's potential of motor skill performance, an individual's potential of developing musculoskeletal problems, including poor posture, and an individual's potential of performing activities of daily living.

SKILL 31.11 Design physical fitness programs incorporating the health-related components to meet the needs of students.

Fitness programs are designed incorporating: mode, frequency, intensity, and time; progression.

A **cardio-respiratory fitness** program is designed by:

* *mode:* aerobic activities (i.e. walking, jogging, swimming, cycling, rowing)

* *frequency:* 3 to 5 days/week

* *intensity:* 60% to 90% of maximum oxygen uptake or 60% to 80% THR

* *time:* 20 to 60 minutes of continuous or interval (non-continuous) activity [time is dependent on intensity level]

* *progression:* prescription is adjusted according to an individual's fitness level and conditioning effects

A **muscle strength** program is designed by:

* *mode:* weight training (isotonic/dynamic)

* *frequency:* minimum 3 days/week to a maximum of every other day

* *intensity:* 60% to 90% of maximum muscle strength (1-RM)

* *time:* 3 sets with 3 to 8 reps and a 60 second rest interval

* *progression:* increase workload (overload) when individual can perform 15 reps at 10 RM level

A **muscle endurance** program is designed by:

- *mode:* weight training

- *frequency:* minimum 3 days/week up to every other day

- *intensity:* 30% to 60% of maximum muscle strength (1-RM)

- *time:* 3 sets with 12 to 20 reps or until point of muscle fatigue with a 15 to 60 second rest interval

- *progression:* increase workload (overload) periodically based on number of continuous repetitions

A **flexibility** program is designed by:

- *mode:* stretching

- *frequency:* 3 to 7 days/week

- *intensity:* just below individual's threshold of pain

- *time:* 3 sets with 3 reps holding stretches 15 to 30 seconds with a 60 rest interval between sets

A **body composition** program is designed by:

- *mode:* combining aerobic exercise and weight training and a moderate reduction of caloric intake

- *frequency:* minimum of 3 days/week; however, daily is best

- *intensity:* low intensity; long duration

- *time:* 45 to 60 minutes of aerobic activity; 3 sets with a minimum of 6 reps for weights every other day

- *progression:* periodically increase as individual improves

SKILL 31.12 Evaluate personal fitness programs and recommend changes where needed

After assessing an individual's fitness level, a personal fitness program can be prescribed. Prescription of a fitness program begins with:

1. identifying the components of fitness that need changing (via assessment),

2. establishing short-term goals,

3. developing a plan to meet the established goals,

4. keeping records to record progress;

5. evaluating progress of goals and making changes based on success or failure.

COMPETENCY 32.0

EXERCISE TRAINING

When you have a choice between taking the escalator
or the stairs, take the stairs.

COMPETENCY 32.0   KNOWLEDGE OF EXERCISE TRAINING PRINCIPLES

SKILL 32.1 Identify basic training principles.

The *Overload Principle* is exercising at a level above normal to improve a physical or physiologic capacity (working a load that is more than normal).

The *Specificity Principle* is overloading specifically for a particular fitness component. In order for a component of fitness to be improved, it must be, specifically worked on. Metabolic and physiologic adaptations are dependent on the type of overload; hence, specific exercise produces specific adaptations creating specific training effects.

The *Progression Principle* states that once the body adapts to the original load/stress, no further improvement of a component of fitness will occur unless an additional load is added.

There is also a *Reversibility-of-Training Principle* in which all gains in fitness will be lost with the discontinuance of a training program.

SKILL 32.2 Identify the variables by which overload can be modified. .

Overload can be modified by varying *frequency, intensity, and time.*

SKILL 32.3 Compute the target heart rate zone.

There are three ways to calculate the target heart rate. Target heart rate (THR) can be calculated by:

1. METs (maximum oxygen uptake) which is 60% to 90% of functional capacity.

2. Karvonean Formula = (MHR - RHR) x intensity + RHR
       MHR= 220 - Age
       RHR = Resting heart range
       Intensity = Target Heart Range (which is 60% - 80% of MHR - RHR + RHR)
       THR = (MHR - RHR) x .60 + RHR to (MHR - RHR) x .80 + RHR

3. Cooper's Formula to determine target heart range is:
       THR = (220 - AGE) x .60 to (220 - AGE) x .80

SKILL 32.4 Identify the relationship of body type to body composition and motor performance.

The ectomorph body type is lean and is more capable of motor performance that involves endurance.

The mesomorph body type is muscular and more capable of motor performance that involves strength and power. The endomorph body type is over fat/obese. Certainly makes motor performance more challenging. More credit to those that do well and rise to the challenge. It is their best hope of maintaining higher levels of health.

SKILL 32.5 Identify common signs of stress

Emotional signs of stress include: depression, lethargy, aggressiveness, irritability, anxiety, edginess, fearfulness, impulsiveness, chronic fatigue hyper excitability, inability to concentrate, frequent feelings of boredom, feeling overwhelmed, apathy, impatience, pessimism, sarcasm, humorlessness, confusion, helplessness, melancholy, alienation, isolation, numbness, purposelessness, isolation, numbness, self-consciousness; inability to maintain an intimate relationship.

Behavioral signs of stress include: elevated use of substances (alcohol, drugs; tobacco), crying, yelling, insomnia or excessive sleep, excessive TV watching, school/job burnout, panic attacks, poor problems solving capability, avoidance of people, aberrant behavior, procrastination, accident proneness, restlessness, loss of memory, indecisiveness, aggressiveness, inflexibility, phobic responses, tardiness, disorganization; sexual problems.

Physical signs of stress: pounding heart, stuttering, trembling/nervous tics, excessive perspiration, teeth grinding, gastrointestinal problems (constipation, indigestion, diarrhea, queasy stomach), dry mouth, aching lower back, migraine/tension headaches, stiff neck, asthma attacks, allergy attacks, skin problems, frequent colds or low grade fevers, muscle tension, hyperventilation, high blood pressure, amenorrhea, nightmares; cold intolerance.

SKILL 32.6   Identify common "stressors" which may affect individuals.

Individuals are affected by the following common stressors: death of a spouse, death of a close family member or a close personal friend, divorce or separation from a significant other, divorce of parents, addition of a new family member, personal injury/illness, unintentional pregnancy, getting married, jail term, dysfunctional family and social ties, financial problems, fired from a job, moving, poor time management, overcrowding, expectations of others, workaholic personality, lack of self-control and self confidence and self-efficacy, low self-esteem, lack of social support, general insecurity, change, heat/cold extremes, poor living conditions, unsafe work environment, one's occupation, retirement, academic/business readjustment, taking out a major loan, discrimination, being a victim of a crime, exposure to water borne or air borne chemicals, and noise.

SKILL 32.7   Identify both positive and negative coping strategies for individuals under stress.

Positive coping strategies to cope with stress include: using one's social support system, spiritual support, managing time, initiating direct action, re-examining priorities, active thinking, acceptance, meditation, imagery, biofeedback, progressive relaxation, deep breathing, massage, sauna, Jacuzzi, humor, recreation and diversions, and exercise.

Negative coping strategies to cope with stress include: using alcohol or other mind altering substances, smoking, excessive caffeine intake, poor eating habits, negative "self-talk" expressing feelings of distress, anger, and other feelings in a destructive manner.

COMPETENCY 33.0

WEIGHT CONTROL

Today is the first day of the rest of your life. Carpe Diem – seize the day.

An unknown theorist

COMPETENCY 33.0   KNOWLEDGE OF NUTRTION AND WEIGHT CONTROL

SKILL 33.1 Identify the components of nutrition.

The components of nutrition are *carbohydrates, proteins, fats, vitamins, minerals, and water.*

SKILL 33.2 Determine the adequacy of diets in meeting the nutritional needs of students.

Nutritional requirements *vary from person-to-person.* General guidelines for meeting adequate nutritional needs are as follows: *no more than 30% total caloric intake from fats* (preferably 10% from saturated fats, 10% from monounsaturated fats; 10% from polyunsaturated fats), *no more than 15% total caloric intake from protein* (complete), *and at least 55% of caloric intake from carbohydrates* (mainly complex carbohydrates).

SKILL 33.3 Determine the role of exercise and diet in the maintenance of proper weight management.

Exercise and diet maintains proper body weight by equalizing caloric intake to caloric output achieved by a permanent change in behavior.

SKILL 33.4 Recognize fallacies and dangers underlying selected diet plans.

Let me take this opportunity to inform you that the goal of using the word diet is not a bad thing. It generally means you step on the scale and don't like the number you see. Lying beneath that calibration is more information on muscle weight, bone weight, water weight, organs of the body weight. Much more sophisticated scales costing 1,500 dollars will give that data through clinics. It is then that your efforts to exercise a lot one week will accurately measure a GAIN in weight due to muscles weighing more than fat. One week if you diet properly and do little exercise you will see a smaller loss. The amount of water you have in your body can influence your weight by a significant amount such as a pound in a 130 pound person. As we age we loose bone mass and at 50 for women especially, their height is dramatically impacted up to an inch and a half because the vertebrae are collapsing. Weight loss with no effort at all is due to hormonal changes in estrogen levels for both men and women. Children on the other hand are making stronger bones and milk and calcium plays an important role in that as well as brain functioning. Calcium is needed for muscles to contract. If you are an elementary teacher PUSH MILK, chocolate was always a favorite.

ELEMENTARY EDUCATION   231

While the following paragraphs may seem negative as each extreme diet is described please keep in mind that there is a scientific diet that is HEALTHY. Weight watchers has been helpful for years in training in these concepts. The person that puts more but smaller meals is increasing the heat of the body called metabolism.

High Carbohydrate diets (i.e. Pritikin; Bloomingdale's) can produce rapid or gradual weight loss, depending on caloric intake. Vitamin and mineral supplements are usually recommended because protein intake is low - which can be difficult to maintain. These diets may/may not recommend exercising or permanent lifestyle changes which are necessary to maintain one's weight.

High Protein Diets, basically, have the same myths, fallacies , and results as high carbohydrate diets. High protein diets also require vitamin and mineral supplements. In addition, these diets are usually high in saturated fats and cholesterol because of the emphasis on protein which, naturally, are found in meat products. There is also a risk of kidney failure.

Liquid Formulas that are <u>physician/hospital run</u> (i.e. Medifast; Optifast) provide 800 or less calories a day that are consumed in liquid form. Dieters forgo food intake for 12 to 16 weeks in lieu of the protein supplement. Vitamin and mineral supplements and close medical supervision are required. Food is gradually reintroduced after the initial fast. These diets can result in severe and/or dangerous metabolic problems in addition to an irregular heartbeat, kidney infections and failure, hair loss, and sensation of feeling cold and/or cold intolerance. These are very expensive and have a high rate of failure.

Over-The-Counter Liquid Diets (i.e. Shakes ie. Slimfast) are liquid/food bar supplements are taken in place of one or more meals per day and advocate and intake of 1,000 calories daily. Carbohydrates, protein, vitamins, and minerals may be so low that they can be as dangerous as the medically supervised liquid diets when relied on for the only source of nutrition. Because of no medical supervision, the side-effects can be even more dangerous.

Over-The-Counter Diet Pills/Aids and Prescription Diet Pills (appetite suppressants) have as their main ingredient phenyl propanolamine hydrochloride [PPA], which has reported, contradictory, effectiveness. Keeping weight off by the use of these products is difficult. Dizziness, sleeplessness, high blood pressure, palpitation, headaches, and tachycardia have been reported with the use of these products. Moreover, prescription diet pills can be addictive.

Low Calorie Diets (caloric restricted) are the most misunderstood way individuals lose weight; however, restricting the intake of calories is the way most people choose to lose weight. All the focus is on food creating anxiety over the restriction of food - especially favorite foods. These diets are also difficult to maintain and have a high failure rate. Like the other diets, once the diet is over, weight is regained because of not making permanent behavior changes. Side-effects of caloric restriction include: diarrhea, constipation, Ketosis, a lower basal metabolic rate, blood sugar imbalances, loss of lean body tissue, fatigue, weakness, and emotional problems. Dietary supplements are needed.

Those who choose *Fasting* to lose weight can deplete enough of the body's energy stores that the result can be death.

SKILL 33.5 Identify the physiological, psychological, and sociological benefits of physical activity.

Physiological benefits of physical activity include the following: improved cardio-respiratory fitness, improved muscle strength, improved muscle endurance, improved flexibility, more lean muscle mass and less body fat, quicker recovery rate, improves the body's ability to utilize oxygen, lowers the resting heart rate, increases cardiac output, improves venous return and peripheral circulation, reduces the risk of musculoskeletal injuries, improves bone mass, cardiac hypertrophy, size and strength of blood vessels, increases the number red cells, improves blood-sugar regulation, improves efficiency of thyroid gland, improves energy regulation, and increases life expectancy.

Psychological benefits of physical activity include the following: relieves stress, improved mental health via better physical health, reduces mental tension (relieves depression, improves sleeping patterns; less stress symptoms), better resistance to fatigue, better quality of life, more enjoyment of leisure, better capability to handle some stressors, opportunity of successful experiences, better Self-concept, better ability to recognize and accept limitations, improved appearance and sense of well-being, better ability to meet challenges, and better sense of accomplishments.

Sociological benefits of physical activity include: the opportunity to spend time with family and friend, making new friends, the opportunity to be part of a team, the opportunity to participate in competitive experiences; the opportunity to experience the thrill of victories.

COMPETENCY 34.0

SOCIAL ASPECTS OF PHYSICAL EDUCATION

It is that openness and awareness and innocence of sorts that I try to cultivate in my dancers. Although, as the Latin verb to educate, educere, indicates, it is not a question of putting something in but drawing it out, if it is there to begin with...I want all of my students and all of my dancers to be aware of the poignancy of life at that moment. I would like to feel that I had, in some way, given them the gift of themselves.

Martha Graham

COMPETENCY 34.0   KNOWLEDGE OF SOCIOLOGICAL ASPECTS OF PHYSICAL EDUCATION

SKILL 34.1   Identify the <u>social skills</u> and values from participation in physical activities.

The social skills and values gained from participation in physical activities are as follows:

- The ability to make adjustments to both self and others by an integration of the individual to society and the environment

- The ability to make judgments in a group situation

- Learning to communicate with others and be cooperative

- The development of the social phases of personality, attitudes, and values in order to become a functioning member of society such as being considerate

- The development of a sense of belonging and acceptance by society

- The development of positive personality traits

- Learning for constructive use of leisure time

- A development of attitude that reflects good moral character

- Respect of school rules and property

SKILL 34.2   Identify <u>activities</u> that enhance socialization.

At the junior high level students indicate a desire to play on a team. They also emphasize that they want to learn activities that would prove useful in their leisure hours.

The senior high level students desire to play harmoniously with others and to participate in team play. Students view activities such as dance and sports as a place to learn respect for their fellow students. The change of pace that physical education classes from academic offerings provides opportunities for enhanced socialization.

Basketball, baseball, football, soccer, and volleyball are social, team activities. Tennis and golf are social activities that are useful in leisure hours.

SKILL 34.3 **Identify the positive and negative influences of participation in physical activity on psycho-social factors.**

Positive Individual Influences:

Feeling better, reduces tension and depression, means of affiliation with others, offers exhilarating experiences, aesthetic experiences, positive body image, controls aggression, relaxation and a change of pace from long hours of work, study, or stresses; provides challenge and sense of accomplishment; provides a way to be healthy and fit, improves self-esteem by mastering skills, provides creative experiences; positive addiction to exercise in contrast to negative substances.

Positive Group Influences:

Cooperation, acceptance of all persons regardless of race, creed or origin, respect for others, assimilate the group attitude, encouragement, develop relationship of self to a group, develop spirit of fairness, developing traits of good citizenship, developing leadership and following qualities, self-discipline, provides additional avenues for social acquaintances, social poise and self-understanding, social consciousness with an accompanying sense of values, individual and social development.

Negative influences: ego-centered athletes, winning at all costs, false values, harmful pressures, lose of identity, role conflict, aggression and violence, compulsiveness, over-competitiveness, addiction to exercise (where commitment to exercise has a higher priority than commitments to family, interpersonal relationships, work, and medical advice), escape or avoidance of problems exacerbation of anorexia nervosa, exercise deprivation effects, fatigue, overexertion, poor eating habits, self-centeredness, preoccupation with fitness, diet, and body image.

COMPETENCY 35.0

INSTRUCTIONAL PRACTICES

Great art brings the head and the heart together.

COMPETENCY 35.0 KNOWLEDGE OF EFFECTIVE INSTRUCTIONAL PRACTICES

SKILL 35.1 Recognize and apply theories of learning in the teaching/ learning process.

INTRODUCTION

A thorough knowledge of the role of **human learning** in the teaching/learning process is foundational knowledge for planning for instruction.

Human learning reflects the complexity of human behavior as a whole.

-Each learner may have a unique set of learning style preferences.
-The tasks of learning differ.
  -For example, learning to drive a car requires both different physical and mental skills than learning to speak another language.

-Teachers must identify and break down for their students the cognitive and physical processes that are involved in a successful acquisition of each kind of learning.

There are general patterns of human learning that have been identified as general principles.

-Principles, gathered and ordered, become the "stuff" of various learning
  -Learning theories can provide helpful frameworks of understanding for teachers to use in planning instruction.
  -Learning theories can aid teachers in anticipating how the learner might respond to instruction.
  -"A characteristic of learning theories is that they address the underlying psychological dynamics of events. Thus, they provide a mechanism for understanding the implications of events related to learning in both formal and informal settings" (Gredler,1997, p. 11).

With a thorough knowledge of learning theory the reflective teacher is better equipped to:

-plan for instruction
-evaluate products for classroom use and to evaluate classroom teaching practice
-diagnose problems in the classroom
-evaluate new research on learning (Gredler, 1997).

Background on the Development of **Learning Theories**

Edward L. Thorndike is referred to as "the father of educational psychology". In 1898 he completed his dissertation on "An Experimental Study of the Associative Process in Animals." Thorndike led the way in research on learning. Thorndike believed earlier methods of studying human learning by way of "introspection" were unscientific.

> "Introspection" is a method in which people would be asked to recall or recount their thinking through looking inwardly at their thoughts.

> Thorndike was a "Behaviorist". Thorndike claimed human learning should be studied by observation and description of relationships among observable events; i.e., by observing "behavior."

The behaviorist approach to the study of learning produced an extensive number of concepts and principles of learning. This approach dominated American psychology for almost 50 years. During this time another approach to the study of learning, called "Gestalt Theory," was also making substantial contributions to research on learning.

Gestalt theory approached learning from a cognitive perspective. It's fundamental proposition was that learning involves a sudden change or reorganization of one's perception of a problem situation. This cognitive process was termed "insight." Ultimately, the behaviorist approach to learning has had more extensive influence in education.

Today the field of learning theory reflects a wide range of approaches. It is helpful to teachers to be knowledgeable of all these approaches. The ability to effectively adapt instruction to the needs of individual learners requires such knowledge.

The **Major Theories of Learning** Introduced

The *behaviorist approach.*

> This approach begins with the following assumptions:

> 1) Human behaviors are largely the result of their environments.
> 2) Learning should be described in terms of relationships among observable events; i.e. stimuli and responses.
> 3) Learning involves a change in behavior.
> 4) Learning occurs when certain events occur in conjunction with other events.
> 5) Many animal species (including humans) learn in similar ways.

Behaviorists have done a substantial amount of research done on animal behavior. Behaviorists used experiments with pigeons and rats to develop extensive number of learning principles. Many of these principles can be applied to human learning.

An emphasis in behavioral theory on the influence of the environment in learning has led to clearer understanding of how human behaviors are reinforced, once they have been emitted. This understanding is essential to teachers who want to help students strengthen a desirable behavior.

Behavioral theory is of limited help in explaining the nature of complex learning.

Cognitive theory.

The **assumptions** of *cognitive theory* counter the assumptions of behavioral theory on significant points.

1) People impose their own meanings on environmental events.
2) By observing how people respond to particular stimuli, we can draw inference about cognitive processes.
3) Learning is an internal process that may or may not result in a behavior change.
4) Cognitive processes play a critical role in determining what is learned.
5) Some learning processes may be unique to human beings.
6) People are actively involved in their own learning.
7) People are selective about the things they process and learn.(Ormrod, 1995)

Cognitive theory is more acceptable to those who see the learner as an agent of his or her own learning, actively constructing meaning from the environment. The emphasis in cognitive theory on cognitive processes has led to understanding of <u>fundamental</u> cognitive processes including:

1) perception and encoding
2) storing information in long-term memory
3) retrieval of stored information.
4) Teachers must understand these processes to be effective in their presentation of lesson material
5) Student difficulties in learning are often identifiable as a breakdown of one of these processes.

Cognitive theory has also aided in our understanding of <u>complex</u> cognitive processes including:

1) concept learning
2) transfer
3) meta-cognition
4) problem solving
5) Understanding of these processes is essential for teachers who are seeking to teach concepts effectively, help students to see application of learning to new contexts, assist students in regulating their own learning, and facilitate students' development of problem solving skills.

Social learning theory

The basic assumptions of *social learning theory* are the following:

1) People can learn by observing others.
2) Learning is an internal process that may or nay not result in behavior change.
3) Cognitive processes play a critical role in determining what is learned.
4) Behavior is directed toward particular goals that people have set for themselves.
5) Behavior eventually becomes self-regulated.
6) Reinforcement and punishment have several indirect effects (rather than a direct effect) on learning and behavior.(Ormrod, 1995)

This approach combines the approaches of behavioral and cognitive learning theories. Some view it as an offshoot of behaviorism. Others emphasize its cognitive aspects.

Social learning theory's contributions:

1) It has contributed to our understanding of learning by observation.
2) It has identified the possible effects of modeled behaviors.
3) It has also contributed to understanding of self-regulation of behavior. In this respect it moves beyond the behaviorist paradigm.

COMPETENCY 36.0

CHILD GROWTH AND DEVELOPMENT

There is but one interpretation of high standards in teaching: standards are highest where the maximum number of students – slow learners and fast learners alike – develop to their maximal capacity.

Joseph Seidlin

COMPETENCY 36.0   KNOWLEDGE OF CHILD GROWTH AND DEVELOPMENT

SKILL 36.1   Describe the developmental stages of children: Intellectual, moral, physical, and social.

Piaget's Theory of Intellectual Development - He studied how human beings organized knowledge at different times in their lives. Specifically, he studied how children attempted to make "sense" of the world in which they lived.

Assumptions in Thinking that are Basic to Jean Piaget's Theory:

1. **Organization** -This is an ongoing process of arranging information/experiences in order to organize thoughts into psychological schemes or categories through the process of
2. **Adaption** to the environment. Children adapt to their world by:

    a. **Assimilation** -integrating new information into existing ones and when the new information doesn't fit **disequalibrium** happens which leads to

3. **Accommodation** -modifying and adjusting our schemata so that the new information will fit into patterns of thinking in an orderly way thus resulting in

4. **Equilibrium** - a balance among organization, assimilation and accommodation.

Piaget Identified 4 Stages of Cognitive Development:

1. **Sensorimotor Stage** (birth - 2 years)

    -Development based on reflex actions (body movement), information is gained through the senses.
    Child understands object permanence. Knowing an object exists even when it is out of sight. (peek-a-boo)
    Development of problem solving behavior through trial and error.

2. **Preoperational Stage** (ages 2-7) Early childhood into the primary grades Children develop the ability to share their experiences with others and to use symbols. During this stage logical mental operations begin.

-Children this age have problems with:

Conservation -Certain properties of an object do not change even though the appearance of an object has changed. (pouring equal amounts of soda into a tall glass and a smaller glass. The child will insist the taller glass has more soda.)

Concentration -because the child is only focusing on one aspect - the height of the glasses.

Reversibility -The child in this stage is unable to back up and rethink an operation, such as thinking about pouring the soda into a glass after the soda has been poured.

3. **Concrete Operational Stage** (ages 7 - 11) Primary- intermediate grades During this stage the child:

-understands the operations of conservation, concentration and reversibility.
-masters the operations of classification - identifying characteristics (size, color) and seriation.
-capable of inferences.

Children in the preoperational stage respond to perceived appearances and those in the concrete operational phase respond to inferred reality or facts.

4. **Formal Operational Stage** (ages 11-adult) intermediate grades and beyond During this stage students are:
-capable of abstract thinking.
-can deal with hypothetical situations
-exercise higher order thinking including synthesis and evaluation.

Application of Piaget's Theory for the Classroom:

    1. Influence on instruction:

        -maintain a healthy balance of disequilibrium to insure
         growth in achievement
        -students must be involved in the learning process
        -the teacher should note students' logic and solutions in their
         thinking as they solve problems.

    2. Influence on curriculum:

        -the students should be at a level of cognitive development to
         be able to understand the concepts being taught
        -students interest and motivation in the lessons are important to
         consider
        -the material in the lessons should relate to the students' lives

Limitations of Piaget's Theory:

    1. Children's development does not consistently fit into neat patterns or stages.
    2. Piaget did not consider the effect of culture and the social group on the child's development.

Lev Vygotsky's Sociocultural View - an alternative to Piaget

Unlike Piaget, Vygotsky emphasized the important role of children's language, private speech and how they use language to interact in their culture. Children first use spoken language to identify their thinking and behavior as they grow and mature. In other words they think out loud. This changes at a later stage to inner speech which aids in critical thinking and solving problems.

 Zone of Proximal Development -Vygotsky identified the "zone" as the optimal time for teaching and learning. This is when a child cannot solve a problem alone but with instructional support from an adult (teacher) learning can take place. This structural assistance is called **scaffolding.**

Influence on Instruction

1. Using the zone of proximal development in teaching allows the teacher to assess the level of the child's thinking, provide appropriate teaching strategies and support materials so that the child will progress smoothly through the zone.
2. During this time the teacher provides instructional scaffolding through probing questions, modeling the learning task, thinking out loud and providing prompts and cues.

D. Influence on Curriculum

1. Curriculum needs to be designed so that the level of difficulty does not exceed the child's zone of proximal development.
2. Instructional materials should be carefully selected for each individual student to reinforce the learning of the new concepts being taught.

Both Piaget and Vygotsky support Constructivism

Constructivism is a view of the learner that states that the child is actively constructing knowledge based on his/her view and interaction with the environment. Constructionists stress the activity of the learner who is linking new knowledge to what he/she already knows and then applying this knowledge to new situations. Piaget emphasized the child creating new knowledge' and Vytgotsky stressed the importance of the tools of knowledge - culture and language.

The child develops cognitively by using:

1. cognitive strategies - organizing material and relating it to what one already knows.
2. metacognition - understanding how his/her mind works, how he/she solves problems and how he/she selects alternatives.
3. Metacognitive strategies - selecting a strategy to use which will aid in obtaining further information.

LANGUAGE DEVELOPMENT

Theories of language acquisition are:

1. **Behaviorists** believe that language develops when the adults reinforce sounds by the infant that eventually leads to words.

2. **Social cognitive theorists** believe that language develops in infants through modeling adult sounds and receiving corrective feedback from the adults.

3. **Psycholinguistics** believe that the infant is born with an innate ability and drive to acquire a language.

4. **Constructivists** believe that language is developed as the adults learn to adjust their language to the child's zone of proximal development.

Stages of Development in Language Acquisition

1. Initial words: **Holo phrases** -Children over generalize and use one word to represent a range of concepts or they under generalize and they use words too exact.

2. Beginning sentences: **Telegraphic Speech** which is sometimes referred to as the two-word stage. Only essential words are used thus the reference to a telegram. Semantics (meanings) used during this stage are complex.

3. Grammar development: Over regularization - The child applies rules when they do not apply i.e. Mommy goed, or adds s too many words. The sentences are simple to understand and the order of words in the sentence is correct.

4. Vocabulary development: Between two and four the child's vocabulary doubles every six months. Between five and six years of age most children have mastered the basic rules of the language. The meanings of words may continue to be egocentric.

5. Appropriate use of language in context: **Pragmatics** is when the child is able to understand the perceptions of others and he/she is able to discuss and defend his/her viewpoint in conversations on the same topic.

Instructional Implications of Language Development:

1. It is important for teachers to have meta-linguistic awareness of language and how it develops in order to assist their students to become proficient in their language ability and thought.

2. Teachers need to be careful in their verbal interactions with young children to focus on the ideas expressed and not on correcting usage. They need to work with their students on an individual basis to probe and extend students' thoughts.

PSYCHOSOCIAL DEVELOPMENT

Children mature socially by developing self concepts, attitudes and interpersonal skills. The term psychosocial describes the relationship between culture and the social environment with the emotional needs of the child.

Erik Erikson based his study of personality by hypothesizing that humans pass through eight psychosocial stages of development. At each stage there are crises or critical issues that need to be resolved in a positive way so that one can move to the next stage and develop a healthy personality. He provided a framework for understanding the needs of students in relation to the larger society in which they live.

The Preschool Years

Stage 1: **Trust vs. Mistrust** (birth to approximately 18 months)
Infants needs are satisfied for nourishment and care. The response to these needs must be consistent so that the infant develops a sense of trust and attachment to one or two adults.

Stage 2: **Autonomy vs. Shame and Doubt** (1 -2 years of age)
The child develops early signs of independence and a sense of some control of his/her environment. This independence is manifested by self-feeding, dressing, toileting, etc. In this stage the children need reassurance and support from the adults around them. Adults need to avoid being too overprotective.

Stage 3: **Initiative vs. Guilt** (2 - 6 years of age)
The child has a great imagination and enjoys play-acting adult roles. Children in this stage are learning to perform more grown up roles and they also realize that certain restraints are necessary.

Elementary and Middle School Years

Stage 4: **Industry vs. Inferiority**
Children in this stage are curious and need to explore and manipulate their environment. They develop competency through their accomplishments. They are more aware of peer interactions, school and their neighborhood. If they do not develop this sense of competence and they have feelings of inferiority it will be difficult for them to adjust to the adult world. Teachers need to encourage and provide opportunities for this "industry" to be reached in a positive way.

Adolescence

Stage 5 **Identity vs. Role Confusion**
The adolescent is attempting to answer the question "Who am I?" They need to achieve a satisfying sense of self worth that includes their values, beliefs, drives and their abilities. The basis for this sense of identity is the satisfactorily resolution of the previous stages.

Beyond the School Years

Stage 6: **Intimacy vs. Isolation**
In this stage the adult demonstrates a willingness to be open about oneself and willing to commit to a close personal relationship.
Stage 7: **Generativity vs. Stagnation**
The adults in this stage express concern and care for future generations.

Stage 8: **Integrity vs. Despair**
In this stage there is a sense of fulfillment that one has led a satisfied life.

MORAL DEVELOPMENT

In studying children's reasoning about moral problems, Jean Piaget and Lawrence Kholberg developed theories on moral growth based on stages of development. They hypothesized that children must pass through each stage and their cognitive growth determined the level of mature reasoning that will be attained.

Piaget's Stages of Moral Reasoning are:

Stage 1: **Moral Realism** (Heteronomy)
Children judge whether an act is right or wrong by the visible consequences of the act. Intention is not considered and rules are never broken. Thus the child who broke four cups setting the table for his/her mother is guilty of doing wrong over the child who broke one cup stealing a cookie from the cookie jar.

Stage 2: **Moral Relativism** (Autonomy)
In this stage children do consider the intentions of the person...In order for this shift from moral realism to moral relativism to take place changes in cognitive development must happen.

Kohlberg's Six Stages of Moral Development:

Preconventional Level
Stage 1: **Punishment and Obedience**
In this stage the motivation is to avoid punishment. There is an unquestioning acceptance of those in authority.

Stage 2: **Instrumental Relativist Orientation**
Action is determined by one's own needs and the desire for rewards. Sometimes the needs of others are considered.

Conventional Level
Stage 3: **Interpersonal Concordia** (Good-Boy)
The need in this stage is to please others. For the first time behavior is judged by intentions.

Stage 4: **Authority - Maintaining Morality**
In this stage social order must be maintained by following fixed rules and respect for authority.

(Kohlberg found that the majority of the people he studied were in the Conventional Level of morally reasoning.)

Post Conventional Level
Stage 5**: Social Contract Legalistic Orientation**
Actions are considered carefully in light of one's self respect and maintaining the rights of others. Laws should be obeyed because they represent a social contract developed by society. However, laws may need to be changed to be more flexible in light of changing circumstances.

Stage 6: **Universal Ethical Principle**
Individuals consider their personal principles (conscience) based on their value system to determine their moral reasoning. In order to uphold their beliefs, they may find it necessary to deviate from the rules (laws) when the rules conflict with their moral principles.

Sex Differences in Moral Development

Kohlberg reported in his studies that males were able to function at the post conventional level (stages 5 & 6) but females reasoned at the lower stages.
Carol Gilligan proposed a theory that views females as taking a different course in their moral reasoning from their male counterparts. Females develop a morality of care and responsibility versus the male morality of justice.

From all three theorists on moral development, Piaget, Kohlberg and Gilligan, we have developed a greater understanding on how humans' moral reasoning changes as cognitive growth takes place.

PHYSICAL DEVELOPMENT

Influence of Heredity and Environment on Physical Growth

The biological processes including one's genetic make-up and hormonal influences are vital to the development of the child particularly for motor skill development. Simultaneously the effects of the many influences by the caregivers and the child's personal experiences stimulate the growth of the child from an immature infant to a competent child, and adolescent. This stimulation includes providing quality nutritional, emotional, and social support so that the child's physical growth, motor skills and talents will fully develop.

Physical Growth and the Sociocultural Environment

In many ways the pattern of the child's physical growth and motor skill development are determined by the setting, resources and beliefs of the society in which he/she lives. What the society identifies as important skills will determine the goals to reach - athletic ability, slenderness, for example.

ELEMENTARY EDUCATION

The Child as an Active Participant in Physical Growth

The infant is innately motivated to exercise basic motor skills. As the infant becomes increasingly mobile other skills develop particularly as the child receives reinforcement and feedback from the adults around him/her.

Rate of Physical Growth

Physical growth, including brain development and the maturation of motor skills manifest themselves in growth spurts usually during infancy and adolescence. Even with these obvious growth spurts there is always present a continuous level of physical growth and   motor skill development until the body has reached its potential. When bones have ossified the child is considered to have reached physical maturity.

Preschool years: For both males and females physical growth is constant and predictable. There is increased control over gross-motor skills and fine-motor skills are also developing.

Elementary years: Height and weight increases and there is a marked awareness of physical differences. In more recent years there is a noted increase trend in obesity.

Individual Differences and Physical Growth

Individual differences in physical growth and motor skill development have a definite affect on the child. These individual differences can cause a significant reaction to the child by those in his/her environment. Whether one is an early or a late bloomer, precocious or one is delayed in his/her growth, this will greatly affect how the child is treated and this in turn will influence the behavior of the child.

 Physical Growth and Its Influence on Other Domains

The child's physical size and weight and his/her coordination of motor skills will have a tremendous affect on the responses and expectations of adults and peers. This will also influence the child's identity of him/herself since it is intricately tied to his/her personal view of his/her physical appearance and abilities. Maturing physically earlier can result in higher expectations of behavior and responsibilities. Males who mature earlier are likely to be more accepted and popular than males who mature later. Females who mature earlier may be at a disadvantage.

SKILL 36.2   Recognize young children as individuals with feelings, attitudes and emotions that shape their behavioral responses.

As children progress through the various domains of development -cognitive, social, physical and moral, they are each developing as unique individuals. This individuality is manifested in the child's self concept and his/her self esteem.

Self-Concept: This is the child's perception of his/her beliefs, knowledge, and feelings that are used to explain who he/she is. As Piaget would say, the child is developing schemata that organize his/her feelings, attitudes, and emotions so that he/she is able to describe him/herself. This self-concept is represented by how the child views him/herself academically, socially and physically. It is based largely on the child's experiences.

Self-esteem: This is the value each child places on his/her self concept. This is the assessment of the child's worth as he/she interacts in the environment. This measure includes whether the child is accepted socially, is successful in school and has overall good mental health. This evaluation results in a comparison of the ideal self with the real self.

Preschool Years
Early on the child gains a sense of individuality. Around 18 months the child will recognize him/herself in a mirror. This sense of self is based on observable physical characteristics and features and immediate behaviors. As the child grows and matures he/she becomes aware that others have separate identities and different interpretations and perceptions on. Knowledge of self moves beyond physical features to include relationships, activities and possessions.

The Elementary Years
Children entering school generally have a very positive self concept and they expect to be successful. As they grow and mature they become more aware of their individual traits and will say that they are smart, funny, shy. They will also identify themselves in relation to being a team member or a member of the Scouts, etc. It is during this time that children begin to make social comparisons of themselves with their peers. These inner thoughts and feelings about themselves as they are making these comparisons is the criteria for the child's claim to uniqueness.

The Adolescent Years
During the adolescent years children are able to define themselves by more abstract values and attitudes. They can see themselves from many perspectives and even opposing ones. They project into the future and consider larger goals in their lives. As they become more competent in their activities they rely more on their own self.

SKILL 36.3 Demonstrate a understanding that a child's prior experiences contribute to individual differences in all areas of development.

As children grow and mature their uniqueness is greatly influenced by the experiences they have and the environment in which they live. Children's differences are a result of differences in cognitive ability, language acquisition, socioeconomic status, culture, and gender.

1. **Cognitive Ability**: Most experts in the area of cognition agree that both heredity and environment play an important role in how well a child will be able to think abstractly, reason, acquire new knowledge and solve problems. Piaget stated that the demands of the environment determines how well children will adapt to new situations and organize their thoughts into logical patterns. The behaviorists like Skinner, and the social learning theorists like Bandura, recognized the critical role of the environment in shaping and modifying behavior.

2. **Language Acquisition**: Acquiring a language and being skilled in verbal communication serves an important function in how well the child will not only communicate the values and expectations of his/her culture but also the level of sophistication of his/her thinking. Language serves to identify the behavior of the child first in private speech and then in inner speech as he/she attempts to complete new tasks and solve problems. Language has a direct effect on cognitive processes such as memory or classification. The adults in the child's environment provide the necessary feedback and role models as they verbalize with the child. The more enriching and challenging the communication the more competent the child will be in using language as a communication tool.

3. **Socioeconomic Status**: The socioeconomic status of the child's parents which is measured by occupation, income, and education level has a very strong affect on the child's values, attitudes, background experiences and academic success. The school dropout rate of students from poor families is twice that of the general population. Both economic and social forces are creating many students who are physically and mentally ill-prepared to be successful in school. The following statistics emphasize this point:

> a. One-fourth of U.S. children currently live below the poverty level.
> b. Fifteen million children are being raised by single mothers whose family income is below the poverty level.
> c. Forty-four percent of African American children and 36% of Latino children live in poverty.
> d. Between one fourth and one third of the children have no adult at home when they return home from school (U.S. Department of Education, 1993). Socioeconomic status (SES) is an important source of individual differences.

4. **Culture**: The attitudes, beliefs, customs, values and behavioral patterns of the social group in which the child lives has an enormous impact on how the child develops as a unique individual. For example, if the culture values school success this is transmitted to the children and they see it as an important aspect of their world. If the culture in the school is significantly different from the learning experiences of the child's culture this may interfere with the child's motivation to learn. Children from different cultures interact with adults in different ways and this too can either be a hindrance or a help as the children enter school.

5. **Gender**: Research studies have indicated that there are no significant differences in intelligence or aptitudes between males and females. Any noted differences seem to be caused by environmental influences. From birth males and females are treated differently. Parents' expectations, whether consciously or unconsciously, are different for daughters and sons. These different social patterns continue in school where teachers have different expectations for their male and female students. These differences stand out particularly in the teaching of mathematics and science. In science classes the boys were more apt to be allowed to use the science equipment and asked to complete the lab demonstrations. In mathematics the difference is attributed to higher expectations for the males by the teachers. This greatly influences career choices and there is a continued decline in females entering professions requiring a major in science or mathematics.

SKILL 36.4 Demonstrate sensitivity to multicultural children and provide for their needs

Traditional View

1. New immigrant children must adapt to the new culture - the culture of the Anglo-middle class (the melting pot theory).
2. Schools expected these immigrant children to reflect the white, Anglo-Saxon middle-class values for academic success and achievement.
3. Student's home life was considered inferior (the cultural deficit model).

The Multicultural Education View

1. Each student regardless of ethnic or cultural background, economic status, gender or differences in learning abilities should have the opportunity to reach his/her full potential.
2. Education reform is needed to remove any prejudice or stereotyping based on race, culture, economic status, gender or varying abilities.

The Role of the Teacher

1. The teacher must understand and accept that students come to school with values and attitudes they have learned in their culture. These attitudes and values may be compatible with school learning or they may be incompatible with the style of learning found in American classes.
2. The teacher has to help the student to be successful in school without the child feeling that he/she has to reject his/her native culture. To accomplish this the teacher has to be sensitive and knowledgeable about the culture of the students in the class and recognize that:
    * Children from different cultures may interact with adults that could appear inappropriate in the school culture.
    * The American classrooms with the emphasis on individual responsibility and competition may be very difficult for children whose culture emphasizes cooperation, group work and helping each other.
    * There may be students in the class whose native   language or dialect is different from standard English. The school may have to offer:

        1. **Bilingual Education** -In these classes the   students and teacher are communicating using two languages.
        2. **English as a Second Language (ESL) or Limited English Proficiency (LEP)** - In these classes the teachers are required to be fluent only in English. The students in the class may represent a variety of languages. The teacher's role is to teach English.

Teaching Strategies

1. Use the student's experiential backgrounds and tie it to the content being taught. Fill in the basic skills and knowledge when needed.
2. Assist the students to understand the traditional education goals by providing the bridge between the student's knowledge/skills and the demands of the school system.
3. Recognize the variety of students' learning styles and build on these by providing strategies that will assist them to catch up.
4. Use instructional materials that show various cultures as part of the mainstream of society.
5. Involve lower SES parents and minority parents in supporting classroom activities and in working with the school.

By being inclusive of all differences -race, culture, gender, handicapping conditions, language, economic status, the teacher can promote a positive cooperative learning climate for each student in his/her class.

SKILL 36.5 Demonstrate the ability to utilize principles of child growth and development for appropriate teaching/learning processes.

Cognitive Development

1. Consider the child's current stage of development.. For example, if the child is at the concrete stage use manipulatives rather than abstract word problems.
2. The knowledge the child possess will determine what new information will be assimilated. Plan lessons to meet the individual needs of each student as much as possible, be flexible. The lesson should be stretched just beyond what the student knows.
3. Help the child to develop his/her meta-cognitive ability by encouraging self talk as he/she attempts to solve a problem.

Language Development

1. To encourage students to enrich their language it is important to focus on the ideas expressed rather than correcting usage. Provide corrective feedback by restating what the student has said.
2. Through probing and extending the student's thoughts the teacher will encourage language development.
3. Read aloud to students to promote language growth.
4. As often as possible provide opportunities for the students to have conversations with adults This will increase their understanding of the meaning of words.
5. As time permits interact with each child one-to-one.

Psychosocial Development

1. Provide activities in the class where preschool children can show initiative. This is important to offset guilt that could develop if the child is constantly being reprimanded.
2. During the elementary years it is important that the students have opportunities to complete projects in which they will have a sense of pride in their accomplishments. The learning environment should allow each students to feel successful. If this does not happen then the student is apt to develop an inferiority complex that may lead to inappropriate behaviors t hat will continue throughout adulthood.
3. Provide opportunities for students to develop positive peer relationships and acceptable social behavior by working together in cooperative learning groups.
4. Allow the students to share their different cultures and ethnicity by selecting appropriate materials, strategies, and by involving family members.

Self Concept Development

1. The learning environment should provide opportunities for the student to have success in school. This success has a direct relationship to self-esteem and positive attitudes of the student.
2. Teachers can provide success for each student by creating a climate that is physically and psychological safe for all students.
3. Encourage students to compete with their own levels of achievement rather than promoting an atmosphere of destructive competition.
4. Accept students even when a particular behavior may be unacceptable. The children should know that being "corrected" in class does not make them a 'bad' person.
5. Establish cooperative learning groups in class whereby students will help each other to learn.
6. Highlight the various cultural groups in your classes and in society as to their value and accomplishments.

Moral Development

1. By providing role playing situations the teacher can help students to develop the morality of caring and having empathy for others.
2. Through the selection of various stories the teacher can direct discussions as to the behavior of the characters portrayed in the readings.
3. Articulate the cultural differences in moral reasoning.
4. Encourage cooperation among the students to offset aggressive behavior.

Physical Development

1. Guarantee that each child's physical comfort is being met so that learning can take place.
2. Note any changes in a child's behavior and notify either the parents or school nurse. For example, squinting to see the board, or turning the head to hear.
3. School materials should be appropriate to the motor skill development of the child.
4. Model accepting and caring behavior by treating each child equally.

SKILL 36.6 Demonstrate the ability to assist students in interacting constructively with their peers.

Studies have shown that peer interaction can have a positive affect on motivation and student achievement. Two major cognitive psychologists also theorized as to the positive effect of peer learning.

1. Jean Piaget - He noted that the disequilibrium created when new information was introduced by peers resulted in a reorganization of the child's thinking.

2. Lev Vygotsky - He believed that children operate in similar *zones of proximal development* but they provide enough differences to stimulate cognitive growth in each other. They can provide the *scaffolding* for another student.

Teaching Strategies to Enhance Peer Interactions:

1. Peer Tutoring - In peer tutoring one student teaches the material to another student. There are two types of peer tutoring:

   a. **cross-age tutoring**: This is when older students work with younger students. This is beneficial because the older students would be familiar with the material. It is not unusual to have a total grade, for example a sixth grade, work with the students in a third grade.

   b. **same age tutoring**: This is when students in the same class assist each other. This is easier to arrange and researchers feel that it is effective. When classmates of the same age and performance level tutor each other taking turns there is an increase in student learning.

2. Cooperative Learning - In cooperative learning a group of students work together as a team to solve academic problems or to complete assignments. Students are rewarded for encouraging each team member to learn. These teams have worked effectively at all grade levels and content areas. Not only has academic achievement improved but attitudes toward students at risk, minorities, and gender differences resulted in greater acceptance in other activities in the class. Researchers, Johnson & Johnson (1994); Slavin (1995), identified the following elements of effective cooperative learning activities:

   a. *positive interdependence:* The teacher sets up activities so that team members must depend on each other to complete the task. Each team member may be given different information or material so that students have to work together to complete the task.

b. *face-to-face interaction:* The teacher has to carefully select the activities so that students will be required to interact with each other. It cannot be an activity one could do alone.

c.*individual accountability:* The main goal of cooperative learning is to improve the achievement of each student. Every member of the team is responsible for learning the material.

d.*interpersonal skills:* The development of interpersonal skills is another key purpose for cooperative learning. Social skills are explicitly taught and monitored.

Two Cooperative Learning Models are:

1. Student Teams Achievement Divisions (STAD) This is a direct instruction model that uses reinforce to improve the learning of concepts, skills and facts. Instead of working individually the team studies and completes the work prepared by the teacher. After comparing their answers with each other and resolving any differences the team members then complete a quiz which is scored like any other quiz. Each member contributes to the team rewards by an improved score over past performances on previous tests or quizzes. This model improves procedural skills.

2. Jigsaw II: In this model each team is responsible for a different piece of information. The team member becomes the "expert" of that piece of information. These "experts" then teach the members of their team. Each member contributes a piece of information to the puzzle and all members are responsible to learn the content of each piece of the puzzle.

SKILL 36.7 Recognize signs of child abuse, substance abuse and severe emotional distress.

	Physical Indicators	Behavioral Indicators
Child Abuse	unexplained bruises, bite marks, burns, fractures, etc.	withdrawn and aggressive, self-destructive, dislike of human contact
	physical neglect-need medical attention, lack of supervision, poor hygiene, hungry	falls asleep, steals food, reports no one at home, self destructive, frequent absences
	sexual abuse-difficulty in sitting or walking, stained clothing, venereal disease, pain or itching in genital area	withdrawn, depressed, low self esteem, massive weight change, peer problems, seductive behavior
Substance Abuse	premature birth, low birth weight, small head size, seizures, strokes, respiratory problems	delay in language development, attention problems, inability to control behavior, coordination problems
Emotional Distress	eating disorders, sleeping problems, loss of energy, chronic complaints	depression, low self esteem, lack of self confidence, poor peer relations, suicidal

COMPETENCY 37.0

ART

The essence of education is not to stuff you with facts but to help you discover your uniqueness, to teach you how to develop it, and then to show you how to give it away.

Leo Buscaglia

COMPETENCY 37.0   VISUAL AND PERFORMING ARTS

SKILL 37.1   Identify the formal elements and principles of the arts.

In the field of the visual arts, artists utilize the formal elements of line, shape (or form), color and texture to create compositions. The artist arranges these elements according to his/her sensitivity to the various principles of design, such as repetition, variation, rhythm, balance (both symmetrical and asymmetrical), unity, movement (or articulation), and center of interest (or focal area).

In the field of architecture, architects deal with the same fundamental elements as above, but also must consider the aspects of materials, structure, function, repetition, balance, scale, proportion, space and climate.

In the field of music, musicians and composers work with the elements of tone, the characteristics of which are pitch, timbre, duration, and intensity. Musical compositions are created when tones are arranged with regard to rhythm, harmony, structure (both open and closed forms), meter and tempo, texture and tonality.

In the field of dance, dancers and choreographers utilize elements of line, form, movement, energy, time and space. The principles are repetition, variation, rhythm, tempo, narration, space, and setting.

In the field of theater, playwrights utilize the elements of language, structure and theme while actors deal with the elements of language, speech, and motivation. (Set, lighting, and costume designers use the elements of the visual arts.)

SKILL 37.2   Identify significant genres (forms) from various visual, musical, and literary examples.

"Genre", originating from the French for "kind", refers to a style or category of work, characterized by content or artistic style. For example, in the visual arts, various genres include, among others, the content areas of seascape, still lives, portraiture, and religious works.

Genres of artistic style include, among others, realism, abstract expressionism, and non-objective compositions.

In the visual arts, "genre" also refers to a specific style of realistic painting which illustrates scenes of everyday life.

In the field of music, various genres include, among others, the forms of cantata, concerto, mass, motet, opera, oratorio, overture, sonata, suite, and symphony.

In the field of literature, a genre is a literary form, such as the novel, the short story, the drama, the epic, the sonnet, the biography, and both formal and informal essays. Other genres include poetry types, such as narrative, lyrical, or dramatic. In addition, works composed in these genres reflect the writing style of the author, and may be classified under headings such as gothic, classic and neo-classic, among others. Works may also be classified by subject matter, such as picaresque, historical, or lyrical.

SKILL 37.3 Identify particular characteristics of various genres.

In the visual arts, one type of genre is based on subject matter, therefore leading to genre headings such as seascape, landscape, still life, portraiture, religious, and interiors, etc. Most of these headings are merely descriptive and self-explanatory. A work of visual art falls into one of these categories merely based on subject content.

Another definition of genre in the field of the visual arts is more specific. A "genre" scene is a realistically portrayed scene that depicts everyday life in a casual, informal, non-monumental way. This type of genre appears throughout the history of art.

Yet another genre in the visual arts is based on the artist's style of work, such as realism, abstraction, impressionism, expressionism, etc. For an example, a painting done by Picasso utilizing the concepts of cubism is said to belong to the cubist genre, while another painting, also by Picasso but reflecting the concepts of neoclassicism, will fall into that genre. (See 1.5 and 2.10 for more information.)

In the fields of music and literature, genre refers to established forms of compositions. Many of these forms have precise definitions and parameters, as given here.

Music

cantata- Developed in the baroque era, these compositions were written for solo and chorus voices, with orchestral accompaniment. With either secular or sacred lyrics, cantatas contain several movements.

concerto- A musical work written for one or more solo instruments with orchestral accompaniment, the concerto usually is comprised of three movements in a fast-slow-fast order.

mass- This choral type is usually associated with the Roman Catholic church service, thus following the form of that service and including six musical parts: the Kyrie Eleison, Gloria in Excelsis Deo, Credo in Unum Deum, Sanctus, Benedictus, and Agnus Dei. Specific masses for the dead are known as "requiem" masses. However, not all masses are written for church services. Since the Medieval period, "concert masses" have been an accepted form of composition.

motet- From the French for "word", a motet is a choral work, utilizing a polyphonic approach. Motets from the thirteenth century were often written for three voices (triplum, motetus, and tenor), and combined texts from both sacred and secular sources. During the fifteenth and sixteenth centuries (Renaissance), the motet expanded to a contrapuntal work for four or five voices a cappella, utilizing a sacred text. The motet also appears in the Baroque and Romantic periods with both orchestral and a cappella variations.

opera- Originating from the Italian word for "work", opera is appropriately named! It is a musical work which, when produced, incorporates many of the other arts as well. Technically, it is a play in which all the dialogue (libretto) is sung, with orchestral accompaniment. The origins of opera were founded in Renaissance Florence by intellectuals reviving Greek and Roman drama. Since then, operatic forms have evolved through many stages. Major ones include "grand opera" or "opera seria", which consists of five acts and is serious in nature, "opera comique", which, regardless of emotional content, has spoken dialogue, "opera buffa" which is the comic opera usually based on farce, and "operetta", also with spoken dialogue and characterized by a light, romantic mood, and popular theme.

oratorio- Developed during the Baroque era, an oratorio is a choral work of large scale, including parts for soloists, chorus and orchestra alike. Themes are usually epic or religious in nature. Although the soloists may take the role of various characters and there may be a plot, an oratorio is usually presented in concert form, without action, costumes or set design.

overture- Usually an overture is the introductory composition to an opera, written to capture the mood of the opera, and even to showcase a musical motif from the opera. However, since in concerts overtures are often performed out-of-context, composers have now begun to write "concert overtures", meant to stand alone, without a larger body of music to follow.

sonata- A sonata is a succession of movements which have loosely related tonalities. The first of these movements usually is composed in a specific pattern, which is known as "sonata form". Sonata form, or sonata-allegro form, follows the pattern of development ABA or AABA, where A is the exposition, B is the development, and the final section of A is the recapitulation.

suite- A musical suite is a group of dances, usually written for keyboards or an ensemble of stringed or wind instruments. The dances are usually unrelated except for a common key.

symphony- Fully refined by the eighteenth century, a symphony is a large scale work composed for a full orchestra. However, the various historic and stylistic periods, in addition to the development of instruments, have produced an evolution of this form. Because of this, "symphony" also refers to compositions for chamber orchestras and string quartets. Although some symphonies vary in the number of movements, in general, the four symphonic movements follow the tempo pattern of fast, slow, moderate, and fast, with a minuet included in the third movement.

Literature

novel- A novel is a fictional narrative of significant length, written in prose and dealing with characters embroiled in a plot Novels are often classified by subject matter, resulting in categories such as:

short story- These fictional works are written in prose, and, due to the limited length, focus on characterization and theme.

drama- This genre refers to a written script upon which a theater performance may be based. Although serious in nature and tone, a drama is usually regarded as a play that is not necessarily a tragedy, and may conclude with a happy ending.

lyric poetry- Deriving it's name from the word "lyre", lyric poetry was originally composed for singing. Generally it is an emotional expression of the poet, subjective in nature and utilizing strong imagery.

sonnet- Refined during the Italian Renaissance by Petrarch, and celebrated by Shakespeare, today a sonnet is fourteen lines of iambic pentameter, a lyric poem that expresses a single idea, theme, or thought, often about love. The many varieties of sonnets stem from the individual styles of well-known writers, thus the categories of Petrarchan, Shakespearean, and Spenserian. Others include Elizabethan, Victorian, and Romantic. The structure of iambic pentameter refers to the accent pattern (alternating stressed and unstressed syllables), and the number of feet in a line or verse (five lines).

epic- This genre of poetry is a long narrative composition, generally documenting traditional heroes and their feats of daring in elevated language. These heroic accomplishments are notable because they have far-reaching ramifications and even significance for the future of the nation or world. The use of symbolism is characteristic in this genre.

biography- Written, factual accounts of people's lives have existed almost as early as writing itself, in as many forms as there are people. Biographies can be as simple as a listing of achievements, or as complex as a psychological analysis. An "autobiography" is written by the author, about himself. A written account of a religious personality or saint is labeled a "hagiography".

essay- An essay is generally a brief, lucid work which presents an author's view on a topic. Factual in nature, essays fall into two groupings: informal or formal. An informal essay is usually short and very personal, reflecting the author's personality and attitude, without necessarily an appeal to logic. A formal essay tends to be longer in length, concisely structured, and more apt to rely on logic and evidence to convince the reader of the worthiness of the opinion.

SAMPLE QUESTIONS

You can't walk out of the church on Sunday morning because you are part of the body all week long. All the parts and details are important and they must function in harmony.

Just know everything and you will be fine. Give your self permission to laugh; your going to need that skill!

Good luck and welcome to the profession.

Sharon A. Wynne

1) If three cups of concentrate are needed to make 2 gallons of fruit punch, how many cups are needed to make 5 gallons?

   A. 6 cups

   B. 7 cups

   C. 7.5 cups

   D. 10 cups

2) If a horse will probably win three races out of ten, what are the odds that he will win?

   A. 3:10

   B. 7:10

   C. 3:7

   D. 7:3

3) The measure of the pull of the earth's gravity on an object is called

   A. mass number

   B. atomic number

   C. mass

   D. weight

4) The law of conservation of energy states that

   A. energy is transformed into matter

   B. the amount of matter is neither created nor destroyed by chemical reaction

   C. energy is neither created nor destroyed by chemical reaction

   D. Mass is created from energy

5) A scientific theory

   A. proves scientific accuracy

   B. is never rejected

   C. results in a medical breakthrough

   D. may be altered at a later time

6) Thunderstorm clouds are called

   A. nimbus

   B. cirrus

   C. stratus

   D. cumulus

7) _____are cracks in the plates of the earth's crust, along which the plates move

   A. faults

   B. ridges

   C. earthquakes

   D. volcanoes

8) Paleontologists who study the history of the earth have divided geologic time into these four large units of time

   A. periods, epochs, eons, era

   B. eons, epochs, periods, era

   C. eons, era, periods, epochs

   D. era, eons, epochs, periods

9) A student scored in the 87th percentile on a standardized test. Which would be the best interpretation of his score?

   A. Only 13% of the students who took the test scored higher.

   B. This student should be getting mostly B's on his report card.

   C. This student performed below average on the test.

   D. This is the equivalent of missing 13 questions on a 100 question exam.

10) Chemicals should be stored

   A. in the principals office

   B. in a dark room

   C. according to their reactivity with other substances

   D. in a double locked room

11) Which of the following best describes current thinking on the major purpose of social science?

   A. Social science is designed primarily for students to acquire facts

   B. Social science should not be taught earlier than the middle school years

   C. A primary purpose of social sciences is the development of good citizens

   D. Social science should be taught as an elective

12) **Economics is best described as:**

A. The study of how money is used in different societies

B. The study of how different political systems produce goods and services

C. The study of how human beings use resources to supply their necessities and wants

D. The study of how human beings have developed trading practices through the years

13) **We can credit modern geography with which of the following?**

A. Building construction practices designed to withstand earthquakes

B. Advances in computer cartography

C. Better methods of linguistic analysis

D. Making it easier to memorize countries and their capitals

14) **Political science is primarily concerned with _____.**

A. Elections

B. Economic Systems

C. Boundaries

D. Public Policy

15) **Which best describes the economic system of the United States?**

A. Most decisions are the result of open markets, with little or no government modification or regulation

B. Most decisions are made by the government, but there is some input by open market forces

C. Most decisions are made by open market factors, with important regulatory functions and other market modifications the result of government activity

D. There is joint decision making by government and private forces, with final decisions resting with the government

16) In the Constitutional system of checks and balances, a primary "check" which accrues to the President is the power of:

A. Executive privilege

B. Approval of judges nominated by the Senate

C. Veto of Congressional legislation

D. Approval of judged nominated by the House of Representatives

17) Which of the following lists elements usually considered to be responsibilities of citizenship under the American system of government?

A. Serving in public office, voluntary government service, military duty

B. Paying taxes, jury duty, upholding the Constitution

C. Maintaining a job, giving to charity, turning in fugitives

D. Quartering of soldiers, bearing arms, government service

18) The Native Americans of the Eastern Woodlands lived on:

A. Buffalo and crops such as corn, beans, and sunflowers

B. Chiefly farming of squash, beans, and corn

C. A variety of game (deer, bear, moose) and crops (squash, pumpkins, corn)

D. Wolves, foxes, polar bears, walruses, and fish

19) Columbus is believed to have first reached Western Hemisphere lands in what is now:

A. Florida

B. Bermuda

C. Puerto Rico

D. Bahamas

20) A major quarrel between colonial Americans and the British concerned a series of British Acts of Parliament dealing with:

A. Taxes

B. Slavery

C. Native Americans

D. Shipbuilding

21) A consequence of the Gold Rush of Americans to California in 1848 and 1849 was that:

A. California spent the minimum amount of time as a territory, and was admitted as a slave state

B. California was denied admission on its first application, since most Americans felt that the settlers were too "uncivilized" to deserve statehood

C. California was purchased from Mexico for the express purpose of gaining immediate statehood

D. California did not go through the normal territorial stage, but applied directly for statehood as a free state

22) Students using the same foot to take off from a surface and land is which locomotor skill?

A. Jumping

B. Vaulting

C. Leaping

D. Hopping

23) Which manipulative skill uses the hands to stop the momentum of an object?

A. Trapping

B. Catching

C. Striking

D. Rolling

24) Having students collapse in their own space or lower themselves as though they are a raindrop or snowflake develops this nonlocomotor skill.

A. Dodging

B. Shaking

C. Swinging

D. Falling

25) Having students move on their hands and knees, moving along lines develops which mechanical principle?

    A. Balance

    B. Timing

    C. Force

    D. Inertia

26) Which movement concept does the game "Simon Says" develop?

    A. Balance

    B. Flexibility

    C. Spatial awareness

    D. Kinesthetic awareness

27) An instructor notices that class participation is much lower than expected. By making changes in equipment and rules, the instructor applied which of the following concepts to enhance participation?

    A. Homogeneous grouping

    B. Heterogeneous grouping

    C. Multi-activity designs

    D. Activity modification

28) Using tactual clues is a functional adaptation that can assist with which type of limitation?

    A. Deaf students

    B. Blind students

    C. Asthmatic students

    D. Physically challenged students

29) Students on a running program to improve cardiorespiratory fitness are applying which exercise principle?

    A. Aerobic

    B. Variety

    C. Specificity

    D. Overload

30) Which of the following health risk factors cannot be improved by physical activity?

    A. Cholesterol levels

    B. Metabolic rate

    C. Stress related disorders

    D. Heart diseases

31) **The most important nutrient the body require, without which life can only be sustained for a few days, is:**

   A. Vitamins

   B. Minerals

   C. Water

   D. Carbohydrates

32) **Engravings and oil painting originated in this country.**

   A. Italy

   B. Japan

   C. Germany

   D. Flanders

33) **A combination of three or more tones sounded at the same time is called a**

   A. Harmony

   B. Consonance

   C. A chord

   D. Dissonance

34) **A series of single tones which add up to a recognizable is called a**

   A. Cadence

   B. Rhythm

   C. Melody

   D. Sequence

35) **Which is a true statement about crafts?**

   A. Students experiment with their own creativity.

   B. Products are unique and different.

   C. Self-expression is encouraged.

   D. Outcome is predetermined

36) The following is not a good activity to encourage 5th graders' artistic creativity:

A. Ask them to make a decorative card for a family member.

B. Have them work as a team to decorate a large wall display.

C. Ask them to copy a drawing from a book, with the higher grades being awarded to those students who come closest to the model.

D. Have each student try to create an outdoor scene with crayons, giving them a choice of scenery.

37) An approach to musical instruction for young children that "combines learning music, movement, singing, and exploration" is

A. Dalcroze Eurthythmics

B. The Kodaly Method

C. The Orff Approach

D. Education Through Music (ETM)

38) Which statement is an example of the identity axiom of addition?

A. 3 + -3 = 0

B. 3x = 3x + 0

C. $3 \cdot \dfrac{1}{3} = 1$

D. 3 + 2x = 2x + 3

39) Two lines that intersect at a 90 degree angle are

A. parallel lines

B. perpendicular lines

C. skew lines

D. alternate exterior lines

40) Given a drawer with 5 black crayons, 3 blue crayons, and 2 red crayons, what is the probability that you will draw two black crayons in two draws in a dark room?

A. 2/9

B. 1/4

C. 17/18

D. 1/18

41) Sandra has $34.00, Carl has $42.00. How much more does Carl have than Sandra?

Which would be the best method for finding the answer?

A. addition

B. subtraction

C. division

D. both A and B are equally correct

42) Which is the least appropriate strategy to emphasize when teaching problem solving?

A. guess and check

B. look for key words to indicate operations such as all together-add, more than-subtract, times-multiply

C. make a diagram

D. solve a simpler version of the problem

43)

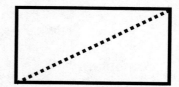

The above diagram most likely be used in deriving a formula for which of the following?

A. the area of a rectangle

B. the area of a triangle

C. the perimeter of a square

D. the surface area of a prism

44) According to Piaget, at which developmental level would a child be able to learn formal algebra?

A. pre-operational

B. sensory-motor

C. formal operational

D. concrete operational

45) Which statement is incorrect?

A. Drill and practice is one good use for classroom computers.

B. Some computer programs can help to teach problem solving.

C. Computers are not effective unless each child in the class has his own workstation.

D. Analyzing science project data on a computer during math class is an excellent use of class time.

46) Each individual speech sound is called a

A. Sight word

B. Grapheme

C. Stimulus

D. Phoneme

47) Kenny, a fourth grader, has trouble comprehending analogies, using comparative, spatial, and temporal words, and multiple meanings. Language interventions for Kenny would focus on

A. Morphology

B. Syntax

C. Pragmatics

D. Semantics

48) When students are encouraged to produce their own spellings or to uses at the spelling of a word in order to promote writing, the students are said to be using

A. Grammar

B. Invented spelling

C. Sight words

D. Linking

49) Identify the correct order for the steps in the writing process

    A. Revising, drafting, prewriting, publishing, editing

    B. Drafting, editing, prewriting, revising, publishing

    C. Prewriting, editing, drafting revising, publishing

    D. Prewriting, drafting, revising, editing, publishing

50) Word recognition through the use of phonics requires the reader to

    A. Determine an approximate pronunciation of the word

    B. Memorize the spelling of a word

    C. Focus only on inflectional endings

    D. Use a dictionary extensively

51) A teaching method which emphasizes before, during, and after reading components is

    A. Echo reading

    B. Repeated reading

    C. A KWL chart

    D. Choral reading

52) The term_____ refers to the process of thinking.

    A. Cognition

    B. Metacognition

    C. Comprehension

    D. Intellect

53) "The" is the most frequently used word in children's books.

    A. True

    B. False

54) Using pictures or illustrations in place of words in a reading passage, is prompting the students to use

    A. Visual discrimination

    B. Sight Vocabulary

    C. Context clues

    D. Homonyms

55) Which of the following is NOT an example of the bottom-up approach?

    A. Whole language

    B. Phonics

    C. Modified alphabet

    D. Linguistic

56) Many basal reading programs recommend the:

   A. Directed reading-thinking program

   B. Directed reading activity procedure

   C. Comprehension procedure

   D. Systematic reading procedure

57) One downfall of the phonics developmental reading approach is:

   A. Word recognition

   B. The student learns the letter sounds first

   C. Letter sounds are integral parts of words

   D. The student focuses more on decoding than on comprehension

58) Which of the following is NOT a developmental reading approach?

   A. Language experience

   B. Whole language

   C. Grapheme-phoneme

   D. Linguistics approach

59) Mercer and Mercer divide the reading experience into two basic processes. What are they?

   A. Word consciousness and functions of print

   B. Fluency and language and conventions of print

   C. Word and lexical knowledge

   D. Word recognition and word and idea comprehension

60) When people read, they utilize four sources of background information to comprehend the meaning behind the literal text. Which of the following is NOT one of the four sources?

   A. Word knowledge

   B. Fluency

   C. Syntax and contextual knowledge

   D. Text organization

61) **According to Rubin, what is the order of the six stages of language development?**

A. Unitary, random, automatic, expansion and delimiting, creative, structural awareness

B. Random, unitary, creative, structural awareness, automatic, expansion and delimiting

C. Expansion and delimiting, automatic, unitary, random, structural awareness, creative

D. Random, unitary, expansion and delimiting, structural awareness, automatic, creative

62) **Which of the following is NOT a step in the listening process?**

A. Receiving

B. Observing

C. Assigning meaning

D. Attending

63) **Which of the following involves correcting or otherwise changing existing information within a current schema?**

A. Assimilation

B. Fluency

C. Accommodation

D. Analyzing

64) **Which of the following is NOT a level of comprehension?**

A. Critical Comprehension

B. Creative Comprehension

C. Interpretive/Inferential comprehension

D. Literal comprehension

65) **Literature based reading instruction**

A. remains the most common source of materials for classroom reading instruction

B. is often used in remedial or clinical settings

C. is a third source of text for reading instruction

D. draws instructional materials from stories and books

66) SQ3R guides the reader through a sequence of steps which are educationally sound.

    A. True

    B. False

67) Ryan is working on a report about dogs. He uses scissors and tape to cut and rearrange sections and paragraphs, then photocopies the paper so he can continue writing. Ryan is in which stage of the writing process?

    A. Final draft

    B. Prewriting

    C. Revision

    D. Drafting

68) Talking into a tape recorder is an example of which writing activity?

    A. Prewriting

    B. Drafting

    C. Final draft

    D. Revision

69) Publishing a class newsletter, looking through catalogues and filling our order form, and playing the role of secretaries and executives are activities designed to teach:

    A. Expressive writing

    B. Transactional writing

    C. Poetic writing

    D. Creative writing

70) Standards of accuracy for a student's spelling should be based on the student's:

    A. Grade level spelling list

    B. Present reading book level

    C. Level of spelling development

    D. Performance on an informal assessment

71) The single most important activity for eventual reading success of young children is:

    A. Giving them books

    B. Watching animated stories

    C. Reading aloud to them

    D. Viewing pictures in books

72) Skilled readers use all but which one of these knowledge sources to construct meanings beyond the literal text:

    A. Text knowledge

    B. Syntactic knowledge

    C. Morphological knowledge

    D. Semantic knowledge

73) Given an hour to write a response to a prompt, what is the maximum time a fourth grader should spend in prewriting?

    A. five minutes

    B. fifteen minutes

    C. ten minutes

    D. twenty minutes

74) The inverted essay introduction requires placing the statement of the main idea (thesis)

    A. at the beginning of the first paragraph

    B. at the middle of the first paragraph

    C. at the end of the first paragraph

    D. in the second paragraph

75) A prewriting technique for using a visual organizer where main ideas with supporting details are arranged around the topic statement is

    A. brainstorming

    B. comparing

    C. analysis

    D. clustering

76) Sam, a 10-year-old fifth grader, has suddenly started to stutter when speaking. What is most likely the speech problem?

    A. A genetic defect

    B. A new habit

    C. Evidence of an emotional conflict

    D. An attention-getting device

77) **What is the learning theorist's view of language acquisition?**

   A. Language is shaped by the reinforcement children receive from their caretakers

   B. Language is the result of innate biological mechanisms

   C. Language results spontaneously

   D. Language is developed through systematic instruction

78) **The teacher states, "We will work on the first page of vocabulary words. On the second page we will work on the structure and meaning of the words. We will go over these together and then you will write out the answers to the exercises on your own. I will be circulating to give help if needed." What is this an example of?**

   A. Evaluation of instructional activity

   B. Analysis of instructional

   C. Identification of expected outcomes

   D. Pacing of instructional activity

79) **What is it called when a teacher uses colored marking pens to color code words with long and short vowels?**

   A. Examples and non-examples

   B. Repetition

   C. Marker technique

   D. Marker expression

80) **Which of the following is NOT a basic assumption of the criteria for teaching mathematics?**

   A. The goal is to help all students develop math power

   B. What students learn is connected to how they learn it.

   C. All students can learn to think mathematically

   D. Teaching is a uniform process best practiced as a recipe or prescription

81) Which of the following is not the most effective math teaching strategy?

    A. To be clear about instructional goals (topics)

    B. To address higher-level, as well as lower-level, lesson objectives

    C. To communicate to students what is expected of them and why

    D. To present math separate from other subject areas

82) Which of the following best promotes understanding of math operations?

    A. The teacher promoting a single best solution

    B. Students verbalizing solutions to problems

    C. Speed tests

    D. Providing solutions to textbook tests

83) Which one of the following is NOT an example of critical thinking in elementary school science?

    A. Conjecturing

    B. Memorizing

    C. Comparing

    D. Concluding

84) Which of the following is NOT an example of critical thinking in elementary school science?

    A. Conjecturing

    B. Memorizing

    C. Comparing

    D. Concluding

85) **Which of the following is a misconception about the task of teaching science in elementary school?**

   A. Teach facts as a priority over teaching how to solve problems

   B. Involve as many senses as possible in the learning experience

   C. Accommodate individual differences in pupils' learning styles

   D. Consider the effect of technology on people rather than on material things.

86) **Which skill refers to quantifying data, performing graphic analysis, making charts, and writing summaries?**

   A. Recording

   B. Data gathering

   C. Data processing

   D. Evaluating

87) **When several computers are connected together by a modem or telephone it is a:**

   A. Processor

   B. Network

   C. Online

   D. Hard drive

88) **The internet has changed the classroom dramatically. This technology allows a teacher to:**

   A. Assign free time to those who finish their work first.

   B. Be exposed to any website of the students choice.

   C. Teach more topics at a faster rate

   D. Combine alternate viewpoints and expertise

89) **Computer simulations are most appropriate for**

   A. replicating dangerous experiments

   B. mastering basic facts

   C. emphasizing competition and entertainment

   D. Providing motivational feedback

90) A fourth grade teacher is presenting the concept of zero in division. The class is not making significant progress. He should

    A. Request the parents teach this to the children for homework. Parents know their children best.

    B. Review the material the next day.

    C. Block schedule a different time of day to present the material

    D. The following day, drop the idea to continue where he left off and present less difficult material that will generate classroom interest.

91) Sue does a lot of attention seeking in Mr. Green's fourth grade class. If she is not she is not saying "cute" remarks, throwing paper, tapping on the desk, or most anything to get the attention of the class to laugh. The most effective non verbal intervention that could be used by Mr. Green would probably be best to apply:

    A. Planned ignoring

    B. Signal interference

    C. Removal of enticing objects

    D. Proximity control

92) A six year old student in Mrs. Brack's first grade class has exhibited a noticeable change in behavior over the last month. The child was usually outgoing, alert, but she has become quiet and withdrawn, and appears to be unable to concentrate on her work. Yesterday, bruises were evident n the child's arm and right eye. Mrs. Brack should:

    A. Ignore the situation

    B. Provide remedial work

    C. Immediately report the suspected abuse to the authorities

    D. Call the girl's parents

93) The duties required of members of the instructional staff of the public school include

    A. Earning an advanced degree

    B. Providing individualized help for students

    C. Using prescribed materials and methods

    D. Participating in all school-related functions

94) A reduction in fluency in reading due to a student confronting unfamiliar words can best be remediated by :

    A. Building Site Words

    B. Phonics

    C. Master phoneme-grapheme relationships

    D. Context cueing

95) When a reading lesson examines the relationship between physical nature of the letters, and the combinations of letters and sounds, the student is drawing heavily from which dimension of reading:

    A. Physiological

    B. Linguistic

    C. Perceptual

    D. Metacognition

96) Understanding intonation, stress, pauses, and tone sequencing that incorporates ideas as they are presented in context such as nonstandard usage, figurative language, and slang requires mastery of:

    A. Social acceptance

    B. Humanities training

    C. Encoding symbols

    D. Linguistic proficiency

97) An element of phonic analysis is the pronunciation of a word by using:

    A. Transitional consonants

    B. Dipthongs

    C. Reinforce psychological clues

    D. Reading comprehension

98) The stated main idea of a paragraph often appears in the _____ sentence:

A. Last sentence

B. Scattered anywhere in the text

C. Always in the first sentence

D. In the title

99) Generally speaking, the writer's main idea is supported by:

A. Many minor details

B. Keyword progressions

C. Major details

D. Publishers

100) Word meanings can be derived by repeating key ideas. "The peaches were succulent—so juicy, sweet and perfectly ripe. " In this case the secret to perfecting and defining the word succulent is to use:

A. A dictionary

B. Adjacent sentence clues

C. Sentence level clues

D. Context clues in entire passage

101) What is not a method you use to find the main idea of a reading selection?

A. Topic/question/answer

B. Journalistic model

C. Restatement of the theme

D. Saccade/fixation pairing

102) Vocabulary can be developed by using word clues such as root words, antonyms, and word forms. If you know that biology is the study of life, musicology has something to do with the study of music, it follows that zoology has something to do with:

A. Zoos

B. Pharmacology

C. The study of animals

D. Farm life

103) A passage may inform, persuade, narrate, describe, or entertain. The criminal justice system seems appropriately named. It really is criminal what the system does to justice. It also seems as though the only one who counts in the system is the criminal. People are outraged at the amount of crime in the streets. They are outraged how quickly criminals are let back on the street. Jails are overcrowded, so bail is set low, court dockets are filled up to eighteen months in advance. The simple fact is that all the solutions the experts are offering have one thing in common is that they are require funding and we don't want to pay for it. We have only to blame ourselves. Everything has a cost. The primary purpose of this paragraph is to:

A. describe a typical outraged reaction to how widespread crime has become

B. convince the reader to support funding for additional jail space

C. explain the rationale behind the practice of plea bargaining

D. relate the process by which criminals go through the judicial system

104) Much has been written about Hemingway's literary style. Few critics fail to notice the brevity of the sentences in many of his works. Sentences are not only short but grammatically uncomplicated, often featuring a bare subject-verb-object structure. While typically spare as far as syntax is concerned, Hemingway's diction is heavily charged with words that create visual and olfactory images. This paragraph organizational style can be described as:

A. Chronological

B. Sequence/Process

C. Spatial/Place Order

D. Simple Listing

105) The literal meaning of a word is:

A. Denotation

B. Connotation

C. Implication

D. Manifestation

106) The national debt is growing continually. In fact, by next year it may be seven trillion dollars. The clue that this is an explicit organizational pattern is:

A. growing

B. in fact

C. seven trillion dollars

D. it is implied

107) The trailer was pulled from its foundation. <u>Nearby</u>, trees snapped and fell. Word clues relating one specific thing to another thing in space reflects:

A. Cause and effect

B. Contrast

C. Comparison

D. Location

108) Jenny said she would come to the party. Danny and Bill said they would also come but much later. How is the second sentence related to the first?

A. It adds to the information presented in the first sentence

B. It qualifies the first sentence with a condition

C. It answers a question raised by the first sentence

D. It restates the central idea of the first sentence

109) The door slammed. Then footsteps thudded down the hallway. Finally, after some silence, a voice came from the kitchen. The events in these sentences are organized according to:

A. degree of uncertainty

B. when they occurred

C. how long they took to happen

D. how loud they were

110) Choose the word that best fills in the blank. Nicki craves macaroni; _____, it gives him hives.

    A. finally

    B. however

    C. in fact

    D. moreover

Elementary Sample Questions Answer Key

1)	C	41)	B	81)	D
2)	C	42)	D	82)	B
3)	D	43)	B	83)	B
4)	C	44)	C	84)	B
5)	D	45)	C	85)	A
6)	A	46)	D	86)	C
7)	A	47)	D	87)	B
8)	C	48)	B	88)	D
9)	A	49)	D	89)	A
10)	C	50)	A	90)	B
11)	C	51)	C	91)	A
12)	C	52)	A	92)	C
13)	B	53)	A	93)	B
14)	D	54)	C	94)	A
15)	C	55)	A	95)	C
16)	C	56)	B	96)	D
17)	B	57)	D	97)	B
18)	C	58)	C	98)	A
19)	D	59)	D	99)	C
20)	A	60)	B	100)	C
21)	D	61)	D	101)	D
22)	D	62)	B	102)	C
23)	B	63)	C	103)	B
24)	D	64)	B	104)	D
25)	A	65)	D	105)	A
26)	C	66)	A	106)	B
27)	D	67)	C	107)	D
28)	B	68)	A	108)	A
29)	C	69)	B	109)	B
30)	B	70)	C	110)	B
31)	C	71)	C		
32)	D	72)	C		
33)	C	73)	B		
34)	C	74)	C		
35)	D	75)	D		
36)	C	76)	C		
37)	D	77)	A		
38)	B	78)	B		
39)	B	79)	C		
40)	A	80)	D		

The Educated Mind

1. He cultivates the open mind

2. He combines the three great heritages of education

3   He always listens to the person who knows

4. He never laughs at new ideas

5. He knows the secret of getting along with other people

6. He cultivates the habit of success

7. He knows that popular notions are sometimes wrong

8. You can't sell him magic

9. He links himself with a great cause.

10. He builds an ambition picture to fit his abilities

11. He always tries to feel the emotion he ought to feel

12. He keeps busy at his highest natural level in order to be happy, useful, and good,

13. He knows it is never to late to learn

14. He never loses faith in the man he might have been

15. He achieves the masteries that make him a world citizen

16. He cultivates the love of the beautiful

17. He lives a great religious life

> The Educated Man
> Copyright 1925
> by William Wiggam

"Are we there yet?"

"Now, we've seen it."